THE EDUCATION OF DISTURBING CHILDREN

THE EDUCATION OF DISTURBING CHILDREN

Pupils with learning and adjustment difficulties

David Galloway and Carole Goodwin

LONGMAN
London and New York

Longman Group UK Limited
Longman House, Burnt Mill, Harlow
Essex CM20 2JE, England
and Associated companies throughout the world.

*Published in the United States of America
by Longman Inc., New York*

© David Galloway and Carole Goodwin 1987

All rights reserved; no part of this publication may be reproduced, stored in a retrieval system, or transmitted in any form or by any means, electronic, mechanical, photocopying, recording, or otherwise, without either the prior written permission of the Publishers or a licence permitting restricted copying in the United Kingdom issued by the Copyright Licensing Agency Ltd, 33-34 Alfred Place, London, WC1E 7DP.

First published 1987
Second impression 1988

British Library Cataloguing in Publication Data

Galloway, David M.
    The education of disturbing children: pupils with learning and adjustment difficulties.
    1. Slow learning children   2. Remedial teaching
    3. Problem children——Education
    I. Title   II. Goodwin, Carole
    371.92   LC4661
ISBN 0-582-49720-5

Library of Congress Cataloging in Publication Data

Galloway, David, 1942–
    The education of disturbing children.

    Bibliography: p.
    Includes index.
    1. Learning disabled children—Education—Great Britain.   2. Problem children—Education—Great Britain.
    3. Mainstreaming in education—Great Britain.
    I. Goodwin, Carole.   II. Title.
    LC4706.G7G35   1987   371.93   86-10444
    ISBN 0-582-49720-5

Set in 10 on 11pt Linotron 202 Times
Produced by Longman Group (FE) Limited
Printed in Hong Kong

CONTENTS

Acknowledgements vii
Disclaimers viii
Note on authorship ix

Introduction: children with learning and adjustment difficulties   x

1. The development of procedures for identifying and educating children with learning and adjustment difficulties   1
    Introduction   1
    Developments up to the 1944 Education Act   2
    The 1944 Education Act   8
    The Warnock Report   12
    The 1981 Education Act: an overview   16
    Whose special education needs?   17
    Assessments and statements: a bureaucrat's dream?   18
    Assessments and statements: a parent's nightmare?   19
    Comment   22
    Conclusions   25

2. Prevalence: do twenty per cent of children really have special educational needs?   26
    Introduction   26
    Evidence from special school rolls   27
    The semantics of behavioural problems   30
    Behaviour and progress: survey evidence   33
    Conclusions from surveys   37
    Which children are said to have special needs?   41
    Conclusions   48

3. The effects of special education   49
    Introduction   49
    Disturbing behaviour: special schools   50
    Disturbing behaviour: other approaches   57
    Counselling, psychotherapy and spontaneous remission   61
    Children with moderate learning difficulties   63
    Children with mild and specific learning difficulties   66
    Conclusions   69

Contents

4. Special education in Norway and the United States 71
   Introduction 71
   Norway 72
   The United States 78
   Conclusions 87

5. Innovations in the education of children with learning difficulties 88
   Introduction 88
   Integration in Bromley: an about-turn in policy? 89
   Developments in Oxfordshire 94
   Countesthorpe College, Leicestershire 99
   Conclusions 104

6. A study of conflicting needs 106
   Introduction 106
   Background 107
   Developments since 1976 109
   Theory into practice? 113
   National and local policies: a critique 115
   Pressures on teachers 120
   Pressures on the support services 125
   Conclusions 129

7. Disturbing children in the ordinary school: problems and possibilities 132
   Introduction 132
   School effectiveness and special educational needs 133
   On-site units 139
   Interaction analysis and behaviour modification 142
   Pastoral care and counselling 146
   Conclusions 151

8. School and LEA policies 153
   Introduction 153
   A whole school approach to special educational needs 155
   A whole school approach to pastoral care 158
   Comment 160
   The LEA's contribution 161
   Developing an integration policy 164
   Conclusions: flexible use of resources? 168

9. Conclusions 172
   Overview: consensus on theory; divergence on practice? 172
   Policy making and planning at four levels 174
   Meeting all pupils' needs 178
   Educational and political priorities 180

References 183
Index 197

ACKNOWLEDGEMENTS

We acknowledge gratefully the numerous but necessarily anonymous schools, teachers, other professional colleagues, pupils and parents, both in Sheffield and elsewhere, whose cooperation helped us to formulate the ideas in this book. The book draws on research in Sheffield, U.K., and in New Zealand. Part of the research in Sheffield was funded by the Department of Education and Science (DES) and in New Zealand by the New Zealand Education Department, the New Zealand Educational Institute and the Mental Health Foundation of New Zealand. Their support is gratefully acknowledged, as is that of those members of Sheffield Education Department and the New Zealand Education Department who made it possible. Chapter 8 contains extracts from an article by David Galloway: 'Meeting special educational needs in the ordinary school: or creating them?' This was published in *Maladjustment and Therapeutic Education* (1985). We are grateful to the editor for permission to reproduce parts of the article.

DISCLAIMERS

The views expressed in this book are the authors' own and should not be taken to reflect those of their employers, nor of individuals or institutions who cooperated with any of the inquiries referred to in the book. When presenting case histories and when quoting teachers or pupils verbatim we have changed names, abbreviations of names, nicknames and other identifying characteristics.

NOTE ON AUTHORSHIP

Planning and writing this book was a cooperative venture. Inevitably, though, with one author working in Cardiff and the other in Sheffield, there was some division of responsibilities. Each chapter went through at least two drafts as we took account of each other's criticisms. For the record, Chapter 1 was written jointly by David Galloway and Carole Goodwin. Chapters 2, 3, 7, 8 and 9 were written mainly by David Galloway. Chapters 4 and 5 were written mainly by Carole Goodwin and Chapter 6 jointly by Carole Goodwin and David Galloway.

INTRODUCTION: CHILDREN WITH LEARNING AND ADJUSTMENT DIFFICULTIES

ORIGIN OF THE BOOK

THE INTEGRATION DEBATE

When we started work on this book our brief was to write a second edition of a book we published in 1979: *Educating Slow-Learning and Maladjusted Children: Integration or Segregation?* But, for reasons we explain below, what has emerged is essentially a new work, in which only a small part of the original text survives.

The earlier volume was published one year after the Warnock Committee had produced its report on special education needs (DES 1978a). This report is widely believed to have supported the integration of children with special needs into the ordinary school system. Its recommendations in this respect were in fact highly equivocal, but they did reflect to a moderate extent the growing international pressure against placing children in separate special schools or classes.

It was our view at the time that the general principle of integration would gradually gain acceptance for children with physical and sensory handicaps. We felt, however, that the debate on integration was bypassing the two largest groups of children with special needs, namely the 'slow learning' and the 'maladjusted'. In addition we considered separate special schooling at least as disadvantageous for these children as for children with physical or sensory disabilities.

We considered the debate important for theoretical, empirical and practical reasons. The theoretical reason was that certain basic needs logically could not be met in separate special schools. The most obvious of these was the need to learn to work and play with ordinary children. Another factor was the restricted curriculum that is unavoidable in a small special school. The empirical reason related to research which, at the most charitable interpretation, failed to support the view that children benefited educationally from attending special schools rather than ordinary schools. The practical reason was based on our own experiences as teachers and as educational psychologists. This suggested that schools which catered well for their most vulnerable children tended also to cater well for the rest of their pupils.

Following on from the last point, there was one level at which we regarded this debate as unproblematic. The choice did not lie between placing children in a separate special school or class and leaving them to sink or swim in the mainstream. We considered the latter course totally unacceptable for the pupils concerned, for their teachers and for all other pupils in the ordinary class who might suffer from the attention given to, or demanded by, the 'special' child. Our argument was rather that teachers in the mainstream should receive the training and the support to enable them to teach pupils with learning or adjustment problems successfully. We knew from our own work with teachers that this could be done. We also recognised that it had implications for teacher training at initial and in-service levels, for the support services and for local education authority (LEA) policy towards children with special needs. Our argument, then, was that special education, in its literal sense, could and should be provided in ordinary schools.

SUBSEQUENT DEVELOPMENTS

While we saw no reason to modify the essential conclusions of the original book, there was an obvious need to update and extend it in the light of subsequent developments. The 1981 Education Act constituted the government's response to the Warnock Report and provided an entirely new legislative framework for special education, with far-reaching implications not only for LEA policy and for members of the support services, but also for teachers in all ordinary schools.

Between them, Warnock and the 1981 Act successfully focused public and professional attention on a previously somewhat neglected minority of children. This attention is reflected in the reports of Her Majesty's Inspectors of Schools (HMI). In 1979 HMI reports on schools might devote a few lines, or even a paragraph to 'peripheral' issues such as pastoral care or remedial teaching. Today headteachers know that a whole section may well be devoted to a school's guidance network and to its provision for children with special educational needs. The days have gone when secondary schools could get away with allocating one part-time teacher to take 'remedial' children for one or two sessions a week.

We soon realised, however, that while developments since 1979 indicated the need for revision and updating of our original book, they also made it impractical. We could no longer accept the terminology of the original title. It reflected an out-moded debate which did not focus on the issue we now considered of most importance.

We shall return to the question of terminology in Chapter 1, but must mention it briefly here. The term 'maladjusted' never, in our view, had much educational or clinical significance. Abolition in the 1981 Act of the former categories of handicap deprived it of any administrative significance either. A slightly different objection applied to the term 'slow learning'. This was not one of the former categories of handicap, in retrospect we would have preferred the broader concept of learning difficulties proposed both by Warnock and by the 1981 Act. Our interest was, and remains, with children whose teachers find their behaviour and/or educational progress *disturbing*. We decided that this focus should be reflected in the title.

A more important issue concerned the changing nature of debate in special education. Coinciding with the increased attention to children with special needs, there is a widespread belief among teachers, members of the support services and HMI, that the proportion of children with special needs remaining in ordinary schools is increasing. This belief applies not only to children with physical and with sensory abilities, but also to children who, allegedly, would formerly have been placed in special schools, classes or units on account of their learning or adjustment difficulties. Most teachers in ordinary schools are convinced not only that they have a larger number of such children than in the past, but also that this results at least in part from a policy of integration.

Yet the almost universal belief that these children are increasingly being integrated within ordinary schools is not borne out by the evidence. The evidence suggests instead that the overall proportion of children placed in separate special schools or classes for slow-learning pupils has remained more or less constant. The evidence also suggests that the proportion placed in separate schools or units because of their disturbing behaviour has actually increased. At least for these two groups of children there is no evidence of increased integration since publication of the Warnock Report. If anything, the reverse is the case. It is true that under the guise of education reform several LEAs have replaced their former educationally subnormal (moderate) (ESN(M)) schools with units for children with moderate learning difficulties, based in ordinary schools. Integration, however, means more than mixing socially in the lunch hour. Units in an ordinary school too often contain the worst of both worlds: the limited curriculum of the special school combined with social and educational isolation in the mainstream.

The question, then, is not whether children with learning and adjustment difficulties are best educated in the mainstream or in

Introduction

separate special schools. There is no longer much debate over this. It is widely assumed that integration is taking place. Moreover, not even the most ardent supporter of separate special schools argues in favour of unnecessary segregation. The question rather is why the widespread assumptions of professionals are not being reflected in practice. To re-phrase the question: why is the proportion of children following separate, and potentially disadvantaging curricula in separate special schools or units remaining constant, if not increasing, when there appears in theory to be a broad professional and political consensus in favour of integration?

A further question concerns the large number of children with learning and adjustment difficulties who have always remained in ordinary schools. The 1981 Education Act probably has led to increased provision for these children within ordinary schools. Unfortunately it does not follow that they will necessarily benefit from the provision that is offered. Already there is disquieting evidence that some schools are identifying a larger number of pupils as having special needs, and giving these pupils a separate curriculum. The problem here is that the separate curriculum may restrict the pupils' life chances rather than extend them. Being identified as having special needs may reduce the pupils' self-esteem, even though the aim in theory is to help the school enhance self-esteem. In a nutshell, special provision within the ordinary school, as in separate special schools, may act as a form of social control by removing slow or disturbing pupils from ordinary classes. In some schools recent legislation may increase the number of pupils thus removed rather than extend the best characteristic of special education into the ordinary class.

We are *not* arguing that this happens in all schools, nor are we arguing that it is in any way inevitable. On the contrary, there is most impressive evidence that some schools are providing education of an outstanding quality for their most vulnerable pupils. The fact remains that the debate on the education of children with learning and adjustment difficulties has lost none of its relevance in the last seven years. This is the case whether one considers the number of children placed in separate schools and units or the number following separate curricula in ordinary schools.

Thus the evolution of special education policy and of our own ideas required a substantially new book, and not just a new title. *The Education of Disturbing Children* may be seen as having developed from *Educating Slow Learning and Maladjusted Children*. We have used parts of the original where they still seem pertinent. These extracts occur mainly, though not entirely, in Chapters 1–3, and account for less than 15 per cent of the total text.

DEFINITION OF TERMS

Commendably, both Warnock and the 1981 Education Act were quite clear that children could not be divided tidily into two groups of handicapped and not-handicapped. They were equally clear that special need must be defined in terms of the child's *educational* needs. It must not be assumed to exist following identification of some physical or sensory disability.

The children with learning difficulties with whom we are primarily concerned in this book were regarded by Warnock as having 'moderate' learning difficulties. This includes, very broadly, the group previously regarded as ESN(M). We would, however, emphasise two points. First, a majority of children who might legitimately have been ascertained as ESN(M) under the 1944 Education Act has in fact always remained in ordinary schools. Second, there is an even larger overlap between these groups and the group which Warnock regarded as having 'mild' learning difficulties.

The latter, according to Warnock, had traditionally been educated in ordinary schools, where they were often regarded as 'remedial' – a term criticised for implying that the children's problem could be cured, even though they might be making excellent progress in the light of their overall development and ability. In practice it is impractical to discuss integrated provision for children with 'moderate' learning difficulties without also discussing provision for 'mild' learning difficulties. Thus, while our primary concern is with children at risk of placement in recognised special schools or classes, we are also concerned, when discussing provision in ordinary schools, with the much larger number who may have learning difficulties without being considered prime candidates for special schooling.

The term 'adjustment difficulties' is equally diffuse. We are concerned, though, with children who may be transferred out of ordinary classes because of their difficult or disturbing behaviour. Some of these pupils are transferred to special schools for 'adjustment difficulties' and others to centres or units for the 'disruptive'. We argue in Chapter 2 that the distinction is based solely on administrative convenience, and lacks clinical or educational credibility. Yet here, too, there is no tidy distinction between pupils who are transferred to special schools or units and pupils who remain in the mainstream. Hence, we are also concerned with the fairly large minority of children whose behaviour causes their teachers anxiety or concern even though the question of their removal from the mainstream may not seriously be considered.

Introduction

SCOPE AND STRUCTURE OF THE BOOK

This book describes different ways in which LEAs, schools and individual teachers may seek to recognise and meet the special needs of a minority of their pupils. We are unashamedly partisan in arguing that these needs are, in principle, better met within the flexible curriculum resources and stable social climate of a successful ordinary school. However, we also discuss the possibilities inherent in special schools and classes, and consider how these may most effectively complement provision in the mainstream.

Chapter 1 deals with the growth of special education for pupils with learning and adjustment difficulties. In this chapter we also describe the principal features of the 1981 Education Act and identify inconsistencies within the Act which may undermine some of its good intentions. This is followed by two chapters dealing with the prevalence of special needs and with research on the effects on children of separate special education. In Chapter 4 we compare developments in Britain with the situation in Scandinavia and in North America, and in Chapters 5 and 6 we describe some British innovations in mainstream provision for the pupils concerned. The final three chapters analyse the implications of our arguments for teachers, with particular reference to LEA policy, school and classroom management, and the development of effective support networks within each school.

We hope that the book will stimulate discussion among teachers in special and ordinary schools. While it is aimed principally at teachers with responsibility for children with special needs, we hope it may also stimulate discussion among educational administrators, advisers, educational psychologists, school medical officers and social workers. From previous experience we are pretty confident that our ideas will not be accepted uncritically. We shall, however, be satisfied if the discussion provoked by the book leads to a rigorous evaluation and review of existing practice in some schools and/or some LEAs. If the evaluation and review help teachers or LEA administrators to plan more effective teaching procedures for their most vulnerable children, we shall be delighted.

David Galloway and Carole Goodwin
September 1985

Chapter one
THE DEVELOPMENT OF PROCEDURES FOR IDENTIFYING AND EDUCATING CHILDREN WITH LEARNING AND ADJUSTMENT DIFFICULTIES

INTRODUCTION

Ever since education in Britain became free and compulsory with the Education Acts of 1870 and 1876 there have been demands for more and better provision for children whose poor progress or behaviour disturbed their teachers. These demands have not gone unheeded by successive governments. In the last ten years, the pressures of economic recession and government attempts to curb public spending have placed a major strain on almost every level in the education system. Yet funding has been made available to increase provision in special education, particularly for pupils whose behaviour disturbs their teachers.

In practice this development has implied an increase in the number of places in special schools or classes, or in units established to cater for particularly disturbing children. We shall show that this situation is not changing as a result of the 1981 Education Act. The principle of comprehensive education is now accepted throughout the country, except in a tiny minority of LEAs. Attempts in some Conservative controlled LEAs to abolish comprehensive schools, reverting to a selective system, have been abandoned following public outcry. Yet in our comprehensive school system a higher proportion of children than ever before is being removed from the mainstream for schooling in separate special schools, classes or units.

This chapter reviews the growth in special education for slow and difficult children up to and following the 1944 Education Act. We examine some of the controversies and tensions which marked the expansion, looking particularly at administrative procedures in the selection of children for special education. We discuss some of the central conclusions and recommendations of the Warnock Report, before taking a critical look at the government's responses, in the 1981 Education Act.

We describe at several points in the chapter what may be called the 'conventional wisdom' of special education. This refers to its stated aims, which in general are based on a broad consensus among special educators about what constitutes good practice. We argue, however, that the broad consensus on good practice is open to different interpretations. The conventional wisdom, for example, holds that children are transferred to special schools for their own benefit. An alternative interpretation sees their transfer as a form of support for their teachers, maintaining standards, stability and control in ordinary schools by removing misfits.

DEVELOPMENTS UP TO THE 1944 EDUCATION ACT

The Education Acts of 1870 and 1876 made no provision for children with learning or adjustment difficulties. A process of rapid natural selection led to their sinking or simply remaining at the bottom end of the lowest classes. Many schools reacted to this situation by creating a Standard 0 taught by pupil teachers, since the few qualified teachers were needed for more 'normal' children. Into Standard 0 sank not only the 'feeble-minded' but also the physically handicapped, partially sighted and delicate children who could not cope with an ordinary class curriculum. Pritchard (1963) notes that with ages ranging from eight to thirteen, 'Together they stagnated'.

This indicates a tension inherent in the education of children with learning or behavioural problems. Children may have sunk into Standard 0 because *they* could not cope with the ordinary class curriculum. Alternatively, Standard 0 could be seen as the tidiest available solution to problems with which *teachers* could not cope. Making these children the responsibility of pupil teachers merely underlined the emphasis on controlling rather than educating them.

We may like to think we have come a long way since these early days of compulsory education, and that children with special needs are no longer treated merely as an administrative nuisance. Yet a survey by HMI published the year after the Warnock Report found that nearly 50 per cent of full-time remedial teachers had less than five years' experience, and that the majority of all remedial teachers were part-timers (DES 1979). Similar problems have also been reported by HMI in Scotland (Scottish Education Department 1978). There has undoubtedly been progress since the days of Standard 0 taught by pupil teachers, yet the administrative expedient of giving low status teachers responsibility for low status pupils is still evident.

Nevertheless, by the early 1890s pressure for special provision for so-called 'feeble-minded' children was growing. A subcommittee of the Charity Organisation Society (1893) supported the principle that a large number of children needed special education outside the ordinary Board schools, and argued that the school boards, and not voluntary bodies, should be responsible for establishing the proposed special schools. They also suggested that schoool boards should be made responsible for providing residential care where necessary. The Charity Organisation Society's recommendations had been anticipated by the Medical Superintendent at the Royal Albert Asylum, G. E. Shuttleworth (1888), who made unfavourable comparison between the limited provision in England with that in less wealthy countries such as Germany and Norway. Pressure on the London School Board also came from within when the Chairman of the Subcommittee on the Education of the Blind and Deaf, Major-General Moberly, urged the Board's School Management Committee in 1890 to open a special school for 'feeble-minded' children (Education Department 1898). This proposal was not accepted, but in the following year the School Board agreed to open three experimental 'Schools for Special Instruction' in the poorest areas of the city. Staff–pupil ratio was not to be above the unthinkably generous level of thirty to one, and the children were to be nominated by the headteacher of their ordinary schools as 'intellectually weak, poorly endowed with perception, memory, reasoning, etc.', a phrase borrowed from Klemm's (1891) book *European Schools*. Before admission each child was to be examined by a committee consisting of an inspector from the School Board, the Board's Medical Officer and the headteacher of the receiving school.

It is of particular interest that the criteria for admission were primarily educational. This was true both of the London School Board's first three schools and of the Milton Street Board School in Leicester where a classroom was made available in 1892 for twelve feeble-minded children. Here, children were selected by a Mr H. Major, a Leicester School Board Inspector, who used a reading book not to see whether the child could read, but rather whether she could explain what was happening in the pictures and answer questions about her environment (Education Department 1898). Another feature of the London schools which is of interest as the first official recognition of a recurring theme was that appointments were initially for five years only, as the Board thought it important that teachers should be able to return to work with normal children.

At this time it was feared that the strain of working with feeble-minded children for a prolonged period might harm the teacher's physical or mental health; more recently the concern has been that a prolonged period in a special school could lead to a lowering of standards, and that a refresher year with normal children might help teachers retain a sense of proportion and realistic educational objectives (Ministry of Education 1954; DES 1973, 1978a).

The education of disturbing children

By 1896, four years after the opening of the Hugh Myddleton School in London, 900 children were attending twenty-four special schools. At the same time schools or classes had opened in Bradford, Birmingham, Nottingham, Bristol and Brighton, and thought was then being given in official quarters to the needs of children who were retarded as well as simply backward. Dr Alfred Eichholz, first Medical Inspector of the Education Department suggested that children requiring special education should be classified into three groups:

1. Those with pronounced mental deficiency.
2. Physically defective and epileptic children.
3. Children who were 'physically and morally healthy – but backward'.

He considered the third group to be very numerous and stated that many should be able to return to their ordinary schools. This notion of some special schools as remedial establishments aiming to prepare children for return to ordinary schools may be seen in two ways. Ostensibly, the proposal was to offer children with problems special help that would enable them to benefit from the educational opportunities offered in an ordinary school. In this sense it could be said to anticipate the debate on 'normalisation' in special education today. The alternative view looks both at the circumstances leading up to a child's removal, and at the motives behind it. If Eichholz was correct in thinking that many children should be able to return to ordinary schools, and presumably to make satisfactory progress, we need to ask why special schooling was necessary in the first place. The implications here are: (a) that special schooling could somehow 'cure' children of their problems; and (b) that children who could not conform to the demands of an ordinary school should be removed.

The trouble with this reasoning is that the concept of cure, like the concept of *remedial* education, implies: 'that these children have something wrong with them that can be put right' (DES 1978a: 47). The reality is that most slow-learning children require continuing support. They may make good progress in a remedial group or in a special school, but if their needs are not recognised on their return, the outlook is poor. It took more than eighty years following Eichholz's recommendations before parents and professionals started seriously to challenge the orthodoxy that special needs should be met in special schools, and to consider the possibility of providing extra help within the ordinary class.

In 1898 the Education Department's Departmental Committee on Defective and Epileptic Children published its report recommending that provision of special education should, when necessary, be compulsory. (Under the 1870 Act parents could place their children beyond the jurisdiction of the School Board by exercising their right to select a voluntary school; owing to anxiety about the stigma attached to special schools, this led to the voluntary schools having more defective children that the Board Schools.) The committee suggested that classes should not generally exceed twenty, and that all heads and the majority of assistants should be qualified. Many of the committee's recommendations were subsequently endorsed in the 1899 Elementary Education (Defective and Epileptic Children) Act, but the Education Department did not accept the principle that local authorities should be obliged to provide special schools. Consequently the Act merely permitted local authorities to make provision for their epileptic and mentally and physically handicapped children. In the following ten years just over one-third of the 328 LEAs used their powers.

This was in part due to the appointment in 1904 of a Royal Commission on the Care and Control of the Feeble-Minded. The Commission heard evidence from the growing eugenicist lobby influenced by the belief of Sir Francis Galton that mental and moral deficiency were, like physical characteristics, hereditary. In addition the developing intelligence test movement held out little hope that the feeble-minded could become self-sufficient; although Binet and Simon (1914) had argued that the feeble-minded should be taught to read and write, they nevertheless remained pessimistic about attempts to educate many of them. Finally, voluntary workers such as Mary Dendy and Dame Ellen Pinsent were arguing in favour of the lifelong segregation of the feeble-minded, thus obviating the need for day special schools, and were exerting considerable influence in the National Association for Promoting the Welfare of the Feeble-Minded, which was founded in 1897. Thus when the Royal Commission reported in 1908 it recommended that the 1899 Act should be amended to exclude mentally defective children who should henceforth be the statutory responsibility of local mental deficiency committees; LEAs which had exercised their right under the 1899 Act to establish special schools for such children should either transfer them to the mental deficiency committees or continue to operate them under their direction. Not surprisingly, the Royal Commission's report provided an active disincentive to LEAs exercising their powers under the 1899 Act.

Two points should be made at this stage. First, giving LEAs powers to provide a certain service, but no obligation, is generally a satisfactory way of ensuring that the service will not be widely provided. Even when the economic climate is favourable, public bodies are understandably more concerned to achieve a high standard in their statutory responsibilities than to spend money on services that are not formally required. Second, and more important, the Royal Commission's recommendations reflected the ideology of the people who advised it. The fact that this was expressed as a humanitarian concern for the less fortunate merely legitimised an ideology in which the 'feeble-minded' were seen as a threat to the structure of society and must therefore be segregated, not only for their own good, but for the welfare of society in general.

The pessimism about the possibility of useful education for the feeble-minded nevertheless encouraged supporters of existing schools to publicise their successes. As a result the Mental Deficiency Act of 1913 required LEAs (as opposed to simply empowering them) to ascertain those children aged seven to sixteen who were mentally defective. The only children who would be passed on to the mental deficiency committees would be those who were incapable of benefiting from education in a special school, in other words the group which would today be regarded as having severe learning difficulties, or ESN(S). The following year the Elementary Education (Defective and Epileptic Children) Act made the 1899 Act mandatory as far as defective children were concerned.

The Act did not lead to the escalation of special educational provision that might have been predicted. In 1914 there were 13,563 children in the mental defective schools, but by 1939 the number was still less than 17,000. There were three principal reasons for this lack of growth.

1. During and immediately after the First World War the country had other things to think about.
2. From 1924 to 1929 a committee chaired by A. H. Wood was investigating the educational needs of the feeble-minded, and LEAs were understandably reluctant to use existing legislation to increase their provision when the committee might recommend a change in the basic structure of special education.
3. By the time the Wood Committee reported the United Kingdom was joining America and other European countries in the recession of the 1930s. In this climate no form of expansion could be contemplated.

The Wood Committee's first brief was to examine the incidence of feeble-mindedness, and the second to propose changes in the present system of educating feeble-minded children in the light of experience gained since the 1899 Act. The committee's investigations into the incidence of feeble-mindedness are discussed in more detail in Chapter 2. What is important here is that the committee, whose members included Cyril Burt and Ellen Pinsent, commented that existing special schools were catering for only one-sixth of the estimated number of feeble-minded children in the country and no formal provision was being made for the even larger group of retarded children who did not technically fill the criteria for certification as feeble-minded. This group was estimated to include about 10 per cent of the population, but could not under existing

Development of procedures

legislation be admitted to special schools as they were not mentally defective. The committee's recommendations, published as the Report of the Joint Departmental Committee on Mental Deficiency (Board of Education and Board of Control 1929), were that certification of the feeble-minded should be abolished, so that the feeble-minded and the retarded might be catered for in one comprehensive scheme. The report referred to children who were 'educable in a true sense' but could not benefit from an ordinary school; thus the group we would now know as SLD was deliberately excluded. The committee hoped, however, that abolition of certification would remove the lifelong stigma attached to attendance at a school for the feeble-minded and enable parents to feel that they were being offered 'a helpful variation of the ordinary school'.

With what could be seen as commendable far-sightedness they hoped that rural areas and small towns would establish special classes (as there would be an insufficient number of children for a special school), but that even in the large towns there would be special classes for less severely retarded children in ordinary schools. As always, the recommendations could be interpreted more than one way.

The severely intellectually handicapped remained outside the education system altogether. This might be seen as reflecting the current state of knowledge about their education. There was little concept at the time of what might constitute a suitable educational programme. On the other hand, placing them in lifelong medical care also suited an ideology which saw them as a threat to the safety of society and regarded measures such as sterilisation as entirely appropriate. It is worth recalling that as late as the 1970s an eleven year-old girl's sterilisation by hysterectomy was recommended by a consultant paediatrician on purely social grounds and was prevented only by a High Court action brought by an educational psychologist (Johnson, 1975).

The recommended abolition of certification for children with what we might today term moderate learning difficulties was a welcome step forward. The emphasis, though, remained quite explicitly on establishing separate special schools or classes for these children. Moreover, the committee anticipated the expansion in separate remedial deparments in its recommendation for special classes for less retarded children in ordinary schools. Here too the emphasis was on removal from the mainstream. Alongside the humanitarian concerns evident in the report there is an underlying theme of segregation and control.

For a variety of reasons, notably the depression of the 1930s, the Wood Committee's recommendations did not receive statutory recognition until the 1944 Education Act. It was in this Act that the structure of special education was based until the 1981 Act.

THE 1944 EDUCATION ACT

The 1944 Education Act was heavily influenced not only by the Wood Committee but also by the reports of committees which inquired into the education of partially hearing and partially sighted children (Board of Education 1934, 1938). All these reports called for special schools to be incorporated within the mainstream of the education system as a way of reducing the stigma atttached to attending them. Section 34 of the Act placed a duty on every LEA 'to ascertain what children in their area require special educational treatment', but other parts of the Act made clear that this need not be in special schools; indeed it was stated explicitly that special schools should be provided for children with serious disabilities, while those whose disability was less serious could be catered for in any maintained or assisted school. In practice this meant that special education could be provided in the ordinary classes of ordinary schools, not only in special classes of ordinary schools. The intention was laudable but, as we shall see later, it led to a number of anomalies.

Under Section 33 of the Act the Minister of Education (now called the Secretary of State for Education and Science) was empowered to issue regulations regarding the categories of pupils requiring special education with additional recommendations on the appropriate provision for each category. In fact, the 1945 Regulations (Ministry of Education 1945) recognised eleven categories of handicap: educationally subnormal, blind, deaf, epileptic, partially sighted, partially deaf, physically handicapped, delicate, diabetic, children with speech defects, and the maladjusted.

Of these only the ESN and the maladjusted directly concern us here. The term 'feeble-minded' ceased to have any administrative significance, at least so far as school-age children were concerned, and children who were *retarded* in their educational attainments were included with the generally backward in the new concept of *educational* subnormality. In other words *any* child whose educational attainments fell significantly below the norm could be included, whatever her developmental level in other respects. As we shall see in more detail in the next chapter, this definition included some 10 to 14 per cent of the school population. Indeed, this proportion must have been included since the criteria for selection were to be relative rather than absolute, a point which is considered in more detail later in this chapter.

The 1945 Regulations issued under the 1944 Act (Ministry of Education 1945) placed a *duty* on LEAs for the first time to provide special education for maladjusted children. Official recognition of the needs of the maladjusted had been granted in the 1930s in financial support for the pioneer child guidance clinics; in addition the 1921

Education Act enabled a few conscientious authorities to pay the fees of maladjusted children attending voluntary homes or schools on the grounds that they were empowered by the rather vague wording of Section 80 to cater for children's health and physical education. Following evacuation of children from inner city areas during the Second World War the authorities became painfully aware that many could not or would not conform to the expectations and requirements of the families on whom they were billeted. Just as it took the Boer War to persuade the authorities that something must be done about the health of the nation's children (it was very inconvenient that only one in every three potential recruits was physically fit enough to be enlisted), so it took evacuation and billeting in the Second World War to persuade them to recognise the needs of the disturbed, or perhaps simply disturbing, children who could not or would not cope with a 'normal' education or family life. Under the 1945 Regulations special schools and 'boarding homes' could be approved by the Minister.

ADMINISTRATIVE PROCEDURES IN SELECTION

The Act abolished certification of 'mentally defective' or 'feeble-minded' children but retained the possibility for LEAs to compel a child to attend a special school. Education had to be appropriate to 'age, ability and aptitude', so if an authority could only provide this in a special school it was logical that it should be given the power to fulfil its responsibilities. Section 34 of the Act stated that the medical officer who had examined the child should, 'if required by the parent or by the authority to do so, issue to the authority and to the parent a certificate in the prescribed form showing whether the child is suffering from any such disability as aforesaid and, if so, the nature and extent thereof'. This seems to be perfectly clear; the authority was empowered, but not compelled to request a formal certificate of ascertainment. Yet to make the point absolutely explicit, Section 34 continued:

> Provided that a local education authority shall not require the issue of such a certificate in respect of any child unless the certificate is, in their opinion, necessary for the purposes of securing the attendance of the child at a special school in accordance with the provision of this Act relating to compulsory attendance at primary and secondary schools.

From this wording it is clear that formal ascertainment should have been needed only when a child's parents wished to resist the LEA's decision to provide special education. Unfortunately many authorities ignored both the letter and the spirit of the Act by formally ascertaining *all* children as suffering from one of the statutory categories of handicap before placing them in a special school. Prior to 1944 medical officers could make the educational decision that a child should attend a special school by the simple act of certifying him mentally defective. For over thirty years after 1944 they continued in many areas to do exactly the same, signing the necessary certificate (Form 1HP) after completing Forms 2HP, 3HP, or 4HP (see below). Hence formal ascertainment replaced certification and the elements of compulsion and stigma remained largely unaltered in spite of occasional efforts by the Ministry to alter the situation. The problem arose to some extent from genuine confusion over the forms issued by the Ministry for completion by medical officers. The first of these, Form 1HP, was the certificate prescribed for use when the authority wished to enforce attendance at a special school. However, 1HP went further than the 1944 Act intended by calling on doctors to make an educational judgement by certifying the category or categories of handicap in which they believed the child should be placed. The remaining forms were not statutory; they were: From 2HP ('report on a child examined for a disability of mind'); Form 3HP ('report by headteacher on a backward child'); Form 4HP ('report on delicate or physically handicapped pupil'); and Form 5HP ('handicapped children of parents serving in the Armed Forces'). A further confusing factor was the statutory nature of the medical examination; since the examination was one which imposed a legal obligation on parents it seemed anomalous not to complete the process by issuing the prescribed certificate if the results indicated a need for special education.

Another problem concerned the role in the assessment process of teachers and of educational psychologists. This problem was recognised both by educationalists and by senior medical officers. The Chief Medical Officer of the Ministry of Education suggested in 1958, for example, that recommendations on the admission of children to an ESN(M) school should be the responsibility of a panel comprising a school medical officer, a representative of the Chief Education Officer, an educational psychologist and the head of the present and/or proposed school. In 1961 the Ministry of Education went a stage further by issuing a circular to all LEAs on special educational treatment for educationally subnormal pupils. The circular recognised that the formal procedures set out in Section 34 of the 1944 Act were not legally necessary providing the parents agreed to a special school place for their child: 'There need . . . be no formality about the offer of a place in a special school if the child needs it or about his admission if the parents accept such an offer, although it is essential to ensure that the parents know that the minimum leaving age from a special school is sixteen.' (The latter was a piece of 'positive discrimination' in the 1944 Act which caused intense resentment among those it was intended to help; a majority of children in schools for

Development of procedures

ESN(M) and maladjusted children have always come from Social Classes IV and V, for whom another year of compulsory schooling increased what they often regarded as the stigma of special education.)

Unfortunately Circular 11/61 went on to recommend that the medical examination prior to admission, which it rightly regarded as essential, should be held in the formal manner prescribed by Section 34. The effect of this recommendation was to reduce the influence of other suggestions in the circular regarding the importance of teachers' views and those of educational psychologists; in many areas LEAs refused to appoint educational psychologists who might offer more specialist advice on the *educational* needs of handicapped and problem children and left responsibility for selection (with formal ascertainment a frequent result) largely in the hands of medical officers. As a result it gradually became clear that the procedures for selecting children for special education needed a more radical overhaul.

This was carried out in another circular, issued by the DES in 1975, which set out to clarify the uncertainty which had arisen 'about the circumstances in which medical examinations can be controlled without formal procedures and about the status of examinations by an educational psychologist'. The circular advised that formal medical examinations prescribed in Section 34 should no longer be held except in the extremely rare cases where parents resisted the local authority's decision that their child should attend a special school. This did not mean that medical examinations should cease, but simply that they should take place at an early stage in an informal atmosphere in which the child's needs could be fully discussed with the parents. Further, the circular recommended that the medical examination should precede assessment by an educational psychologist, and that the educational psychologist should be the person responsible 'for conveying to the authority a recommendation about the nature of the special education required and where it should be provided'. The old Forms 1HP to 5HP were withdrawn and replaced by a new series: Form SE1 (for completion by the child's teacher); Form SE2 (for completion by a school doctor); Form SE3 (for completion by an educational psychologist); Form SE4 (a summary and return sheet describing the needs of a child requiring special education); Form SE5 (containing the essential elements of Form 1HP, for use only when the authority wished to enforce attendance against a parent's will); and Form SE6 (an up-to-date version of form 5HP about handicapped children of parents serving in the Armed Forces).

Circular 2/75 formed the administrative basis for the selection of children for special education until the 1981 Education Act created an entirely new framework. Although the circular lacked statutory force, it was implemented, at least in part, by most LEAs. In theory its effect was to ensure that decisions regarding special education were made on educational rather than medical grounds. In practice this was not always the case, as medical or ancillary resources were often based in special schools. The child had, therefore, to attend the special school in order to benefit from the resources, even if her educational needs could have been better met in an ordinary school.

The circular overcame none of the problems concerning the use of IQ or personality tests in the selection process, nor did it resolve anomalies and inconsistencies in the concept of maladjustment (See Ch. 2). What it did achieve was to broaden the scope of assessment processes, and place greater emphasis on the child's educational needs. Medical diagnoses could then be considered strictly in the light of their implications for the child's future teaching. This, of course, meant that children should be placed in special schools because the special school could offer them something more than an ordinary school and not simply because they had a medical condition or an IQ below 70. The emphasis was clearly shifting from medical to educational needs.

THE WARNOCK REPORT

BACKGROUND

Circular 2/75 was seen from the outset as an interim measure. It reflected a growing consensus among administrators, doctors, educational psychologists and teachers that the framework for special education in the 1944 Act had outlived its usefulness. The circular introduced new procedures for selection, thereby giving greater prominence to educational criteria. It did not, and could not, change the underlying legislative framework, but rather attempted to bypass it by reserving formal ascertainment for the tiny minority of children whose parents opposed their transfer to a special school. In this respect the circular also reflected: (a) a growing respect for parents' rights to be actively involved in decisions about their children; (b) a feeling that everyone concerned – teachers in ordinary and in special schools as well as children – would benefit from easy and informal transfer between the two systems.

This was the climate in which the Warnock Committee started its work. It was in fact in November 1974, before the publication of Circular 2/75, that Margaret Thatcher, then Secretary of State for Education and Science, announced that she proposed to appoint a committee:

to review educational provision in England, Scotland and Wales for children and young people handicapped by disabilities of body or mind, taking account of the medical aspects of their needs, together with arrangements to prepare them for entering into employment; to consider the most effective use of resources for these purposes; and to make recommendations.

The committee was appointed with Mary Warnock in the chair, and submitted its report four years later (DES 1978a). Members of the committee were appointed by the Secretary of State who presumably took advice from HMI and from senior civil servants in the DES. Only one of the committee's twenty-six members was a parent of a handicapped child. In spite of the disproportionate number of children from ethnic minorities in special schools, no black person served on the committee. Nor did any handicapped person. Indeed almost the only non-specialist outside the civil service, the teaching profession, and the ancillary or support services was the chairperson, an Oxford philosophy don. The committee's membership reflected the prevalent view that decisions on special education were best left to professionals. Consumers, in the form of parents or young people, could not be expected to know what was best for their children.

From the outset it was inevitable that the committee would face massive, and often conflicting, demands from the multitude of interests involved in special education. The committee must also have had to take account of the government's own thinking about special education. Circular 2/75 could be seen as a polite way of saying: 'we can't wait while you deliberate; we've got to do something about the system now'. Even more obviously, Section 10 of the 1976 Education Act required special education to be provided in ordinary schools unless this would be impracticable, incompatible with the efficiency of the school, or would involve unreasonable public expenditure. Although Section 10 was never implemented it very clearly signalled to the committee the government's intentions towards a highly contentious subject.

INTEGRATION

The committee took the qualifications on integration in Section 10 as indicating concern for the quality of special education as well as the location. The report argued that special schools would continue to be needed for three groups. In summary these were as follows:

1. Children with severe or complex physical, sensory or intellectual disabilities.
2. Children with severe emotional or behavioural disorders.
3. Children with less severe disabilities who do not perform well in an ordinary school.

Without coming down firmly against any kind of integration, the committee could hardly have been less enthusiastic in its support for integration. There was never any doubt that *every* child ever admitted to special schools under the 1944 Act could have been included in at least one of the groups for whom special schools would continue to be needed. The effect of the committee's recommendation was to hold out the faint possibility of integration for children whose parents were sufficiently well informed and articulate to insist on it. In practice this meant children with physical and sensory disabilities, whose parents could draw on the support of determined independent pressure groups. For most children with learning and adjustment difficulties no such support was available. For them there was never any rational basis for a belief that the Warnock Report recommendation would lead to increased integration in ordinary schools. Indeed the reverse was the case since two out of the three groups for whom continued special schooling was anticipated consisted of children with behavioural problems and children who 'do not perform well in an ordinary school'. This point becomes clearer by considering Warnock's terminology.

CONCEPT OF SPECIAL EDUCATIONAL NEED AND TERMINOLOGY

The committee was concerned with three broad areas of special educational need. The first centred on provision of special means of access to the curriculum. For example, a deaf child will need some form of specialist teaching in receptive and expressive language. The second area was the need for 'a special or modified curriculum' and the third for 'particular attention to the social structure and emotional climate in which education takes place'.

The committee recommended abolition of the categories recognised under the 1944 Education Act, and their replacement with the generic concept of learning difficulties. In this way attention would focus explicitly on the child's *educational* needs. The reason, of course, was that medical disability and educational need could not be equated in the manner implied by the statutory categories. From an educational point of view a child who has permanently injured his writing hand may be more handicapped than a paraplegic child. Not only were the statutory categories illogical; they did not fit many of the pupils shown to have special educational needs.

Learning difficulties, according to Warnock, should be distinguished between mild, moderate and severe. The moderate and severe approximated broadly to the existing special school population, whereas children with mild learning difficulties would be found in every ordinary school. The committee concluded after reviewing the research that up to 20 per cent of children would have some form of special educational need at some stage in their school career.

Oddly, while rejecting the term ESN, the committee decided to retain the equally objectionable label of maladjusted, on the grounds that 'the implication of this term (namely that behaviour can sometimes be meaningfully considered only in relation to the circumstances in which it occurs) is an advantage rather than a disadvantage'. While this is certainly true, it overlooks the fact that in practice the term has seldom been used in this discriminating way. Instead it had become, and remained, a label useful principally for the purposes of removing children to special schools.

Perhaps the committee's problem lay in finding a suitable alternative word to describe the children currently regarded as maladjusted. It is also possible, though, that the retention of the term reflected an ideological belief that teachers in ordinary schools should not be expected to cope with troublesome pupils. That, certainly, seems to be behind the caveat that special schools would continue to be needed for children with severe emotional or behavioural problems.

The committee could have adopted the easy, and honest, solution of calling these children 'disturbing' rather than 'maladjusted'. By definition, children who are called maladjusted or disturbed attract these labels because they have disturbed adults. The adult's disturbance may be at the level of frustration or anxiety at not 'getting through to' the child, or it may be sheer physical fear of violence. The term 'disturbing' implies a recognition of the children's effects on adults, while the terms maladjusted and disturbed are too often taken to imply psychological or social characteristics in the child. The committee appeared to give little serious thought to the alternative possibility that children's behaviour might to a considerable extent reflect their experiences at school (see Ch. 7).

Warnock's emphasis on recognising and meeting special educational needs merely continued the humanitarian tradition in special education. Yet all traditions have their own ideologies which are based on premises which should not go unquestioned. The Warnock Commitee recommendations on children with learning and adjustment difficulties held out no realistic hope of increased integration. Consciously or otherwise, they were based on an ideology which considered the removal from ordinary schools of pupils presenting educational or behavioural problems necessary for the good of all concerned. This ideology in turn was based on a view which sought the causes of learning or behavioural problems in the child and/or in the child's family background rather than in the child's social and educational experiences at school.

These are not, of course, incompatible. In our view it is as misguided to ignore the possible importance of cognitive factors in the child or social factors or the child's background as to ignore the importance of the school's social and educational climate. The points we wish to emphasise are simply: (a) that the importance of school factors in the origin of learning and behavioural problems was consistently under-estimated in the report; and (b) that the report held out no realistic prospect of integration for these children; if anything the extended concept of special educational need should have been expected to result in increased numbers in separate special schools or classes. This, then, was the background to the 1981 Education Act.

THE 1981 EDUCATION ACT: AN OVERVIEW

The 1981 Education Act was the government's response to the Warnock Report and provides an entirely new legislative basis for special educational provision. The Act does not specify *how* special needs should be met. In this sense, like most education law, it is enabling rather than prescriptive. In retrospect two broad aims can be seen to underpin virtually every aspect of the Act:

1. To reflect the current conventional wisdom on what constituted good practice, with particular reference to the Warnock Report.
2. To do so without allocating any extra money from public funds.

The Act abolished the categories of handicap recognised under the 1944 Education Act, replacing them with the generic concept of special educational need. It also acknowledged Warnock's extended concept of special needs encompassing up to 20 per cent of the school population. Elaborate new procedures were laid down for assessment and for specifying how children's special needs should be met.

In this connection an important feature of the Act was to *require* LEAs to identify children with special needs. In addition the Act required governors of all maintained and voluntary schools 'to use their best endeavours' to ensure that teachers recognised a child's special needs and were able to make the necessary provision to meet them. This was the first time that a formal obligation for special education had been placed on ordinary schools. Parents were given new and explicit rights to participate in the process of assessment, and to appeal against the LEA's decisions concerning their child. The Act acknowledged the principle of integration by requiring that a child's special needs should be met in ordinary schools except in certain specified circumstances. In addition, children attending an ordinary school were to 'engage in the activities of the school together with children who do not have special educational needs' as far as was 'reasonably practical'.

The Act has been hailed by Mary Warnock (1982) as 'a great step forward'. Is it? In the next section we discuss some of the tensions and anomalies arising from the Act.

WHOSE SPECIAL EDUCATIONAL NEEDS?

ATTRIBUTING SPECIAL NEED

Superficially the statement that a backward reader has special educational needs is not controversial. Clearly the child 'needs' special help in reading. The position is less straightforward, though, than it appears. In general special educational needs are identified by teachers, usually without consulting children. Formal assessment under the 1981 Act requires teachers to comment on the child's own perception of her needs. In practice this section is usually left blank, or filled with some bland comment such as: 'the child will do what is best for him', or: 'the child is not in any position to make a reasonable decision'. Thus, attempts to include children's perceptions of their own needs are often left entirely to the discretion of the teachers and other professionals involved. The problem, though, goes deeper than this.

'NEEDS' AND 'WANTS'

Logically, a person cannot say he needs something without in some sense also wanting it. I might say that I need dental treatment but don't want it. Yet even here, the fact that I claim to 'need' the treatment implies that I want to be free of the discomfort that lack of treatment is causing me or may cause me in the future. In the same way, when teachers talk of a child having special educational needs they are necessarily referring, often in very general terms, to something *they* want to be provided on the child's behalf.

To complicate matters still further, a teacher's statement that a child has special needs is unlikely to be based solely on observation of the child's progress or behaviour. Quite legitimately the teacher may feel that the child's presence is having a detrimental effect on other children in the class. Hence, the basis for claiming that the *child* has special needs may be logically independent of any aspect of the child's progress or behaviour. In these circumstances the *individual child's* progress or behaviour may be little more than a *post hoc* rationalisation of the *teacher's* absolutely reasonable concern about the progress of *other* children. Logically, the teacher's concern about these other children implies a wish to give them more time and attention. The points at issue here are simply:

17

1. When teachers say that a child has special educational needs they are implying that they want something to happen.
2. Their wishes may not coincide with those of the children themselves or of their parents, who may see their needs in a different light.
3. The teacher's conclusions may be based on the interests of other children, not of the children labelled as having special needs.

These points become clearer when we look at the Act's assessment procedures.

ASSESSMENTS AND STATEMENTS: A BUREAUCRAT'S DREAM?

Both the advice the LEA must obtain when assessing a child under the 1981 Education Act and the sequence of procedures to be followed are specified in detail. Teachers, parents, doctors and members of the education support services may request a child's formal assessment. Parents must be given the chance to object, unless, of course, they make the request. Having decided to accept the request, the LEA has to obtain written requests from the child's teachers, a school medical officer and an educational psychologist. If other agencies are involved they should also be invited to comment. The reports are supposed to indicate the nature of a child's needs, but not to specify precisely how or where they should be met.

An officer of the LEA then has to collate all the reports and decide whether to prepare a 'Statement' indicating the special educational provision that should be made for the child. Parents can appeal against a decision not to issue a Statement. Having decided to issue one, though, the LEA must prepare a draft for consideration by the child's parents who can make representations about its content. The draft must include copies of the reports from the school, the school medical officer and the educational psychologist. Having considered the parents' representations, or ascertained that they are happy with the draft, the LEA prepares the final statement either in its original form or amended. If they are still not satisfied, the parents can then appeal to a local Appeals Committee. This has no power to overrule the LEA's recommendations in the Statement, but can ask the LEA to reconsider them. If this fails parents may, as a last resort, appeal to the Secretary of State for Education and Science.

The amount of paper-work in this process is staggering. Any parents who go through all the appeal procedures will receive over fifty letters in connection with their child's assessment. This naturally does not include all the correspondence within the LEA, for example from administrators to school medical officers and educational psychologists requesting them to carry out an assessment. The implication is clearly that the Act may be creating new layers of bureaucracy without corresponding educational benefits. One early report suggests strongly that this is the case.

Adams (1984) studied the way nine LEAs had implemented the Act during its first year of operation. The main thrust of his study did not criticise the content of the new procedures. Instead he drew attention to their elaborate nature and their time-consuming requirements. Most LEAs were making little attempt to restructure or extend special educational provision in ordinary schools in order to reduce the number of pupils put forward for assessment because of their inability to cope, either socially or educationally. Their priority seemed rather to be to maintain the *status quo* at a time of acute government imposed restrictions on local authority spending. Consequently the major task was to establish a system for administering the Act. One LEA provided no extra resources for this. Another, at the other end of the spectrum, appointed three extra educational psychologists, one adviser, additional teachers, clerical and auxiliary staff, and no fewer than six administrative staff. Of these only the psychologists would have been actively involved in actually assessing children. The adviser would presumably have been involved in preparation of Statements and in discussion of difficult cases. The six administrators would have been occupied mainly in sorting out all the paper-work.

ASSESSMENTS AND STATEMENTS: A PARENT'S NIGHTMARE?

THE RIGHT TO PARTICIPATE

We have already outlined the rights of parents to initiate, or object to, their child's assessment, to comment on the draft Statement and to appeal against the Statement which the LEA eventually issues. The Act gives them the right to copies of professionals' reports on their child. In addition they can be present at all stages in the assessment process except in the cases of: 'assessment over a time in the classroom or other setting' and: 'some forms of psychological testing that may need to be carried out without the presence of observers, including parents'. Yet the Act is far from being a parent's charter.

Formal assessments and Statements are obligatory only in the case of children in designated special schools or classes. In many LEAs teachers only request an assessment when they think special schooling may be appropriate. This poses a dilemma for parents. If they request assessment, the LEA is not likely to refuse. In practice, many LEAs are unlikely to issue a draft Statement unless special schooling is considered appropriate. There are two main reasons.

1. Placing a child with a Statement in an ordinary school may commit the LEA to providing that school with additional resources, which may be unavailable, or available only in special schools.
2. Accepting a child with a Statement commits the headteacher to review his progress each year, and potentially involves him and his staff in considerable extra work. Without an assurance of support from the LEA, many heads may be unwilling to accept the child.

Parents who want their child's special needs to be met in the ordinary school may find formal assessment a risky business. Far from securing additional resources for their child in the mainstream they may end up with a Statement specifying education in a special school. Moreover the Statement will be legally binding unless reversed following an appeal.

Even when present at parts of their child's assessment, parents are at a disadvantage. The DES (1983) guidelines contain a checklist for professionals to bear in mind, with three main headings: (a) description of the child's functioning; (b) the aims of special educational provision; and (c) the facilities and resources necessary to provide it.

From a parent's point of view there are two problems. First, much of the 'description of the child's functioning' will be based on the teacher's and possibly the educational psychologist's observation in the classroom, to which they have no access. Second, and more serious, the assessment process focuses almost exclusively on the child, apparently taking for granted the school or classroom context in which the child's needs have become apparent. Parents are hardly in a position to comment on ways in which the school or the teacher may have contributed to the child's problems. Yet this contribution may be the crucial factor (see Ch. 7).

RETURN TO THE MAINSTREAM

Nor does the Act offer any comfort to parents whose children are attending special schools and wish them to transfer to the mainstream. Indeed the reverse is the case. Between publication of the DES circular on discovery and assessment of children requiring special education in 1975 and implementation of the 1981 Education Act in 1983, the overwhelming majority of children entering and leaving special schools did so on an informal basis. The circular explicitly advised against formal ascertainment under the 1944 Act unless the LEA wished to enforce special school attendance against the parents' wishes. Following assessment children were admitted to special schools informally by mutual agreement between their parents and the LEA. They could return to the mainstream on the same basis. If parents wished to insist on return to the mainstream they could simply remove their child. The LEA would then have to place the child in an ordinary school or carry out a formal ascertainment in order to enforce special school attendance. Local education authorities seldom followed the second course.

The 1981 Act reversed the trend towards the informal and flexible use of resources that had gradually been developing since 1944. Parents no longer have the right to remove their child from a special school without the LEA's agreement. As this does not apply to parents of children in ordinary schools it appears discriminatory. Nor can return to the mainstream now be arranged on a simple informal basis. Instead return must be preceded by a formal reassessment, using the same elaborate, complex procedures as the original assessment. Far from promoting integration, the Act's assessment procedures make it more difficult.

INTEGRATION

One of the odder pieces of mythology to surround the 1981 Education Act is that it encourages integration. Even the most cursory reading will show that while it empowers LEAs to integrate children with special needs, it does not encourage, let alone require, them to do so. The Act says that children's special needs should be met in ordinary schools subject to:

1. Parental wishes.
2. The possibility of meeting the child's needs in an ordinary school.
3. 'Provision of efficient education for the children with whom he will be educated'.
4. 'The efficient use of resources'.

The last two of these clauses could have been invoked for every child ever placed in every special school in the country. Once an LEA has separate special schools, it is obviously 'inefficient' not to use them, especially as they cannot be closed without the Secretary of State's approval. Further, many children with learning or adjustment problems are referred for assessment *because* of their effect on other children. By thus encouraging LEAs, albeit indirectly, to maintain the *status quo* the Act may effectively discourage them from considering how 'efficient education' might be provided for *all* children in the mainstream.

COMMENT

The 1981 Act continues the humanitarian tradition of concern for children with special needs which can be traced back to the first special schools at the end of the last century. When discussing the Warnock Report we concluded that all traditions have their own ideologies, which should not go unquestioned. They also have their 'hidden agenda'.

Tomlinson (1982) notes that A. F. Tredgold could support euthenasia for idiots and imbeciles yet dedicated his book on *Mental Deficiency* in 1908 to 'all those of sound mind who are interested in the welfare of their less fortunate fellow creatures'. The contradictions today are just as stark. A major government report followed by an Eduction Act received widespread acclaim as important contributions to the educational well-being of children with special needs. Both are widely, if not quite unanimously, believed not only to encourage the principle that children with special needs should be educated in ordinary schools, but also to have resulted in this actually happening. Numerically by far the largest groups of children with special needs are those with moderate learning difficulties (who include the former ESN(M)) and with adjustment difficulties (the former maladjusted and/or disruptive). Yet neither the Warnock Report nor the 1981 Education Act held out any immediate prospect of integration for these groups.

In one sense this was probably inevitable. Most education law in Britain, as we have noted, is broadly enabling rather than narrowly prescriptive. It reflects a general consensus on good practice, but does not tell LEAs how to run their schools and even allows considerable latitude for choice in the types of school that are provided. Compared with most other countries Britain has a decentralised education system. A strength of this system lies in the scope for variation and innovation within it. Giving LEAs clear criteria for assessing children's special needs was presumably seen as no more than formalising good practice. To tell LEAs how and where to meet the needs they identified would have been a different matter altogether. Indeed, this could have been virtually impossible given the regional variations in the quantity and quality of special education services.

The Act, then, remained faithful to the traditions of British educational legislation. As a result it provided loop-holes which enabled LEAs to conform to the letter of the law while ignoring what may have been the underlying intentions. Local education authorities should not be unduly criticised for their lack of response. The Act imposed major additional burdens on professional and administrative services that were already over-stretched. Yet Parliament provided no additional funds to help LEAs to respond constructively.

The problem for the 1981 Education Act, and for the children whose needs it was designed to meet, is a deceptively simply one. Conforming to the letter of the law is not particularly difficult provided essentially administrative procedures are followed. These procedures have implications for school and classroom practice, but as we have argued elsewhere neither LEAs nor individual schools will have much difficulty in evading them (Galloway 1985b). The intentions behind the Act, however, require a wide-ranging review within each LEA of responses to the 20 per cent of children considered to have special needs. Parliament did not, and arguably could not, legislate for this. Any major policy changes such as a decision to educate children with learning and adjustment difficulties in ordinary classes of ordinary schools rather than special schools or units, needs a decision in the education committee of each LEA.

The Act undoubtedly provides a helpful framework for any LEA wishing to adopt an integration policy. The statement of a child's special needs may even be seen as a way of ensuring that appropriate resources are provided, though this is easily evaded as formal assessment is only mandatory for children in designated schools or units. Unfortunately, few LEAs have availed themselves of the opportunity implicit in the Act to carry out a wide-ranging and critical review of their existing provision. We discuss some of the reasons later (see Chs. 5 and 6). There is, however, one initiative which must be mentioned here.

When they were elected in 1981, members of the Inner London Education Authority (ILEA) committed themselves to a review of under-achievement in education, with particular reference to working-class children and to girls. As part of this review they set up three committees of inquiry. The first was a review of secondary schools (ILEA 1984), the second of primary schools (ILEA 1985b) and the third of special schools (ILEA 1985a).

THE FISH REPORT (ILEA 1985a)

With John Fish, a former HMI staff inspector for special education in the chair, the brief of this third committee set up by ILEA was:

> To review the range, quality and coherence of provision to meet special educational needs in the Authority . . . particularly in the light of the Warnock Report and the 1981 Education Act and the Authority's initiative to promote equal opportunities and combat under-achievement of children from all backgrounds . . . (p. 1).

The emphasis in these terms of reference on equal opportunities and under-achievement provides a context which was strikingly absent from the Warnock Report and from the 1981 Education Act. Without being explicit, they implied: (a) that existing special education services might not be providing pupils with the same opportunities that they might have in the mainstream; (b) that the well-documented disproportionate representation in special schools of boys and of minority ethnic groups might reflect unequal opportunities; (c) that the need for special education might result from under-achievement.

The importance of the report here lies in its unambiguous statement of underlying principles. The committee was quite clear that:

> The aims of education for children and young people with disabilities and significant difficulties are the same as those for all children and young people. . . . Disabilities and significant difficulties do not diminish the right to equal access to, and participation in, society (para. 1.1.22).

It followed from this statement that equal opportunities to participate in and contribute to society should be provided irrespective of children's special educational needs, as well as of their race, social class and gender. The committee was equally explicit in recognising that:

> Disabilities and difficulties become more or less handicapping depending on the expectations of others and on social contexts (para. 1.1.25).

Special school placement, clearly, cannot provide equal opportunity to participate in and contribute to the life and work of an ordinary school. The committee was in no doubt that the proper place to educate children with special needs was the ordinary school, asking rather pointedly: 'If the Authority strongly endorses the comprehensive principle, why has it no stated policy on the integration of children and young people with special educational needs in schools and colleges for all?' (para. 3.16.8). The report recognised, though, that children could be socially isolated in ordinary as well as in special schools. To be effective, integration requires that the child should as far as possible be taught in an ordinary class and that any additional provision should be directed towards this aim. Teachers, though, would need support in coping with new demands. A key recommendation was that:

> . . . all teachers accept responsibility for meeting as far as possible the special educational needs which may arise in their classrooms and be enabled to do so in collaboration with the network of advisory and support services available to them (para. 3.16.20).

We shall return to the Fish Report later. Some of its detailed recommendations, particularly the education of children with adjustment difficulties, lacked the coherence and clarity of the underlying principles and aims. The report has nevertheless provided an impressive and detailed framework within which the ILEA could plan radical changes in the education of all children with special educational needs. There is no reason to doubt that these changes would be consistent both with the letter and with the spirit of the 1981 Education Act.

CONCLUSIONS

The Inner London Education Authority's response to the Fish Report will presumably become apparent gradually. The wide-ranging changes which the report calls for will require lengthy negotiations with all interested groups, with the consequent possibility of compromise and delay. The fact remains that ILEA's elected members have welcomed the report, and have thus taken the first step in a radical re-orientation of special education policy. Few other LEAs have got as far. We know of none which has so publicly or so comprehensively reviewed their policies for meeting special educational needs. Nor do we know of any which have so firmly adapted a commitment to equal opportunities and opposition to discrimination.

So far we have asserted, without providing evidence, that neither the Warnock Report nor the 1981 Education Act was likely to lead to increasing integration in ordinary schools for children with learning and adjustment difficulties. We have also implied that as a result these children have been badly served both by Warnock and by the Act. These assumptions should not go unquestioned. In the next chapter we consider whether there is any evidence that separate special schools and units are now less numerous than in the pre-Warnock era. In Chapter 3 we ask whether children benefit from attending them.

Chapter two

PREVALENCE: DO TWENTY PER CENT OF CHILDREN REALLY HAVE SPECIAL EDUCATIONAL NEEDS?

INTRODUCTION

Probably the most widely remembered recommendation in the Warnock Report is that services for children with special educational needs should be based on the assumption that up to 20 per cent will require special help at some stage in their school career. It is known that no more than 2 per cent of these children have ever been placed in recognised special schools or classes. We also know that educational backwardness and behavioural problems are by far the most frequent reasons for placement. It is clear that these are also the problems presented by a majority of pupils with special needs who remain in ordinary schools. Nevertheless, our analysis of information from special school rolls will show that the steady increase in special school placements since 1944 has continued since the Warnock Report and introduction of the 1981 Act.

Commendably, the Warnock Committee was also concerned with other pupils, for example pupils who might be under-achieving, even though their overall level was well above average. It is clear, though, from the research on which the committee based its conclusions that backwardness and problem behaviour accounted for a large majority of children considered to have special needs. In this chapter we describe some of the major studies.

We argue that some of these studies have made a valuable contribution to our understanding of learning and behavioural problems. On the other hand, in arguing that up to 20 per cent of children may have special educational needs, both Warnock and the architects of the 1981 Education Act reached a conclusion that is not justified by the research. We argue that the conclusion was essentially a political one, based on a statistical artefact. In the second half of the chapter we review some of the research on these children, with particular reference to medical factors that may contribute to the problems they present and to social factors in their families. We show that the children come overwhelmingly from working-class and socially disadvantaged families with a disproportionate representation of minority ethnic groups.

EVIDENCE FROM SPECIAL SCHOOL ROLLS

THE POLITICS OF 'DISCOVERY'

In theory, admission to special schools for children with moderate learning difficulties has never been based solely, or even primarily, on IQ. As early as 1953, Regulation 14 of the Ministry of Education's School Health Service and Handicapped Pupils Regulations defined ESN pupils as those who 'by reason of limited ability or other conditions resulting in educational retardation require some specialised form of education wholly or partly in substitution for the education normally given in ordinary schools'. Thus the term was explicitly intended to include children whose educational attainments were retarded for reasons *other* than lack of cognitive ability. With great optimism the Ministry had earlier suggested that special educational treatment would be appropriate for any children whose educational attainments lagged 20 per cent or more behind the average for their age.

One wonders whether the Minister and his advisers recognised the number of children for whom they were recommending a statutory form of special education. It would have taken (and in spite of subsequent increase in provision would still take) a tiny proportion of the children covered by this definition to fill every recognised special school or class. Hence, school medical officers, and later educational psychologists resorted to the principle of supply and demand. In other words, children were 'discovered' only after a supply of places had become available.

This last statement is not quite true. Children could also be 'discovered' as a political weapon to induce a reluctant authority to increase its provision. Once a child was ascertained under the 1944 Education Act, the LEA was legally obliged to provide the appropriate form of special schooling. By ascertaining more children than could be catered for in existing special schools, an LEA could be induced to consider opening new ones. What tended to happen in practice was the demand tended fairly consistently to exceed supply, but only by a moderate amount.

Professionals, as we argue later in the book, are themselves subject to powerful pressures from their employers to work within the constraints of the existing system. Professionals who frequently cause their employers embarrassment by recommending facilities that do not exist locally rapidly become unpopular, and are seen as unrealistic, even disruptive. On the other hand, moderate requests for additional places in special schools or classes are seen as constructive for at least three reasons: (a) they draw attention to needs which are not currently being met, but without too seriously upsetting the LEA's *status quo*; (b) implicitly they legitimise the LEA's decision to establish its existing special schools, since doctors or psychologists would only ask for more places if the present facilities were proving successful; (c) they strengthen the hand of special education administrators and advisers when demanding a larger share of resources.

There is nothing surprising, then, in the observation that demand for places in special schools or classes consistently outstrips supply. If we also consider the effect of pressure from hard-pressed teachers in ordinary schools, this becomes even more understandable. When the behaviour problems and learning difficulties of certain pupils are generating acute stress for them and their colleagues, headteachers would be less than human if they did not demand places in separate special schools or units. Yet they, too, are realistic, and consequently hesitate to make demands that might be rejected as exorbitant. This explains the wide regional variations in special school places.

REGIONAL VARIATIONS

These have always been very marked. In 1966 the number of children being educated or awaiting placement in special schools or classes, hostels, or hospital schools for the maladjusted ranged from 3.4 per 10,000 in the North of England to 28.3 per 10,000 for the metropolitan area of London (DES 1966).

With respect to Northerners, this must reflect more than regional variation in the incidence of maladjustment. The Warnock Report made clear that the situation had not changed, noting that in 1977 ten times as many children had been ascertained as maladjusted in one London borough as in another.

Though the range is smaller, regional variations are also evident in provision for children with moderate learning difficulties (DES 1966, 1978a). In Wales 2,262 children (49.9 per 10,000) were being educated, or were awaiting places in special schools or classes, while the comparable figure for the South East of England was 4,435 (92.1 per 10,000). The range was smaller than for maladjusted children. Only the North West region joined the South East in having more than 90 children per 10,000 in or awaiting places in ESN schools; in contrast the Eastern region of England had ascertained 5,056 pupils, representing a mere 59.9 per 10,000 children of school age. While not quoting regional rates for ESN(M) pupils specifically, the Warnock Report notes that ascertainment for special education – in which the ESN(M) was, of course, by far the largest single category – ranged from below 120 per 10,000 of the school population in a few rural areas to above 300 in a few large cities. The range was further shown from the fact that only 44 out of 105 authorities in England and Wales fell within a range 10 per cent above or below the average of 183.

The prevalence of special educational needs

Somewhat dryly, the report comments: 'Some of the variations between authorities may reflect variations in local policy and the strength of assessment services, but they also suggest a relationship between the rate of ascertainment and the availability of special provision.' While it is logically possible, though improbable in practice, that selection criteria might be consistent within each LEA, the regional variations make an absolute nonsense of any claim for consistent criteria between LEAs.

SPECIAL SCHOOL ROLLS

Numbers of children in primary, secondary and special schools are published annually. Until 1978 information from England and Wales was merged and published in the DES *Statistics of Education* series. Since 1978 figures for Wales have been published separately as *Statistics of Education in Wales*. Until 1984 figures were published for children in each category of handicap recognised under the 1944 Education Act. This enables us to make comparisions over a period of time. Since January 1984 a new, more complicated classification has been used which makes comparision with previous years impossible.

At the outbreak of the Second World War fewer than 17,000 children were receiving education in what were subsequently called ESN(M) schools. There were no recognised special schools for maladjusted children, though a handful was catered for under a clause of the 1921 Education Act. Special schools, as an expensive resource, suffered during the war, so that by 1946 there were only 11,000 children in ESN(M) schools. Figures for maladjusted and ESN(M) children from 1950 onwards are shown in Table 2.1. For the years 1978 and 1982 the figures are obtained by summing relevant data in the Welsh and the English statistics of Education.

TABLE 2.1: Full-time pupils in special schools for maladjusted and ESN(M) pupils in England and Wales

	1950	*1960*	*1965*	*1970*	*1974*	*1978*	*1982*
Maladjusted	587	1,742	2,904	6,093	11,583	14,406	14,017
ESN(M)	15,173	32,815	42,670	51,768	53,353	62,697	63,981

Sources: Department of Education & Science (1966, Table 36; 1977, Table 27; 1978, Table 24; 1982, Table A22/82); Welsh Office (1978b, Table 7.01; 1982, Table 7.01).

The minimal changes in special school enrolments between 1978 and 1982 must be seen against a marked decline in overall school rolls. Discussing figures for England, Swann (1985) shows that the proportion of children aged five to fifteen in ESN(M) schools actually increased by 13.5 per cent. In the case of ESN(M) children the increase was most marked among five-year-olds. Swann attributes this to:

> ... the expansion of nursery classes in special schools and other forms of preschool intervention which bring very young children to the attention of education authorities, notably home-visiting schemes based on the Portage Project. (p. 12)

In the case of maladjusted pupils the percentage increase was only slightly higher for primary pupils (12.1 per cent compared with 9.3 per cent for secondary pupils). Here, though, the figures are misleading as they do not include the growing number, mainly from secondary schools, who are placed in centres for disruptive pupils. In a survey in which just over half the LEAs cooperated, the Advisory Centre for Education (1980) found that 439 units had places for 6,791 pupils, or nearly half the total number of pupils in schools for the maladjusted in 1976. It seems highly probable that this form of provision will increase still further following the gradual phasing out of corporal punishment as a result of decisions in the European Court of Human Rights.

Swann shows that the increase in separate provision for children with moderate learning difficulties and with adjustment difficulties has not occured in the case of children with sensory disabilities. For these children, as for children categorised as delicate, epileptic or having speech defects, special school enrolments have declined. Overall, the conclusion is quite clear: at a time, according to popular rhetoric, of increasing integration, the opposite was occurring for the two largest groups for whom special schooling had been provided since 1944. This situation is unlikely to change as a result of the 1981 Education Act. Using information from seventy LEAs, the Advisory Centre for Education and the Spastics Society (1983) found that only 9 per cent anticipated a significant drop in special school enrolments. Even these LEAs thought the drop would apply mainly to children with sensory or physical disabilities.

THE SEMANTICS OF BEHAVIOURAL PROBLEMS

We have argued that the 'discovery' of children requiring special education generally follows the opening of a school or unit to cater for them. We are not, of course, arguing that opening a special school for children with adjustment problems created 'unmanageable' pupils who were previously contained satisfactorily in ordinary schools. Until the 1981 Act abolished the categories of handicap, there was, however, a very real sense in which the opening of a special school created *maladjusted* children, namely that maladjustment was neither a clinical diagnosis nor even a descriptive term but an administrative category. As Graham and Rutter (1970) pointed out, the chief purpose of the term 'has been to provide a label under which special education may be provided according to the *Handicapped Pupils and School Health Service Regulations* (Ministry of Education 1945, 1959)'. The 1945 Regulations defined maladjusted pupils as those 'who show evidence of emotional instability or psychological disturbance and who require special educational treatment in order to effect their personal, social and educational readjustment'. The problem was not simply that the terms 'emotional instability' and 'psychological disturbance' stood as much in need of clarification as 'maladjusted'; the definition implied, illogically, that special *educational* treatment was needed for some (but not all) children with the quasi-*medical* symptoms of emotional instability and psychological disturbance. Further, all teachers in special schools know many children whose disturbing behaviour can reasonably be viewed as a normal, or even healthy, reaction to highly abnormal and stressful conditions in their families or even in their previous schools. Not surprisingly, maladjustment is not recognised as a clinical condition in the most widely used systems for categorising children's psychiatric disorders.

Thus Rutter (1965) classified psychiatric disorders as either neurotic disorders, antisocial or conduct disorders, a mixed group in which both neurotic and conduct disorders are present, developmental disorders (such as enuresis or speech problems) the 'hyperkinetic syndrome', child psychosis, psychoses originating at or after puberty, mental subnormality, and educational retardation as a primary problem. Subsequently Rutter *et al.* (1974) proposed a three-part classification in which the first part related to the clinical psychiatric syndrome such as 'specific developmental disorder', 'neurotic disorder' or 'conduct disorder'; the second related to the child's intellectual level (regardless of aetiology); and the third noted any associated or aetiological factors, such as contributory medical factors, and environmental factors such as parental friction or lack of warmth towards the child. The Underwood Report (Ministry of Education 1955) could hardly avoid the issue by not using the term maladjustment (it was, after all, the Report of the Committee on Maladjusted Children). It anticipated Rutter's classification by grouping the 'symptoms' of maladjustment under six headings: nervous disorders; habit disorders; behaviour disorders; organic disorders; psychotic behaviour; educational and vocational difficulties. Stott (1971), too (from a psychologist's perspective), has sought to identify and describe types of maladjustment by means of teachers' or parents' completion of the Bristol Social Adjustment Guides. In the latest revision of the Bristol Guides behaviours are classified into two main groups: under-active behaviour, which includes problems such as depression, lack of energy, indifference to other people's opinions; and over-reactive behaviour, which includes hostility, 'showing off', distractibility.

The common point to emerge from medical and psychological attempts to classify behaviour disorders or describe types of 'maladjustment' is, as suggested in Chapter 1, that maladjustment is at best a ragbag term for describing *any* type of behaviour which teachers, psychologists or doctors find disturbing. This point is not invalidated by the discovery in recent years of another category of behaviour problem, namely the disruptive pupil.

We have already mentioned the flourishing industry in provision for these pupils. Here we need note only that there have never been any acceptable criteria for distinguishing maladjusted and disruptive pupils. Research on disruptive pupils, whether attending special units or ordinary schools, reveals a wide range of social, personal and education problems. Exactly the same is true of maladjusted pupils. In each case the label is no more than a vague description of the pupil's behaviour with an implication that it is disturbing to others. Every pupil admitted to units for the disruptive could equally well have been labelled maladjusted if it would have served any administrative or educational purpose to have done so. The reverse is not the case, as some pupils admitted to schools for the maladjusted could not appropriately have been placed in units for the disruptive. In so far as any meaningful difference exists, then, it lies in maladjustment being more all-inclusive.

Local education authority administrators and educational psychologists can still get themselves into some curious muddles over this spurious distinction between maladjusted and disruptive children. Recommendations have to be couched in language appropriate to the desired destination. If, for example, a place is to be sought in a unit for disruptive pupils, the child must not be called maladjusted, since this may imply that a recognised special school or class is needed. It will also invoke formal assessment under the 1981 Education Act. Conversely, if a child is called disruptive in a teacher's or psychologist's report, placement in a special school may be difficult to arrange.

The conceptual muddle for administrators, teachers and psychologists results from an even greater muddle in the legal system. As LEAs started to consider the problems presented by their disruptive pupils:

> Education officers gradually realised that it was usually cheaper and always administratively easier to open special centres for disruptive adolescents than expand the special school system. The reasons lie in the small print of the 1944 Education Act, and need not concern us here. The

distinction was largely administrative. Units were faced with fewer staffing constraints in the form of recommendations on pupil : teacher ratios in special schools. They could be more flexible in their admission and discharge procedures. Pupils could always remain on the roll of their original school to which it was theoretically hoped they would return (Galloway *et al.* 1982: 60).

The 1981 Education Act has compounded the problem rather than clarified it by excluding centres or units from the formal assessment procedure. Whereas pupils attending all recognised special schools or classes must have the 'protection' of a Statement this is not the case for disruptive pupils. This clause may be seen in two ways. Cynically it could be seen as an indication of the government's recognition that the primary function of special education, at least for one group of pupils, is to assist the smooth administration of the ordinary school system. Critics of special schooling and of remedial departments in ordinary schools have long argued that the provision exists more for the benefit of teachers and pupils in the mainstream than for that of pupils removed from the mainstream.

Slightly more charitably, the government could have intended that there should be a quick turnover in units for disruptive pupils. After the proverbial short sharp shock, or, depending on the teachers' and the LEA's ideology, intensive remediation and therapy, pupils would return to their original schools chastened and well adjusted. The labyrinthine complexity of formal assessment and statementing procedures would make short-term admission very difficult, if not impossible, to arrange. Hence, disruptive pupils must be excluded from it.

The most probable explanation is that the government just did not recognise the nonsense inherent in attempts to distinguish on administrative grounds between disruptive pupils and pupils whose behaviour required special schooling. Presumably the government was advised by civil servants, HMI and LEAs. Yet these were precisely the people who, purely for administrative convenience, had been drawing this distinction under the provision of the 1944 Education Act. The effect of the 1981 Act was to enshrine in law a spurious distinction that had developed previously on an *ad hoc* basis.

BEHAVIOUR AND PROGRESS: SURVEY EVIDENCE

OVERVIEW

It is clear both from regional variations and from the problems of definition that the number of children attending special schools or classes can give us no accurate picture of the total numbers presenting behavioural or educational difficulties. This is why the results of major surveys including *all* children in a given population can be useful. The most detailed studies to have been carried out in Britain are the National Child Development Study (Kellmer Pringle et al. 1966; Davie et al. 1972; Fogelman 1976) and the surveys carried out by Rutter and his colleagues on the Isle of Wight (Rutter et al. 1970) and in an Inner London Borough (Rutter et al. 1975a; Berger et al. 1975; Rutter et al. 1975b).

THE NATIONAL CHILD DEVELOPMENT STUDY

The National Child Development Study investigated all children born between 3 and 9 March 1958. Each child's teacher was asked to complete an early version of Stott's Bristol Social Adjustment Guide; in this the teacher is given a large number of statements about children's behaviour and asked to underline the ones which describe the child in question most accurately. When the Guide is scored the items which indicate some degree of deviance are given codes: coded items are then summed to obtain an overall total. Stott described children with scores from 0 to 9 as 'stable', those with scores from 10–19 as 'unstable', and those with scores above 19 as 'maladjusted'. On this basis teachers assessed 64 per cent of the children as stable; 22 per cent as unsettled and 14 per cent as maladjusted. Davie et al. (1972), emphasised that 'the terminology is not necessarily applicable in, say, a clinical context', since the assessment was carried out solely by the class teacher. In addition it is now known from other studies (Rutter et al. 1970) that a majority of children with emotional or behavioural problems display them either at home or at school, but not both. Had it been possible to ask parents for similar information about their children's behaviour the results might have been quite different. In the same study teachers thought that 13 per cent of the children would benefit from special educational help, mainly on account of their educational attainments, but only 5 per cent were actually receiving it. However, the form of special educational help under consideration was in the ordinary school. When they were asked which children 'would benefit *now* from attendance at a special school', only 2 per cent fell into this category. Preliminary findings from the third follow-up of the National Child Development Study (Fogelman 1976) showed that 17 per cent of sixteen-year-olds were thought by their teachers to have 'little, if any, ability' in mathematics. The corresponding figure for English was 11 per cent. Those receiving special help within the school on account of 'educational or mental backwardness' amounted to 7 per cent; this help was considered inadequate for 2 per cent, and teachers indicated that help was needed, but not being provided, for a further 2 per cent.

The prevalence of special educational needs

The design of the National Child Development Study made broad regional comparison possible, but prevented a detailed study either of behavioural disorders or learning difficulties. With a sample of over 11,000 children, the project clearly had to rely heavily on screening techniques and questionnaires completed by (or under the supervision of) professional personnel on the spot. Problems over the definition of maladjustment have already been noted, and equally valid objections can be raised against the subjective manner in which both educational attainments and a need for special educational help were assessed. For the most detailed and scientifically most rigorous picture of the educational and behavioural problems of English children we must turn to the surveys conducted by Rutter on the Isle of Wight and an Inner London Borough.

INNER LONDON AND THE ISLE OF WIGHT:
(a) BEHAVIOUR PROBLEMS

The Isle of Wight survey included all ten-year-olds with homes on the island who attended local authority schools, or special schools whose fees were paid by the local authority. The Inner London Borough study included all children attending schools within the Borough. For the purpose of comparison with the Isle of Wight survey, all immigrant children and all children with immigrant parents were excluded from the Inner London Borough. This was to ensure that differences could not be attributed to the higher number of immigrants in London; the immigrant children (mainly West Indian) were in fact covered by the survey, but the results were described separately (see below). Almost identical methods were used in each of the surveys. All children were screened in the summer term of their penultimate year at junior school by means of group tests of non-verbal intelligence and reading. In addition the teachers completed the Rutter Scale for Teachers (Rutter 1967), a questionnaire in the form of twenty-six statements about behaviour in which the teacher is asked to state whether each behaviour occurs, sometimes occurs, or is absent. Children were selected for individual study on the basis of high scores on the Rutter Scale and low scores on the group reading test. They were compared with randomly selected control groups to allow comparisons within each area as well as between the two areas. The mothers of children selected for individual study on the basis of the Rutter Scale (or because they were in the random control group) were interviewed for two to three hours by a social scientist or psychiatrist. The reliability of this interview had been investigated in the Isle of Wight Study (Graham and Rutter 1968a). This contained a series of set questionnaires about emotional or behavioural problems in the preceding year; family relationships and interactions were assessed in the same interview. A much shorter interview was carried out with the father, and both parents were asked to complete a health questionnaire which focused on symptoms associated with psychiatric illness or stress. In London, but not in the Isle of Wight, the Rutter Scale results were checked by means of an interview with the child's current teacher (not usually the one who completed the questionnaire), in which questions concentrated specifically on emotional disturbance, conduct disorder, and disturbances in relationships with peers and staff. Children selected for individual study on the basis of the group reading test scores were tested on the short form of the Wechsler Intelligence Scale for Children (Wechsler 1949) and the Neale Analysis of Reading Ability (Neale 1958) which measures children's comprehension and accuracy and fluency.

Psychiatric disorder was assessed from the information provided by teachers and parents as described above. There is a semantic problem here, and it is essential to be clear about the limitations of the term. Rutter and Graham (1968) are explicit on this point:

> Psychiatric disorder . . . refers to abnormalities of emotions, behaviour or relationships which are developmentally inappropriate and of sufficient duration and severity to cause persistent suffering or handicap to the child and/or distress or disturbance to the family or community. Our use of the term does not involve any concept of disease or illness, nor does it necessarily assume that psychiatrists are the right people to treat such disorders.

This definition clearly distinguishes psychiatric disorder from other medical conditions, yet discussion of diagnosis generally implies a medical condition. Some people might prefer another term, such as maladjustment, but this would suffer from similar objections.

That a child is said to have psychiatric disorder in this context implies that he has, or simply is, a problem; it does not imply that the problem lies primarily with the child, nor does it imply that this emotion or behaviour is necessarily in any way unreasonable, unpredictable or abnormal in the light of his current and past experiences. The results should be seen in the light of these comments.

Almost twice as many children were said to be 'deviant' on the basis of the Rutter Scale in London as on the Isle of Wight (19 per cent and 11 per cent respectively). The total number of children with psychiatric disorder in each area was estimated from the numbers diagnosed in the control group and in the group selected by screening; again the London rate was twice that of the Isle of Wight (25 per cent against 12 per cent). The higher London rate applied to both sexes, but was much more marked in girls (26 per cent against 8 per cent). This was largely due to the high number of London girls who were not selected by the teacher's questionnaire, mainly because their problems were confined to home.

INNER LONDON AND THE ISLE OF WIGHT:
(b) READING BACKWARDNESS AND SPECIFIC READING RETARDATION

It is known that reading standards vary in different parts of the country. Scotland, for instance, has rather higher standards than England (Davie *et al.* 1972) and evidence obtained by Berger *et al.* (1975) showed the reading ability of London primary school children to be below the national average. In Kent, Morris (1959, 1966) demonstrated that attainments varied according to the characteristics of the schools the children attended. Unfortunately none of these studies took intelligence into account. On commonsense grounds one might suppose that children whose reading is retarded relative to their general level of cognitive development (as measured by an individual IQ test) might have different characteristics and different teaching needs from children who are backward but not retarded relative to measured intelligence. The statistical technique of regression analysis was used in the surveys to identify severely retarded children whose scores on either the accuracy or comprehension scale of the Neale Test fell some thirty months or more below the score predicted from their age and IQ (Yule *et al.* 1975).

On this basis (which excluded other data available from the original Isle of Wight survey), just under 3 per cent of Isle of Wight children were considered to suffer from specific reading retardation. In London the equivalent figure was just under 10 per cent. Backward readers (twenty-eight months or more backward on either accuracy or comprehension), accounted for 8 per cent of the Isle of Wight children (11 per cent of the boys and 6 per cent of the girls) but 19 per cent of the London children (22 per cent of the boys and 16 per cent of the girls). There was, of course, very considerable overlap between the specific reading retardation and the general reading backwardness groups. (In the original Isle of Wight research, all but ten of the eighty-six children in the former were also in the latter.) Nevertheless, it is safe to assume that one ten-year-old in five, excluding immigrants, in the London Borough was reading below the seven-year-old level nationally.

CONCLUSIONS FROM SURVEYS

WARNOCK'S 20 PER CENT

At first sight Warnock's conclusion that up to 20 per cent of children will have special educational needs at some stage in their school career seems to be amply born out by research. Given the publicity surrounding this recommendation, and its recognition in a DES (1981a) circular, one might think: (a) that it was a recent discovery; (b) that it had a sound statistical basis; (c) that it was essentially a statement about educational need rather than about political priorities. In fact it was nothing of the sort.

HISTORICAL BACKGROUND

Warnock's conclusion could have been reached on perfectly adequate research evidence at any time in the previous fifty years. The evidence is uncontroversial and readily accessible. In his book *The Backward Child* Cyril Burt (1937) reported evidence that one child in ten above the 'educable defective' level could be considered backward. In addition, only one in six of the so-called educable defectives – later labelled ESN(M) – was actually attending a special school.

Even government reports were accepting this point nearly fifty years before Warnock. Largely on Burt's advice, the Wood Committee on the educational needs of the feeble-minded (later ESN(M)), noted that roughly 10 per cent of children not classified as feeble-minded would need additional help (Board of Education and Board of Control 1929).

In the field of behaviour problems the position was just as clear. Milner (1938) found that teachers in girls public day schools referred 17 per cent of pupils for difficult behaviour. In the state system, McFie (1934) reported London elementary school teachers noting at least one of four 'behaviour deviations' in 46 per cent of pupils. Just in case it is thought that problems were confined to Britain, North American teachers found cause for complaint about the behaviour of more than 50 per cent of their pupils (Haggerty 1925). At the risk of labouring the point, it is worth recalling that Dickens described the educational standards in some nineteenth-century independent schools, and that the army was required to quell pupil riots at some of the country's most famous public schools (Gathorne-Hardy 1977).

STATISTICAL CERTAINTY, POLITICAL COMPROMISE OR MORAL JUDGEMENT?

Criteria which have been used to identify children with learning difficulties have been an IQ below 70, a reading age 28 months or more below chronological age (reading backwardness), a reading age 28 months or more below the level that would be predicted from the child's IQ (reading retardation) and psychiatric disorder. Rutter *et al.* (1970) found that at least one of these conditions applied to 16 per cent of ten-year-olds on the Isle of Wight, and more than one to 4 per cent. In other surveys the criteria of psychiatric disorder has been extended to include children identified as deviant on questionnaires completed by teachers.

Warnock regarded these criteria as 'handicaps'. There has been little serious discussion of the assumption that they constitute evidence of special educational need. We need therefore to consider the underlying assumptions.

Gipps and Goldstein (1984) have shown that the criterion of IQ 70 was based on earlier work by Cyril Burt who in turn had selected it purely for administrative convenience. Burt was quite adamant that:

> For immediate practical purposes the only satisfactory definition of mental deficiency is a percentage definition based on the amount of existing accommodation (Quoted by Gipps and Goldstein 1984: 15).

The position has clearly changed radically since then, both in terms of test construction and in terms of available provision. Nevertheless, that in itself answers none of the problems.

To interpret IQ scores it is necessary to understand the way tests are constructed. Typically, an intelligence test is expressed as an intelligence quotient (IQ) with a mean of 100 and a standard deviation of 15. By generalising from the groups on whom the test was developed to the population at large, it is possible to predict the proportion whose scores are likely to fall in a given range. Thus, 68.2 per cent of the population obtain scores which fall within one standard deviation of the mean (IQ 85–115); 95.4 per cent obtain scores within two standard deviations of the mean (IQ 70–130), and a mere 0.2 per cent is expected to obtain scores over three standard deviations from the mean (IQ above 145 or below 55). On this basis 2.3 per cent would be expected to score below 70 with the same number scoring above 130 on an instrument such as the Wechsler Intelligence Scale for Children.

Results of reading tests are more often expressed as reading ages. Yule (1973) has shown that for statistical reasons reading quotients can be misleading, especially at the extremes. Yet the criteria of twenty-eight months remains an arbitrary one. This is not a criticism of the research. When classifying research results for a professional audience some kind of grouping is necessary. Quite rightly, teachers want to know what proportion of children score within a given range. The cut-off cannot, however, be absolute. This becomes clear when we consider other possibilities.

It would have been quite reasonable for Warnock to have argued that children with a reading age more than eighteen months below their chronological age had special educational needs. Alternatively the committee could have selected a cut-off point of thirty-six months. In the first example the proportion with special needs would have risen sharply. In the second it would have declined. In both cases solid research evidence would have been at hand to legitimise the conclusion. The reason is simply that tests of intelligence and educational attainment are designed to identify children within given ranges.

The same argument applies to children presenting behavioural problems. In Britain the most widely used screening instruments are Rutter's (1967) Scale and Stott's (1971) Bristol Social Adjustment Guides. These owe their popularity to the fact that they contain items familiar to teachers. If they did not, teachers would refuse, not unreasonably, to waste time completing them. Yet by containing items familiar to teachers the design of the instruments ensures that they will identify a substantial minority of children. The size of this minority depends entirely on the selected cut-off point, which can be raised or lowered at will. Again, defining and justifying a cut-off point is not just a legitimate exercise for researchers, but a necessary one.

For the Warnock Committee, however, the problem was rather more complex. They could identify any cut-off points to justify the recommendation that services should be based on the assumption that a certain proportion of children had special educational needs. Whether the proportion was 5 per cent or 35 per cent, research could be produced to justify the recommendation. In this sense the figure of 20 was based on a statistical certainty. This tells us nothing, though, about the probable reason for selecting this figure of 20 per cent. Our contention is that this can only be understood, and justified, by reference to a political compromise and a moral judgement.

As a body established by the government of the day, the Warnock Committee had to make recommendations for the government's consideration. Neither individuals nor committees make recommendations in a vacuum. All recommendations are influenced by an assessment of how they will be received. There are few benefits in being ridiculed by politicians and by professionals for unrealistic recommendations. To have recommended that services should be based on an assumption that 35 per cent would have special needs at some stage in their school careers might indeed have invited ridicule as unrealistic. Conversely, to have concentrated only on services for the 2 per cent currently attending special schools would have invited ridicule for ignoring overwhelming evidence about children with special needs in ordinary schools. The figure of 20 per cent may thus be seen as a political compromise. It may also be seen as a moral judgement.

This becomes apparent when we consider the implication of a statement that a child has special educational needs. Clearly, the statement implies that the child requires some kind of help over and above what a class teacher in a primary school or subject teacher in a secondary school could reasonably be expected to provide. It follows that when we say up to 20 per cent of children will have special educational needs at some stage in their school careers we are making a statement about the children that teachers 'ought' or 'ought not' to be expected to teach without extra help. This can be seen as a political point, with implications for government funding of special education. It can be seen as a professional point, with implications both for the initial and in-service training of teachers. Neither of these points should obscure the fact that the statement also makes a moral judgement. This relates simply to the size of the minority that teachers should regard, on behavioural or scholastic criteria, as in some way deviant, exceptional and in need of extra help.

Our argument is essentially a philosophical one, but it can have very important practical implications. Logically, the statement that 20 per cent of children have special needs says nothing about where or how these needs should be met. In fact, both Warnock and the 1981 Education Act assume that the majority of special needs can be met in ordinary classes. The problem is that teachers may use this figure to argue that they cannot be expected to cope with a child, who should therefore be receiving 'help' elsewhere. This is why some commentators on the 1981 Education Act have argued that it will lead to a larger number of children than previously receiving a separate and potentially disadvantaging curriculum (e.g. Tomlinson 1982).

WHICH CHILDREN ARE SAID TO HAVE SPECIAL NEEDS?

No critique of the statistical or conceptual background to the claim that up to 20 per cent of children have special educational needs should overlook the fact that teaching these children is always challenging and often stressful. Nor should it obscure the need for information about the children and the problems they present. The temptation is to describe the children in purely individualistic terms, with reference to behaviour, attainments, intelligence, factors in the family background that may affect progress in school and so on. This is fine as far as it goes. The danger is that individualistic explanations overlook underlying trends which may also reveal hidden functions of special education, as opposed to its stated functions. In this section we first consider the importance of ethnic, sex and social class factors in selection for special schooling. We then review evidence on family background and on medical factors which may contribute to behaviour or learning problems that are taken as evidence of special needs.

ETHNIC MINORITIES

A continuing source of controversy in special education for children with learning and behavioural problems is the presence in special schools of a disproportionate number of children from ethnic minority groups. Since Coard's (1971) book, *How the West Indian Child is Made Educationally Sub-Normal in the British School System*, this has remained a sensitive issue. Using DES statistics Tomlinson (1982) shows that in 1972 2.9 per cent of West Indian children were placed in ESN(M) classes compared with 0.66 per cent of all children. In 1976 the numbers had fallen to 2.4 per cent and 0.55 per cent respectively. Education statistics are no longer collected by ethnic origin. There is little evidence, however, that this situation has changed radically.

Tomlinson suggests that West Indian children are also likely to be placed in special schools and units for disruptive pupils. Again, hard evidence is lacking. However, in Sheffield children from ethnic minorities were not over-represented in a sample of children suspended from school (Galloway 1982) nor in special groups for problem children in ordinary schools (Galloway *et al*. 1982). Yet the overall picture was neither straightforward nor altogether encouraging.

In 1973–74 the LEA's psychological service had carried out a survey of West Indian children in ESN(M) schools. The results showed a considerable over-representation and led to a good deal of discussion within the LEA. By 1978–79 West Indian children were no longer over-represented in schools for the ESN(M). On the other hand they accounted for nearly one-third of all pupils in the LEA's special schools for the maladjusted and in its special school for pupils who were ESN(M) and maladjusted. In other words the evidence suggested that pupils who would once have been referred to ESN(M) schools were now being sent to schools for the maladjusted.

This naturally raises some important questions about the needs of pupils from ethnic minorities, especially Afro-Caribbean children. Two groups of explanation have been put forward. One focuses on the pupils and their families, while the other emphasises factors in schools and in society, particularly the effects of teachers' attitudes towards children from minority groups.

Tomlinson (1980) reviewed studies of Afro-Caribbean children's school performance. In twenty-seven of these, Afro-Caribbean children had lower attainments than whites. For present purposes one of the most useful of these was Rutter's Inner London study, in which information from West Indian immigrants and British born children of West Indian parents was analysed separately (Rutter *et al*. 1974; Yule *et al*. 1975; Rutter *et al*. 1975c).

The behaviour questionnaire completed by teachers (Rutter 1967) distinguishes between 'conduct' disorder, 'emotional' or 'neurotic' disorder and 'mixed' disorder. In both the mixed and the neurotic types of behaviour problems no differences were found between the West Indian and the non-immigrant groups. In contrast, conduct disorder was much more common among the West Indian groups. A different pattern was found between West Indian and non-immigrant girls. In the latter emotional problems were more common than conduct or behaviour problems. In contrast, conduct problems were many times more common in West Indian girls, as in West Indian boys. Yet although *teachers* apparently found West Indian children more troublesome, evidence from *parents* suggested a lower rate of behaviour problems than reported by parents of white children. This suggests quite strongly that highly subjective factors are likely to influence the ways in which white teachers assess black children.

By implication individualistic explanations focusing solely on the pupils themselves are inadequate. Factors at school may also contribute to the problems reported by teachers. The results of reading and intelligence tests (Neale 1958; Wechsler 1949) further illustrate the importance of looking at a wide range of data.

On the reading test the immigrant group as a whole scored about two years below their age level, or just over one year below the non-immigrant controls who were themselves well below the national average. Similarly, the mean verbal and peformance scale IQs for the West Indian immigrant group were 87 and 90 compared with 101 and 104 respectively for the controls. Taken in isolation these figures are misleading as the authors are at pains to point out. For example, children who were born in the West Indies were considerably less successful on both intelligence and attainment tests than children born in Britain to West Indian parents. This is, of course, scarcely surprising as the tests were standardised on a non-immigrant population.

However, there were also many reasons for West Indian children born in Britian having attainments below the indigenous population. There was a tendency for the West Indian children to attend less favourable schools. They were more likely to live in overcrowded homes with poor facilities. Their fathers were more likely to be semi-skilled or unskilled manual workers. They were more likely to have had child-minding by non-relatives in their early years, and other studies had shown a tendency for them to have had fewer toys and less interaction with their parents (Pollack 1972).

On their own none of these points is particularly contentious though their interpretation most certainly is. Many of the studies reviewed by Tomlinson (1980) raised similar issues. From the Afro-Caribbean perspective, though, much of the social and educational disadvantage they experience results from conscious or unconscious discrimination in housing and employment as well as in the education system. Developing the last point, a majority of psychologists would not seriously dispute the view that there are serious doubts about the suitability of IQ tests for predicting the educational attainments of West Indian children. As these tests have in the past constituted an important, if not central, component in the assessment of slow-learning children for special schooling it is not hard to see why the Afro-Caribbean community is concerned. As the DES (1983) continues to advocate their use in formal assessments carried out under the 1981 Education Act, continuing concern is both understandable and legitimate.

This leads us to a more contentious issue. Faced with evidence of Afro-Caribbean pupils under-achieving in the school system, and being referred to special schools in disproportionate numbers, teachers and other educationists tend to seek explanations in terms of deficiences in the pupils and in their family backgrounds. The Afro-Caribbean community sees the explanation in a very different way. The view here is that the explanation lies partly in culturally biased tests, but to a much greater extent in teachers' stereotypes of black children and low expectations of what they 'ought' to be achieving (Coard 1971; Tomlinson 1981, 1982).

Controversy over the existence of racially prejudiced attitudes in schools dogged the chequered history of the government's inquiry into ethnic minority education (DES/1981b, 1985). To a large extent this controversy reflected the lack of awareness in many teachers of their own racial identity and attitudes. In the early days of the committee's work the word racism elicited intense anger and defensiveness. By publication of the final report the possibility of discussing the topic in a more rational manner was gradually becoming accepted. This reflected an awareness that an action seen by one person as an example of blatant racial prejudice might be seen in an entirely different light by other participants. Members of the committee were in no doubt that teachers in some schools failed to recognise racially based attacks on pupils. Moreover, by perpetuating stereotypes of minority ethnic groups, some teachers were maintaining a climate which implicitly condoned discrimination and prejudice.

SEX AND SOCIAL CLASS BIAS

Under the 1944 Education Act it became considerably easier to ascertain children as ESN than it had previously been to certify them as mentally defective. The reason lay in the extended scope of the ESN category to include children who were educationally retarded for reasons other than intellectual backwardness. As Cleugh (1957) pointed out:

The prevalence of special educational needs

Prior to 1944 the transfer to an MD school of Charlie who was a nuisance but whose intelligence quotient was relatively high, could be challenged on the grounds that he was not mentally defective, but now (unless the circumstances were quite exceptional) he would be fairly sure to come under the ESN umbrella.

Of course, Charlie would also be covered by the catch-all clauses in the 1981 Education Act that children should be taught in ordinary schools subject to 'provision of efficient education for the children with whom he will be educated' or to 'efficient use of resources'.

Evidence that children with moderate learning difficulties are placed in special schools for reasons other than their educational backwardness is not hard to find. We have already noted the West Indian community's resentment at their children's high rate of referral to special schools. We have also noted that teachers, though not parents, report a high rate of problem behaviour in Afro-Caribbean children. It seems fairly clear that the two observations are linked.

A second point concerns the disproportionate number of boys in schools for children with moderate learning difficulties. In 1982, 34,441 boys were attending these schools in England, compared with 21,120 girls (DES 1982). Boys tend to vary more than girls at both ends of the intellectual spectrum, but the difference is nothing like sufficient to account for the greater number of boys. The explanation must lie elsewhere. A boy who finds himself failing at school is more likely to show behaviour problems of the 'acting-out' or openly disruptive type than a girl, who is more likely to show her distress in withdrawn behaviour that can easily go unnoticed in a large class. This also explains why boys outnumber girls in schools for the maladjusted (10,533 and 2,644 respectively in 1982) (DES 1982). The evidence suggests very strongly that special school placement is considered appropriate because of problems the pupils present in their ordinary classes. There is nothing inherently wrong in this. Most educational psychologists can think of children for whom they have recommended special schooling because of the damaging effect they were having on the teacher's morale and on the progress of other children in the class. What is utterly unacceptable is to claim that transfer is being recommended in the child's own interests when the evidence, at the most charitable interpretation, is inconclusive (see Ch. 3). A much more plausible conclusion is that transfer is recommended in the interests of the teacher's mental health.

A further point about all kinds of special education for children with behavioural or learning difficulties is the children's social class origins. While it would be an over-statement to say that children from middle-class and professional homes are never placed in special schools or units, it is certainly true that this happens very seldom indeed. A not atypical picture emerged from a study of four schools for maladjusted children:

The most striking feature about the social class distribution within the four schools was its absence. There was, effectively, little or no distribution in the sense that the overwhelming majority of the pupils came from the categories IV and V,* 'semi-skilled' and 'unskilled'. There were only seven identifiable cases of non-manual work and some of these require the benefit of doubt. . . . In these areas at least middle- and upper-class children do not become maladjusted (Ford *et al.* 1982: 136).

An interesting implication here is that the term 'maladjusted' may be seen as a derogatory label used by middle-class professionals on working-class children. Labels which the working class sometimes use on the middle class are 'snooty', 'snobbish', 'stuck up', 'big headed'. It is entertaining to speculate on the reaction if a LEA identified a school as having exceptional problems on account of the number of children to whom these labels applied.

FAMILY BACKGROUND

Until the mid-1960s tensions arising from family background and from disturbed relationships within the family were seen as the principal cause of maladjustment. The pioneers of special schools for the maladjusted discounted almost entirely the effect of experiences at school, seeing a child's learning difficulties as a symptom of personal problems which in turn frequently resulted from problems in the family (e.g. Wills 1941, 1945; Lennhoff 1960; Shaw 1965). Maladjustment, then, was seen essentially as a medical or psychiatric problem. As Laslett (1984) has pointed out, this view gradually changed, with increasing emphasis on the children's educational difficulties and on the educational objectives of special schooling.

We do not dispute that the shift in emphasis was a necessary one. One effect, though, may have been to facilitate referral for special education purely on the grounds of disturbing behaviour at school. This in turn may lead us to under-estimate the importance of contributory factors in the home background.

There is in fact widespread agreement that children referred for special schooling frequently came from highly stressful home backgrounds. Ford *et al.* (1982) collected information about the parents of children attending three schools for the maladjusted. They note the National Child Development Study's observation that one child in nine was not living with both natural parents, but that only 5 per cent were being brought up by one parent alone. Yet in the three schools which the authors investigated, the fathers of 22.5 per cent of children were dead, absent or unknown. It is worth emphasising, however, that growing up in a single parent family is not necessarily stressful. In some circumstances it can be healthier than a conventional two parent family (see Rutter 1972).

* On the Registrar General's Classification on Occupations.

Evidence of stress within the family is also well documented. A study in Sheffield of pupils suspended from school for disciplinary reasons revealed evidence of psychiatric disorder in at least one parent of nearly half of the families interviewed (Galloway 1982). All of these pupils could legitimately have been referred to schools for the maladjusted or units for the disruptive if it would have served any useful administrative or educational purpose to have done so. Using a quite different approach, Rutter (1966) has documented the effect on children's social adjustment of parental ill-health. He found poor psychiatric health a greater risk factor than physical ill-health.

Another way of investigating the role of family background is to identify measures of social disadvantage. In the National Child Development Study, Wedge and Prosser (1973) and Wedge and Essen (1982) described children as disadvantaged when their families:

1. Had only one parent and/or five or more children.
2. Lived in an overcrowded house or a house with no hot water.
3. Received means-tested welfare benefits on account of their low income.

The study found a very marked relationship between family disadvantage and poor educational attainment. As the children grew older the relationship became more marked.

PHYSICAL FACTORS

Evidence on the importance of ethnicity, gender, social class and family background shows quite clearly that factors other than measured intelligence, educational attainments and personality are implicated in the development of moderate learning difficulties and of maladjustment. We should not, however, overlook the possibility that physical factors may also play a part.

In the Isle of Wight study, Graham and Rutter (1968b) noted behaviour problems in 34 per cent of epileptic children. Anderson (1973) studied physically handicapped children attending ordinary classes. She found that children with neurological abnormalities were the only group to show more behaviour problems than able-bodied children in the class. Notwithstanding this result, the connection between neurological problems and behaviour problems is far from straightforward. Harris (1978) was doubtful about the existence of any clear relationships between temporal lobe epilepsy and aggressive behaviour, and found no clear association between EEG abnormalities and specific behavioural symptoms.

At best we may conclude that physical factors may contribute to behavioural or learning problems, but can seldom be said to cause them. This is illustrated from a study in Sheffield of pupils suspended from school (Galloway 1982). Many of the pupils had a history of severe illnesses or accidents. In just over one-fifth of cases these could have been associated with neuropathology. They were far more likely to have suffered severe illnesses or accidents than their siblings. The medical history could have contributed to the behavioural problems these pupils presented, but a large number of other factors was also relevant, principal among which was the schools they attended (see Ch. 6).

CONCLUSIONS

In Chapter 1 we showed that the proportion of children receiving separate special education for behavioural or learning problems has not declined since publication of the Warnock Report, and may even have increased. In this chapter we have reviewed research on the prevalence of children with behavioural or learning problems. We have also discussed anomalies and inconsistencies in the interpretation of the research results.

Children referred for special education are vulnerable on several counts. They may be retarded intellectually and come from families with damaging relationships and/or severe social disadvantage. Physical and constitutional factors may increase their vulnerability to stress at home or at school. We show in Chapter 7 that school may constitute a protective factor in their lives, but that it may also constitute an additional source of stress. Yet by no means all children who are vulnerable by reason of cognitive, educational, personal or family problems are considered for special schooling. This is reserved, in some areas almost exclusively, for children from working-class homes, and generally from working-class homes which are socially disadvantaged. The implication that special schooling is used, at least in part, as a way of removing disturbing misfits from the mainstream cannot be ignored. Nor is it possible to ignore the implication that family factors may sometimes be used to relieve teachers of responsibility for a child's poor progress or behaviour: 'We don't expect too much of Jimmy: we know about the family background.'

Chapter three
THE EFFECTS OF SPECIAL EDUCATION

INTRODUCTION

'It's only the child I'm thinking of.' A look of pained surprise often crosses the face of teachers, psychologists and members of other caring professions at the mere suggestion that their activities may not altogether be in the child's best interests. After all, the function of special education, by definition, is to meet special educational needs. Moreover, the continuing demand for places in special schools, classes or units attests its value. What professional would ever recommend something that was not in the child's interests?

Given our earlier scepticism about the 1981 Education Act and about the prevalence of special educational needs, it will not be surprising that we have reservations about the act of faith implicit in the last paragraph. The caring professions have never excelled in evaluating their own effectiveness. Those professions which specialise in interpersonal relationships and special education seem to have been the least conscientious in this respect. Transferring a child to a special school, or arranging a special curriculum within an ordinary school, may, and usually does, reflect a conscientious attempt to meet the child's needs. It may also include a 'hidden agenda' unrecognised by all participants. The transfer not only legitimises the existing mainstream curriculum by acknowledging that it does not, and implicitly that it should not, cater adequately for 'special' pupils. In addition, transfer may reduce the mainstream teacher's motivation to review the curriculum in order to cater more effectively for all pupils in the class (e.g. Breese 1983). The hidden agenda in special education makes rigorous evaluation all the more essential.

The education of disturbing children

SCOPE

This chapter reviews evidence on the progress of children admitted to residential and day schools for the maladjusted. We also consider the very limited evidence on off-site units for disruptive pupils and on special classes or units within ordinary classes. We take a critical look at the argument that all problems will be solved if only treatment is carried out early enough, and then review the progress of disruptive or maladjusted children in all forms of special education in the light of other available evidence from evaluation studies in counselling and psychotherapy.

The final section of the chapter examines evidence on the progress of children with moderate learning difficulties. We also consider the progress of children with mild learning difficulties in the course of 'remedial' lessons and subsequently.

We are concerned in this chapter with those forms of special education which cater for children with special needs as a group, in special schools, centres or classes. In some forms of provision the children are admitted full-time, as a long-term educational alternative to ordinary schooling. In others they are admitted part-time, with a view to early return to the mainstream.

DISTURBING BEHAVIOUR: SPECIAL SCHOOLS

We consider here the progress and social adjustment of children in two forms of residential schooling and in day schools for the maladjusted. One form of residential provision is for maladjusted pupils, in schools maintained by LEAs or by independent bodies. In general the independent schools only accept pupils referred and paid for by LEAs. The second form caters solely for pupils in the care of local authority social services departments.

RESIDENTIAL SCHOOLING FOR DELINQUENTS

Until the 1969 Children and Young Person's Act, juvenile court magistrates had the power to send children aged 10–16 to approved schools for delinquent behaviour. Following the 1969 Act, approved schools became known as community homes with education on the premises. The change in name was accompanied by an increasing emphasis on providing a more liberal and therapeutic regime than the custodial and often punitive approved schools. Admission was controlled strictly by social services departments who retained res-

The effects of special education

ponsibility for supervising the young person's rehabilitation following discharge. In the last few years the number of community homes with education has fallen sharply. This is due to a policy change involving management of young offenders, and children considered 'at risk' for other reasons, within the community. One reason for this policy change was the recognition that residential schooling for delinquents was strikingly ineffective in changing their behaviour.

Numerous studies have shown that a majority of young people discharged from community homes continue to commit criminal offences following discharge (e.g. HMSO 1972). The subsequent adjustment of young people leaving traditional custodial schools did not seem to differ in any important way from young people leaving schools with family grouping (Craft 1965) or schools run as 'therapeutic' communities (McMichael 1974; Cornish and Clarke 1975). Cornish and Clarke (1975) argue that this was inevitable, since the focus under both regimes was on behaviour within the school. Consequently, little or nothing was done to tackle the family and community pressures which contributed to the pupil's problems in the first place. Nor could anything be done to change the pupil's response to these pressures, since the school was residential and thus far removed from them.

A further problem concerns the educational standards in residential schools administered by social services departments. A report by HMI (1980a) identified major weaknesses in the curriculum at many community homes, and argued that they catered inadequately for many pupils with special educational needs. In theory, social services departments cooperate closely with LEAs. In practice friction is frequent. Teachers often feel professionally isolated both from their colleges in ordinary schools, and from the residential and social work staff. It would be remarkable if educational standards did not suffer.

RESIDENTIAL SCHOOLS FOR MALADJUSTED PUPILS

The evidence from the first residential schools for maladjusted pupils appears at first sight somewhat more encouraging. Shaw (1965) kept a record of the behaviour and adjustment of all pupils passing through Red Hill, his school for intelligent secondary age boys, since 1934. Apart from six pupils who had died since leaving the school and six more whom the school had failed to contact, he regarded 67 per cent as 'radically cured on a completely permanent and adjusted basis', with a further 21 per cent improved. Of the rest 2 per cent were not failures, but could not really qualify for description as improved, and the remaining 10 per cent were regarded as failures. Burn (1964), in his account of George Lyward's school Finchden

Manor, reported that 290 boys had been through the school since 1930. Fifteen boys had attended for brief treatment in the early 1930s and had returned to the ordinary school system, though we have no information on whether or not they succeeded in their ordinary schools. Eighty-three boys were sent away as too difficult, went to mental hospitals, ran away, were withdrawn by their parents or guardians, or left on their own initiative against the school's advice. Of the remaining 192 (66 per cent) nearly all had settled down, often in distinguished careers. Both Shaw's and Burn's claims seem impressive (and many visitors to both schools were also favourably impressed), but neither gave a detailed explanation of how they arrived at the figures; a further problem is that both schools were atypical in only taking boys of high intelligence and frequently keeping them until they were eighteen (at Red Hill) or later (at Finchden Manor). Nevertheless, each school claimed that around 66 per cent of its pupils achieved substantial and lasting improvement. As we shall see, this figure recurs with almost monotonous consistency in studies evaluating the outcome of treatment, though it is more often reached by combining the 'greatly improved' and 'partly improved' groups.

Another study which investigated the subsequent adjustment of boys discharged from residential schools for maladjusted children was Balbernie's (1966). Unlike the bright pupils of Finchden Manor and Red Hill, the boys ranged from below average to above average in general intelligence, and only thirty-two were included in his study. When followed up at the ages of seventeen and a half to twenty-two, only five had been able to settle successfully in their own homes and two of these were unable to hold a regular job. A further eight had achieved some degree of adjustment away from home and eleven were in Borstal, detention centre or mental hospital, or were seeking discharge from the Services after appearing in court. In other words, only 41 per cent of the sample could be rated a success, and this on rather generous criteria. Balbernie made the interesting observation that all the improved boys had made a good relationship with an adult at the school, usually someone outside the professional residential staff, such as a cook or gardener. An equally important point was that continued improvement seemed to be associated with continuance of this relationship, and that neither the boys' degree of disturbance when admitted to the schools nor their disturbance on discharge appeared as important in their subsequent adjustment as the amount of follow-up support they received. This observation held good irrrespective of the boys' diagnosis; so-called psychotic or affectionless boys were as likely to continue to improve as ostensibly less disturbed boys, provided their support after leaving was adequate. From the depressing histories of the majority of the young men in Balbernie's survey, one can only conclude that adequate support was seldom forthcoming. A further and more fundamental point is whether residential placement was necessary in the first place if adjustment at follow-up depended not on the children's state on entering or leaving the school but on subsequent support in the community. This view is supported by Balbernie's observation that for the twenty boys whose families were very definitely rejecting before their admission to a residential school, the relationship problems deteriorated still further in the course of treatment.

All the studies mentioned so far are of independent schools which were among the pioneers of special education for maladjusted children in this country. Their books (Wills 1945, 1960, 1971; Lennhoff 1960; Shaw 1965; Burn 1964) have had a substantial impact on the training and subsequent thinking of teachers in state maintained schools for the maladjusted. Unfortunately, but perhaps inevitably, the enthusiasm of the innovators did not extend to carrying out a detailed investigation of their results in a way which would enable others to see whether similar methods could achieve the same results in different settings. This was particularly necessary as the most rapid expansion since 1944 in places for maladjusted children has been in day schools in the maintained sector. Apart from the question whether approaches which can be implemented successfully in a residential school are also appropriate in a day school, there is the additional question about whether the bureaucracy of an LEA could (or should) allow headteachers the degree of freedom enjoyed by the pioneers of independent boarding schools.

It is disturbing that serious evaluation studies in LEA maintained schools should be so thin on the ground. Roe (1965) studied the progress of children in eight residential schools in the Inner London Education Authority. She found encouraging gains over a twelve-month period in reading ability, but not to the same extent in mathematics. Whereas the average gain in reading age was a year or more, depending on the measure used, this was not the case in maths. It is, of course, reasonable to assume that as the children were maladjusted they might be expected to make less progress than a 'normal' child in the course of a year. On the other hand, we could hope that the effect of smaller classes and, hopefully, more experienced teachers might compensate for their emotional and behavioural problems on admission.

A large number of studies have demonstrated improvement in behaviour following treatment with behaviour modification techniques (e.g. Burland 1979; Wolf *et al.* 1975; Fixsen *et al.* 1973; Brown 1978). Burland (1978) has reported that 73 per cent of children leaving his primary schools for pupils in the IQ range 70–95 returned to 'educational facilities in which they did not need special help for behaviour difficulties' (p. 103), presumably ordinary schools in most cases. He has also described procedures for preparing pupils for their return to their own homes and to ordinary schools (Burland 1985). There appears to be no detailed information, though, on the measures of adjustment used in the ordinary school, nor on the children's adjustment over a period of years.

Other studies have reported a much lower percentage return to ordinary classes. Thus, Cooling (1974) found only 20 per cent of leavers from sixty-eight residential special schools transferring to day or boarding schools for ordinary children. More recently Dawson (1980) suggests that about 24 per cent return to ordinary schools.

The employment history of pupils discharged from residential schools is another area on which we have inadequate information. Cooling (1974) found that just under half the leavers had left to start work. At first sight this appears quite encouraging, but Cooling gave no information on the *reasons* for transfer nor about the pupil's subsequent employment history.

DAY SCHOOLS FOR MALADJUSTED PUPILS

Information on the progress of children attending day special schools is, if anything, even more limited than that of children in residential schools. Roe (1965) found that maladjusted children attending Inner London day special schools generally made less academic progress than children in the residential schools, though this tendency was most marked in mathematics. Only 16 per cent of leavers from five day special schools returned to ordinary schools. It is important to note that this was 16 per cent of *leavers*, *not* 16 per cent of the school's population. Thus, we have no information on the number of pupils spending over, for example, two years in special education who returned to ordinary school. This must have been considerably less than 16 per cent. On the basis of the most pessimistic figures on the 'spontaneous remission' of behavioural problems (i.e. the tendency to clear up without any formal treatment) we should expect a much higher proportion to return to ordinary schools.

The pupils' headteachers generally thought they had improved in the course of the year. Those opinions were not, however, born out by evidence from Bristol Social Adjustment Guides (Stott 1963) which suggested some deterioration in behaviour. Other evidence from one of Roe's schools suggested that children's behaviour might deteriorate in their first year or so at the school, followed by a significant improvement (Simmonds 1965).

The inconsistency in the Inner London study between headteachers' estimates of improvement and the possibly more objective estimates obtained from the Bristol Guides was confirmed in a smaller study by Critchley (1969). He reported on the progress of thirty-two boys of low average intelligence aged from six to twelve in a day special school. Using the Bristol Guides he found that just under two-thirds of the boys had improved, and that the ten boys who did not improve were perceived as hostile to adults by the teachers completing the guides. As in the ILEA study the headteachers thought the majority (twenty-seven of the thirty-two) had improved, but this optimism was not supported by the Bristol Guides. Critchley's findings were also consistent with the ILEA results in that the boys in his sample made more progress in reading than in arithmetic.

As in residential schools, encouraging results have been claimed with behavioural approaches. Atkinson (1975), for example, used a 'token economy' in which tokens earned for good work or behaviour could buy privileges or rewards. Within two and a half years of opening the school was catering for forty-six pupils and sixteen pupils had returned to ordinary school, or in three cases, had entered employment. Unfortunately we do not know what proportion of all admissions these pupils represented, nor for how long their successful progress was maintained.

Looking further at the employment history of pupils leaving day schools, Roe (1965) found that 80 per cent of pupils who left at school leaving age were holding down a job. A more detailed study was carried out by Tuckey et al. (1973) who followed up 788 leavers from special schools for all categories of handicap. Unfortunately this constituted only 58 per cent of their original sample – an unacceptably low proportion in view of what is known about the effect which lost cases (clients who refuse their cooperation) can have on the results (e.g. Rutter 1977). A more basic problem was that the study compared maladjusted school leavers with other categories of handicap; this was understandable, as it was a survey of all special school leavers irrespective of the category of their handicap. However, we have already seen that maladjusted children differed from many similar pupils who remain in ordinary schools only in receiving the administrative label which acted as passport to the special school.

A more useful comparison would have been with similarly disturbed adolescents leaving ordinary schools; the evidence reviewed in Chapter 2 suggests there is no shortage of these. This said, it is of interest that 50 per cent of the maladjusted pupils in Tuckey's survey left school at fifteen (when the statutory age for all special school leavers was sixteen), a feature which distinguished them from all other categories of handicap. All but one had worked since leaving school (97 per cent). Over three-quarters of the maladjusted pupils were considered suitable for further education or training, but of these less than one-third actually received it.

An important incidental finding was that headteachers tended to under-estimate the pupils' chances of success in employment. Heads considered only 14 per cent suitable for employment without further education or training, but 72 per cent obtained jobs direct from school. Headteachers were in fact more pessimistic about employment potential than was justified for all categories of handicap, but especially for the deaf and maladjusted. This lends strong support to the view that special schools may over-protect their pupils. On the other hand there was evidence that the maladjusted group had had a greater number of jobs since leaving school than any other category.

The existence of LEAs with primary special schools, but with no secondary school provision, provides an interesting opportunity to assess subsequent progress. Marshall (1971) found that 80 per cent of leavers from an Outer London Borough special school had been reintegrated into ordinary school, with good subsequent adjustment in all but 8 per cent of cases. Firm conclusions are not possible owing to lack of detailed information on the children's problems on admission to special education and on the procedures for gathering information on their progress after leaving. The evidence suggests, however, that the virtually automatic transfer from primary special schooling to secondary special schooling which exists in some LEAs may be unnecessary at best and actively opposed to the child's interests at worst. More controversially, the evidence also suggests that it may be the anxieties of special school teachers and educational psychologists that keep children segregated in special schools, and not the needs of the children.

CONCLUSIONS

The dearth of information on the progress and subsequent adjustment of pupils in day schools for the maladjusted is exceeded only by the lack of information about the nature of the problems they presented on admission. Roe (1965) found that just over half the children admitted to day schools were considered too timid or withdrawn to cope with the demands of ordinary school. In contrast this applied to only eight out of thirty-four children referred to residential schools. Similarly only two out of twenty-eight day school admissions were thought to be becoming delinquent or 'at risk' in other ways in the community, compared with twenty-five out of forty-two boarding school children. Anecdotal but consistent evidence over the last ten years suggests very strongly that day schools are increasingly being used for disruptive pupils. Residential schools are reserved: (a) for the most severely disturbing pupils of all; (b) for pupils the social services department cannot or will not take into care even though their families are considered by LEA support staff and by teachers unable to cope with them. There is anecdotal evidence that this second group is increasing as a result of social services departments closing down some of their worst institutions and making more determined efforts to provide care and support within the community.

Be this as it may, it illustrates one of the problems in interpreting the research evidence: because the pupils constitute a heterogeneous group, it could be considered inappropriate to expect uniformity in terms of progress. In one sense, though, this is a spurious argument. Whatever else day or residential special schools may attempt to do, they presumably aim: (a) to help their pupils make good *educational* progress; (b) to help them become independent of the special school, either by returning to ordinary school or by successful entry into employment.

Against these criteria, both day and residential schools must be considered expensive, inefficient and ill-conceived. With annual fees of over £15,000 per pupil in many residential schools we need not dwell on the cost. With very few exceptions, residential schools achieve a low rate of return to the mainstream. This is also the case in most day schools, but when transfer occurs out of administrative necessity, for example when there is no school for secondary pupils, successful integration appears to be the norm. Improvements in behaviour seem not to exceed the improvements we should expect on the basis of spontaneous remission. In day schools there is evidence of deterioration in behaviour in the first year, with some subsequent progress. Evidence on employment suggests that most leavers succeed in finding jobs, though not necessarily in holding them, but this pre-dates the massive rise in unemployment of the 1980s. Overall, the available evidence lends no support to the belief that referral to special schools for the maladjusted is likely to benefit the children concerned.

DISTURBING BEHAVIOUR: OTHER APPROACHES

OFF-SITE UNITS

In the late 1960s and early 1970s two separate but related trends led to demands for additional provision for disturbing pupils. One was increasing dissatisfaction with the existing network of child guidance clinics, described in an influential article by Professor Jack Tizard (1973) as wasteful in their use of resources and inefficient in their results. The second was recognition by LEA administrators and politicians that existing special schools could not cope with the older and more openly disruptive pupils who were being referred, often following temporary or permanent exclusion for disciplinary reasons. Off-site units have attracted a great deal of critical attention. We consider here evidence on their organisation, curriculum, the pupils' attendance and rates of return to ordinary schools.

An early survey by HMI criticised the buildings in which many units were housed. It also claimed that some units received inadequate funds, either for capital expenditure or for day-to-day running costs (HMI 1978). Further problems are cited by Francis (1980) as lack of accountability, inadequate criteria for admission and a tendency to admit a disproportionate number of pupils from minority ethnic groups. This tendency was also confirmed in one of the earlier Inner London studies (ILEA 1981).

Her Majesty's Inspectorate of Schools (1978) reported a wide range of academic subjects being offered across the units, but an unacceptably narrow range within most of them. According to Dawson (1980) units had a narrower curriculum than special schools. Given the complexity of the secondary school curriculum and the inevitably small number of teachers in any one unit, a narrow curriculum becomes virtually inevitable. Common sense suggests that this is unlikely to facilitate successful return to the mainstream.

Her Majesty's Inspectorate of Schools found some evidence of improvement in the attendance of pupils at off-site units. A similar tendency was found in a study of ILEA centres (Mortimore *et al.* 1983). This, however, must be set against an HMI appraisal of the ILEA units which criticised the curriculum as 'inevitably limited by accommodation and staff expertise' and concluded that 'the whole programme of off-site units for disruptive pupils needs reappraisal' (HMI 1980b).

In view of the ambiguous and often unstated motives in referring pupils to off-site units, it is perhaps less than surprising that their record in returning pupils to ordinary schools should be extremely poor. The majority of units in Britain were established with the expressed aim of returning pupils to the mainstream. In the overwhelming majority of units this aim was rapidly, if tacitly, abandoned. In his excellent review of all current forms of provision Topping (1983) quotes American studies which reached the same conclusion. The same was true of all off-site units established by the Education Department in New Zealand (Galloway and Barrett 1984).

It is not, however, inevitable. Topping (1983) quotes an unpublished study by Mickleborough (1980) claiming a reintegration rate of 78 per cent. In addition the key centre in Birmingham (Dain 1977) and the Hungerford Centre in London (Lane 1977) have reported high rates of return to mainstream schooling. We return to this question in Chapter 7, when we consider how such units may operate successfully.

There appears to be an almost total lack of information on the progress of pupils leaving off-site units for the world of work.

Galloway and Barrett (1984) found only 22 per cent of leavers from four New Zealand units entering employment. Almost as many were committed to Department of Social Welfare institutions by the courts. We were able to obtain no information, though, on the pupils' eventual employment records. The only thing that could be said with confidence was that a majority did not make a smooth transition from the unit to regular employment.

ON-SITE UNITS

Whereas off-site units generally admit pupils from several schools, units based in an ordinary primary or secondary school generally serve only the host school. The term on-site unit is used here, although they have been described in a wide variety of terms, from 'sin-bins' to 'havens'. The earliest units were seen as a way of extending the work of educational psychologists and child guidance clinics, by providing a consultancy service on schools. The 'adjustment groups' in West Sussex primary schools aimed to provide a therapeutic environment for 'maladjusted' children, who attended the groups on a part-time basis. At around the same time the ILEA was establishing 'nurture groups' for socially disadvantaged children in infant schools (Boxall 1973), with additional support for the children's mothers (Gorrell-Barnes, 1973). Meanwhile a unit at Brislington School in Bristol was attracting attention for its work with difficult secondary age pupils (N. Jones 1973, 1974).

Evaluation of pupils' progress in the West Sussex groups suggested some improvement in relationships with adults and with other children in around two-thirds of pupils. The children least likely to benefit, however, were those whose behaviour was most overtly disruptive. In a review of the American literature Carlberg and Kavale (1980) concluded that 'emotionally disturbed' and 'behaviour disordered' children tended to make better progress in special classes than in ordinary classes. This held true both of achievement and of social behaviour. Unfortunately the nature of the review made it impossible to review the frequency of transfer back to the mainstream. Nor was it possible to assess subsequent progress. One of the best conducted of the studies reviewed by Carlbert and Kavale found striking evidence of improvement while the pupils attended the group (Vacc 1968), but this was not maintained on return to ordinary lessons (Vacc 1972).

In Britain provision in ordinary schools exploded in the 1970s and early 1980s. The early groups were initiated by educational psychologists and attracted a good deal of attention in professional papers and journals. It seems likely that this publicity may have led headteachers and administrators to see on-site units as a convenient way of dealing with the problems generated by problem children.

The education of disturbing children

In Sheffield we studied the seven schools which had established on-site units (Galloway *et al.* 1982). The pupil–teacher ratio was extraordinarily generous, ranging from an average of 5 : 1 to just under 2 : 1, or more generous than would be found in almost all special schools. As with off-site units, though, the curriculum was much narrower than in the mainstream. More worrying, we only observed one unit in which an explicit attempt was made to link the curriculum in the unit with the curriculum in the mainstream.

Behaviour in the groups was generally excellent, but this did *not* generalise to the pupils' behaviour outside the unit itself. Indeed, when we looked at the evidence on exclusion and suspension we found that as many pupils were excluded from school for disciplinary reasons in the first two years of each group's existence as in the previous two years. Whatever else the groups might have been doing, they were not reducing the number of pupils referred for separate special schooling or excluded as unmanageable. They were, however, removing a substantial number of children from ordinary classes and by giving them a different, narrower curriculum were making successful return to ordinary classes unlikely.

CATCH 'EM EARLY: FACT OR FICTION?

At this stage it is worth looking at one of the more persistent red herrings in special education, namely that if problems are recognised and treated early enough they are more likely to be solved quickly and successfully. Illogically, this argument is often invoked in support of pre-school and primary provision. The argument is illogical on at least two grounds.

First, as the Warnock Report pointed out, the problems presented by many pupils are temporary, and clear up without specialist provision. Second, there is evidence that just over half the pupils assessed as displaying signs of psychiatric disorder in adolescence present problems for the first time in adolescence. Just under half have also presented problems as children (Rutter *et al.* 1976). This alone makes nonsense of any argument that resources should be concentrated in younger age-groups in order to prevent more serious problems later.

Day units for pre-school children have mostly been operated by hospital child psychiatry departments, with results that have proved inconclusive. Woolacott *et al.* (1978) found no differences between twenty-five children who attended a day hospital pre-school unit for a year and a control group with a similar pattern of behaviour problems. On follow-up five years later no significant differences were found between children who had received treatment and controls. In contrast Frommer (1967) reported improvement in nearly three-quarters of anxious children attending a day hospital unit, though in fewer than half the aggressive children. Barton (1984) reported a 'good outcome' in thirty-six of sixty-nine children attending a therapeutic pre-school unit, but only seventeen of these (25 per cent of the total) went on to normal play-group or school.

Turning to schools and units for younger children run by LEAs the picture is even more bleakly discouraging. Day and residential special schools have notoriously low rates of return to the mainstream. Primary special schools achieve no better results than secondary, except when integration becomes an administrative necessity through lack of provision for older age-groups. Research from on-site units is equivocal, but there is little evidence to support the view that problems in adolescence have been reduced by treatment at an earlier stage.

COUNSELLING, PSYCHOTHERAPY AND SPONTANEOUS REMISSION

Even if children attending special classes or units invariably made excellent academic and social progress, which manifestly is not the case, we could still not conclude that the improvement resulted from their attendance. We would still need to know how many pupils with similar problems improved without receiving any kind of special education. At present we have no way of answering this question. There has, however, been a considerable volume of research on the effects of counselling and psychotherapy. Not all pupils receiving these forms of treatment would be considered maladjusted or disruptive by teachers. On the other hand, counselling and psychotherapy are possible options for all pupils considered maladjusted or disruptive.

The first major study to question the usefulness of psychotherapy with children found that children who received treatment were no more likely to improve than 'defectors' who were accepted for treatment but never began it (Levitt 1957). In both groups about two-thirds of the children were reported to have improved. This, of course, is the figure quoted with almost monotonous regularity in other research which we have already reported. In a later article Levitt (1963) reviewed twenty-two evaluation studies. He found that children with 'acting out' problems such as delinquency were significantly less likely to improve following psychotherapy than children with identifiable behaviour problems such as enuresis or school phobia.

The poor outlook for children with behavioural problems has been confirmed by Robins (1966, 1972) in a long-term follow-up of children treated at an American child guidance clinic. The children tested for neurotic disturbance had almost as satisfactory adjustment when followed up as adults as a control group matched for neighbourhood, race and age. The children treated for antisocial behaviour, in contrast, were more likely to show a wide range of problems as adults, including trouble with the police, poor employment records and difficulties in family relationships. A long term follow-up to a study of children in Buckinghamshire obtained broadly similar results (Mitchell and Rosa 1981).

The picture from research on counselling and psychotherapy is not uniformly gloomy. Wright *et al.* (1976) re-analysed some of the studies in Levitt's (1957) review. He confirmed that children who received treatment were no more likely than untreated controls to have improved by the end of treatment. Nevertheless, they had improved by the time they were followed up even though they had received no further treatment. A similar finding was obtained from a group therapy programme in secondary schools in the North East of England (Kolvin *et al.* 1981). Six well-qualified social workers conducted 'non-directive' discussion groups using Carl Rogers's group therapy principles with a total of sixty pupils presenting a wide range of problems. The programme ran for one term, and a few differences were found immediately afterwards. Three years later, however, teachers' reports showed significant improvements in behaviour. An earlier follow-up had found academic as well as behavioural gains, but the academic gains were not maintained for the full three years.

OVERVIEW

From a theoretical point of view Wright's and Kolvin's work is of considerable interest. Counsellors, psychologists and psychiatrists may also take comfort in the evidence that children who receive treatment are quite likely to derive some long-term benefit, even though there may be no immediate change in behaviour. Teachers, however, may legitimately be a little cynical. They may feel that two or three years is too long to wait when they are concerned about a child's behaviour *now*. They may even feel justified in concluding: (a) that offering pupils individual or group counselling or psychotherapy has no immediate relevance to their own needs as teachers; (b) that in the absence of anything more constructive they might as well continue to place their trust in special schools or units. These may not do the children any good, but they do at least have the merit of removing a small number of misfits from the mainstream – in most cases permanently. We show in Chapters 5 and 7 that the nihilism of this conclusion is unjustified. Teachers can in fact do a great deal to help

The effects of special education

themselves and their pupils. The evidence we have reviewed so far suggests, however, that most existing special schools and units for children with behaviour problems might realistically be seen as part of the problem rather than as part of the solution. Is the same true of provision for children with learning difficulties?

CHILDREN WITH MODERATE LEARNING DIFFICULTIES

We are concerned here with children who until the 1981 Education Act would have been labelled ESN(M) and in America are still termed the Educable Mentally Retarded. Abolition of the ESN(M) category has not resulted in the closure of special schools or classes that catered for ESN(M) pupils, nor has it resulted in any substantial changes in the pupils referred to them. Hence, we still need to consider whether they benefit the children concerned.

It is a sad reflection on the uncritical attitudes of educationists and administrators in Britain towards children with special needs that almost all the relevant research has been carried out elsewhere. Whether findings on special schools or classes in North America or Scandinavia can generalise to Britain is a matter for debate. What is not a matter for debate is that in the absence of serious attempts to compare the progress and adjustment of children in special schools in Britain with that of similar pupils attending ordinary schools, we have to look overseas.

Nor is it a matter for serious debate that the results lend no support to the lobby for special schools or classes for children with moderate learning difficulties. Research over the last fifty-five years has shown two pretty consistent trends. First, some, but by no means all, studies have shown the children becoming socially better adjusted in special schools. Second, the overwhelming majority of studies show children making at least as much educational progress in ordinary classes.

The debate was opened by Bennett (1932) who found that children in ordinary classes obtained higher scores on reading and spelling and arithmetic tests than other children, matched for age and IQ in special schools. As with almost all the research, however, there were questions as to whether the two groups were really comparable. Thus in Bennett's survey, there were more boys in the ordinary class group and there were further differences in the prevalence of physical factors such as defective hearing and eyesight. Perhaps more important, there was no attempt to control for emotional stability and general motivation towards school when selecting the groups. Thurstone (1959) obtained similar results when she compared children with IQ scores in the 50–79 range. She suggested four possible explanations for the superior educational attainments of the ordinary class children: first it was possible that ESN(M) pupils were stimulated by being in an ordinary class; second it was possible that their motivation decreased in a special class; third, dull children selected for special schools differ from those who are not; finally, teachers in special schools might place less emphasis on improving educational attainments than their colleagues in ordinary schools. All these possibilities merit consideration, but no real conclusions can be drawn without more evidence about the possibility that dull children selected for special education are selected because they have *additional* problems.

Other projects have investigated the children's social adjustment as well as their educational attainments. Ellenbogen (1957) compiled two groups on the basis of age, sex and school district; all the special school children had already received special education for at least two years. The educational attainments of children in ordinary classes were consistently higher than those of special class pupils, but the latter were regarded by their teachers as socially more active and better emotionally adjusted with regard to school and the future. Ann Jordan (1959) also found better general adjustment in special class children, emphasising the social isolation of ESN(M) children in ordinary classes. Cassidy and Stanton (1959), Wrightstone *et al.* (1959) and Johnson (1962) all concluded that special classes promote social adjustment, while ordinary classes promote educational attainments. On the other hand not all studies have found consistent differences between special classes and ordinary classes. Blatt (1958) tried to eliminate selection errors by comparing dull children in a district with special schools with dull children in a district which had no such provision. In other words, he compared a group of children who had been selected for special education with a group consisting not only of children who *would* have been selected if facilities had existed, but also of children who would have been overlooked even if facilities had existed. He found no important differences between the two groups in the results of achievement tests. Similarly, Ainsworth (1959) found no important differences in educational progress or social adjustment.

The consistency with which these early studies showed no educational benefits from special class placement undoubtedly helped to influence public opinion. They led one of North America's leading figures in special education to argue in a much quoted article:

> If I were a Negro from the slums or a disadvantaged parent . . . and knew what I now know about special classes for the educable mentally retarded, other things being equal I would then go to court before allowing the schools to label my child as 'mentally retarded' and place him in a 'self-contained special school or class' (Dunn 1968).

The effects of special education

Subsequent work has done nothing to invalidate this conclusion. Thus, Carlberg and Kavale (1980) concluded from their review of the available literature that special class placement was unlikely to benefit 'Educable Mentally Retarded' (EMR) children. Yet it was another seven years following Dunn's seminal article before the passing of Federal Law 94/142 with its principle of the child's right to education in the 'least restrictive environment' possible (see Ch. 4).

So what of the situation in Britain? In one of the few studies carried out here Maurice Ascher (1970) compared children aged eleven to thirteen in ESN(M) schools with children of similar age and IQ in the remedial departments of ordinary schools. Only children with an IQ in the range 60–90 were selected for inclusion (in either group); in addition they were regarded by their teachers as having 'normal' behaviour, health, physique and attendance for that particular type of school. (Whether special school teachers regard 'normality' in these respects in a different way to ordinary school teachers is not known.) As would be expected from other research, most of the parents were in Social Classes IV and V and lived in council property, mainly flats. The children were tested individually in their first or second year of secondary education, and again a year later. Results showed that the remedial department group had significantly higher scores on vocabulary and reading tests, both on initial testing and re-testing. The number of children improving over the year was also greater in the remedial group. To a lesser extent the same applied to scores in an arithmetic test. Children with the lowest initial scores tended to make the most improvement – an encouraging finding, but disconcerting if there is an inclination to concentrate on practical activities for slow learners.

A battery of tests investigating the children's preferred social contacts out of school and their preferred leisure occupations suggested greater maturity in the children from remedial departments. Unfortunately this aspect of the survey was not discussed in detail. Concluding, Ascher remarks that 'stated in very conservative terms, the special school children showed no particular advantage by the educational placement and also possibly suffered some segregation from children in ordinary schools'.

Ascher's study suffers the same problems concerning selection of children for each group as the American literature; to put it very simply, we should expect the differences if the ESN(M) children had been placed in special schools for reasons other than intellectual dullness and educational backwardness, for instance maladjustment or family problems.

Another English study (Shearer 1977) investigated the way in which ESN(M) provision was perceived by parents, teachers and the children themselves. Over three-quarters of the parents and children said they were happy with their classes or schools, and satisfied with their educational progress. Unfortunately, no conclusions can be drawn from these superficially encouraging results as there was no comparison group of children who remained in ordinary schools. Might parents who were not offered special education (or who refused to accept it) have been equally happy about their children's progress in the local secondary schools? Might the children themselves have told the researchers they were glad they had not been sent to special schools? Equally unsatisfactory is Shearer's evidence on the children's improvement in behaviour, since this was based on informal opinions as to whether the children had improved, remained the same or deteriorated. We have already seen (in relation to maladjusted children) the wide disparity between informal opinions about improvement and slightly more objective assessments with techniques such as the Bristol Guides.

It will be clear from the review so far that a cardinal weakness in all the quoted studies has been the difficulty in comparing two groups. None of the studies was based on a *random* allocation of pupils to special schools or ordinary classes. The idea of allocating children at random to special schools or ordinary schools would cause many teachers and educationalists to throw up their hands in horror. Nevertheless, we have reviewed consistent evidence that 'special' does not necessarily mean 'better'. In spite of the horror of thalidomide, it is doubtful whether the medical profession has ever allowed new drugs on to the market with the same haphazard, random enthusiasm which has characterised the development of special education. As Ford *et al.* (1982) imply, special education may be responsible for 'invisible disasters'. The disasters may be invisible because they happen to children from disadvantaged families who cannot provoke the public and political debate surrounding different forms of medical treatment.

CHILDREN WITH MILD AND SPECIFIC LEARNING DIFFICULTIES

MILD LEARNING DIFFICULTIES

Some children are regarded as backward, but not backward enough to justify full-time special school or special class placement. Broadly, these are children whose educational backwardness is associated with low measured intelligence (see p. 37). Until quite recently many secondary schools and some primaries provided 'remedial' classes in which these pupils spent virtually all their time. As a result of mounting and consistent pressure from HMI (e.g. DES 1972, 1979; Scottish Education Department 1978), the number of full-time 'remedial' classes is probably declining. At least in principle, the special needs departments which are replacing remedial departments seldom withdraw pupils on an indefinite full-time basis. It is still widespread practice, however, to withdraw pupils from ordinary lessons for extra help in basic skills. Hence, there is still a need to evaluate the effects of separate classes for children with mild learning difficulties.

In one of the few well-controlled studies of the effects of special education, Osterling (1967) was able to allocate children in Swedish primary schools to slow-learner or to ordinary classes. The children all had an IQ of at least 70, and could therefore be regarded in Britain as having mild learning difficulties or as 'remedial'.

The children were tested at regular intervals in Swedish and arithmetic; the ordinary class group showed a gradual improvement relative to the slow-learner classes, especially in arithmetic. When Osterling investigated the pupils' social adjustment, he found that both groups experienced a good deal of frustration, mainly due to their sensing the negative expectations of the people around them. Nevertheless, there was an important difference between the two groups. With the ordinary class children, frustration was focused mainly on school, perhaps reflecting their relative failure compared with their peers; in contrast, children in the slow-learner classes tended to experience greater frustration outside school, at home and in the community. Osterling does not comment on which group is likely to have better social adjustment in the long run, but his investigation does place a large question mark on the American studies which found better social adjustment among children in special schools or classes than in ordinary schools. Might the special school children have appeared more disturbed if the inquiry had focused on their behaviour out of school, and might the ordinary class pupils then have appeared less disturbed? Osterling himself points out (in his review on the American literature) that 'since the regular class may be more analogous to post-school life than the artificial environment of the special class, it is conceivable that optimal accommodation for mentally retarded children in school could result in post-school problems of adjustment'.

Another well-controlled study was carried out in New Zealand by Frampton (1981). She was able to compare the progress of pupils in a traditional secondary school slow-learner class with that of pupils admitted the following year when all the slow learners were integrated into ordinary classes. The results showed no significant differences in academic progress, but considerable benefits for the integrated group on a social adjustment scale.

The results were consistent with other studies. Carlberg and Kavale's review, for example, concluded that slow-learning children above the EMR level were likely to make considerably less academic progress in special classes than in ordinary classes. As Frampton argues, there really does not seem to be any need for more research on the subject.

CHILDREN WITH SPECIFIC LEARNING DIFFICULTIES

It is sometimes thought that educationally retarded children whose educational backwardness is *not* associated with low measured intelligence are more likely to respond well to remedial teaching than children whose backwardness *is* associated with low IQ. In fact it is not at all clear that this is the case. The Isle of Wight study found that the second group suffered from more neurological, speeech and motor problems. Yet they made significantly *more* progress than the children whose retardation was more specifically related to reading (Yule 1973). Similar results have been obtained in New Zealand (Silva *et al*. 1985).

This has interesting implications for the selection of children for special education. In the first place it confirms much of the research on remedial reading that IQ does not have a crucial influence on a backward or retarded reader's chances of making progress, at least in the ranges encountered in ordinary schools and in the upper half of schools for children with moderate learning difficulties. Yet it is still not uncommon for educational psychologists to use IQ as the most important single criterion in recommending transfer to a special school or class. An equally important point is the possible inference that resources for special education should be aimed at the group with the worst prognosis, namely children with specific reading difficulties, rather than at more globally retarded children who may have a better outlook in respect of educational progress.

A valid objection to this argument would be that many, if not most, of the children selected for ESN(M) schools are in fact retarded in reading, even when retardation is assessed in relation to age and intelligence level. On the other hand children in ESN(M) schools form a very small proportion of the children with specific reading retardation, and one wonders whether resources might more profitably be directed at reducing this problem than at providing a total educational environment for a minority. There is firm evidence from research on remedial reading that short-term improvement is possible, and several indications that these improvements can be maintained if adequate follow-up support is provided.

REMEDIAL READING

Carlberg and Kavale found some evidence that 'learning disabled' children in America benefited from special class placement. This group would include children considered to have specific learning difficulties, including so-called 'dyslexia' in Britain. Unfortunately it is not clear how far progress achieved in the special class was maintained on return to the mainstream. The question is complicated in Britain by the fact that some remedial groups contain globally backward children *and* children with specific learning difficulties, for example in reading.

Nevertheless short-term gains from remedial reading have been reported quite consistently (Sampson 1975). There has been less agreement about whether this improvement is maintained over the next few years. Lovell *et al.* (1962, 1963) carried out a large-scale investigation of the long-term effects of remedial education on children who were taught individually in child guidance clinics or in small groups at their own schools. Both groups improved initially, but neither group maintained the improvements. Lovell's rather gloomy conclusion was that the results seemed to be more or less the same whether the children were dull or of average intelligence, and whether they were taught singly or in groups.

More optimistically Kellmer Pringle (1961) found that most parents of children who had received remedial teaching at least eighteen months earlier were satisfied with their children's educational progress and social adjustment. Shearer (1967) obtained similarly encouraging results with a smaller group who were taught in a primary school adjustment class; he showed that the loss of progress achieved during remedial teaching could be reduced if the children received adequate follow-up in their ordinary classes. This point was made more clearly by Tobin and Pumfrey (1976) who followed up primary school children who had received remedial education. As usual, the 'tested' children were found to make better progress in the short term, but a disturbing pattern emerged when they entered their secondary schools. The 'untreated' children continued to make progress after leaving their primary schools, while the 'treated' pupils actually regressed, though only marginally in the case of children at Roman Catholic schools; although the 'treated' groups were still showing some benefit, the gap was narrowing. Reinforcing an earlier suggestion (Cashdan and Pumfrey 1969) the authors comment on this rather widespread tendency:

> It has been argued that this is hardly surprising. If a pupil is returned to a situation which initially contributed to his need for remedial help and the situation is essentially the same, then regression seems extremely likely. A strong case can be made for continuing the help that appears to have been effective in the short term.

CONCLUSIONS

Our review of work on the progress of slow-learning and disturbing children makes uncomfortable reading for anyone involved in special education. At the risk of only minor over-simplification the evidence can be summarised in two sentences: (a) all kinds of special schools or units for disturbing pupils have a dismal record in returning pupils successfully to mainstream education, though the extent to which they actually reduce the chances of spontaneous remission of behavioural problems remains an open question; (b) slow-learning children make better progress in ordinary schools than in special schools, and in ordinary classes than in remedial classes. Whatever else most of the forms of special provision that we have reviewed may be doing, there is little evidence that they are meeting children's special needs.

Perhaps the most striking aspect of the research is that so little of it is recent. For at least the last twenty years the evidence, overwhelmingly, has shown that children with moderate learning difficulties are less likely to make progress if transferred to a special school or class in which they follow a separate curriculum. Yet the proportion of children transferred to officially designated special schools and classes shows no signs of reduction. We continue to remove children with mild and/or specific learning difficulties from the mainstream for extra help in 'remedial' or 'special needs' classes. Yet there has been more than ample evidence for at least twenty years that gains from remedial teaching are usually lost on return to the mainstream unless continuing support is provided. Every parent and every teacher knows that children learn from each other, for better or worse. Yet the number of pupils transferred to special schools or units for the maladjusted or disruptive has never been higher.

All these anomalies are carried out by caring, experienced, responsible teachers, psychologists, doctors and administrators, all acting in good faith, in what they genuinely believe to be the best interests of the children concerned! The easy explanation lies in terms of a conspiracy to maintain the *status quo* by removing misfits from ordinary classes. The reasons, however, lie much deeper, in the organisation of special education at national, LEA and school level, and in the wider social and political climate in which teachers are working. To justify this statement we need to look at the policy and practice of special education in some other countries.

Chapter four
SPECIAL EDUCATION IN NORWAY AND THE UNITED STATES

INTRODUCTION

In this chapter we look at special education in two other countries – Norway and the US. This comparative perspective is valuable for three reasons. First, it allows us to question some prevalent assumptions about special education in Britian. Second, it is refreshing to examine the history of educational development in different countries, and look at the underlying attitudes and philosophy towards special education on which present arrangements are based. Finally, a more detailed analysis of how children with special needs are educated – both in ordinary and in special schools – encourages us to reflect on our own educational system in a critical manner.

We have chosen to look at two countries which have both passed legislation on special education in the last ten years. In each case the relevant laws espouse a philosophy which explicitly aims to integrate children with special needs into ordinary schools, and ordinary classrooms. This form of individual integration is particularly interesting as it seeks to avoid many of the pitfalls of special classes or units, in ordinary schools (see Chs. 5 and 6).

We chose to describe Norway because its financial provision for children with special needs exemplifies one way of achieving integration for a child within an ordinary community school. Children in Norway would have to travel long distances to reach a special school. Over the years special education provision which resulted in virtually automatic residential provision became unacceptable to many parents. Parental pressure, combined with progressive political and educational thinking, resulted in legislation in 1976. The new law advocated integration and specified financial provision to encourage this to happen. It anticipated the implementation of the 1981 Education Act in Britain by some seven years.

The education of disturbing children

The US Public Law, 94–142, came into effect in 1978. This, too, was a response to pressure from campaigning groups, and in particular was connected with educational and social thinking stemming from civil rights protests. The ideological foundation of a 'rights' approach within American society and institutions offers a useful contrast to Britain. We emphasise the strengths and advantages of this approach, and contrast it with the model of special education in Britain.

In each country we look at the system of mainstream education, at the development of policies in special education and at the current administration and organisation of special education. We then take a critical look at the contribution made to international debate about integration, with particular reference to comparisons and contrasts with special education in Britain.

NORWAY

Norway is one of the five member countries of the Nordic Council which was formed in 1972 to foster cultural cooperation between Finland, Denmark, Sweden, Norway and Iceland. This council has done a great deal to spread discussion and information about the educational systems of member countries. There are several significant differences between Britain and Norway in the history and organisation of education. Administration is usually centred on smaller units. Communes, for example (equivalent to our LEAs), normally cover a population of 10,000–30,000.

The comprehensive school system is considerably older. The principle of comprehensive schooling dates from 1919 when a seven year comprehensive schooling for all children was first introduced. In 1959 this was extended to nine years of schooling.

Education in Norway starts later than in England, beginning at seven, and ending at 16. Norwegian schools are generally small by our standards. As a matter of educational philosophy Norwegian law restricts new schools to a maximum of 450 pupils. This is because Norwegian educationalists believe that small schools are better at pastoral care and social education than large ones.

Children normally change from primary to secondary school at the age of thirteen. Classes are mainly unstreamed although option choices in the secondary years often lead to selective groupings. Norwegian educationalists are, however, largely committed to avoiding early specialisation because of the restrictions this imposes on later career paths. A high percentage of Norwegian children continue into further education. About 85 per cent of sixteen- to seventeen-year-olds are enrolled in voluntary upper secondary schools.

In general classes are smaller. In Norway class size is around twenty for child up to thirteen years, and twenty-four for children aged thirteen to sixteen (an interesting contrast with British staffing ratios where smaller groups are in the older age ranges).

Norwegian education has a more standardised curriculum than in Britain. Curriculum 'guidelines' are issued to the schools by the central government department. There is also a more explicit emphasis on social education and pastoral care as an integral part of school curricula.

The training of teachers provides another interesting difference from Britain. Most teachers working in comprehensive schools have taken a four-year teacher training course. Those working in upper secondary schools must have a university degree and a postgraduate teaching certificate, or an equivalent degree from teacher training college. Most teachers in the early grades (1–6) are trained to be generalists (that is, to teach most subjects in the curriculum, rather than become subject specialists).

THE ORGANISATION OF SPECIAL EDUCATION

The Ministry of Education in Norway is responsible for the education of all children, including children with severe learning difficulties. Legislation of 1976 established the principle of integration and required that handicapped children should, as far as possible, be sent to a school within their local area. Because of the size of the country and its sparse population distribution, particularly in the north, Norway has emphasised the individual integration of handicapped children within ordinary classes in the local school, in contrast to the 'unit' or group provision of special education in other Scandinavian countries (Sweden being a notable example).

In Norway the principle of integration is seen as part of government policy towards equal opportunities for disabled people. Norwegian communes, or LEAs have interpreted the 1976 Act as implying a need to move resources from the previous system of separate special schools into the ordinary school system. This has sometimes been done by the relocation of teachers, as in the appointment of liaison teachers to work within ordinary schools to provide support to children and their class teachers. It has sometimes been done by emphasising the need to return children back to mainstream education after a period in a separate special school – with some staff being given a specific brief for this work. Thus Haug Special School near Oslo, has a teacher whose specific job is to return children back to the ordinary school system and support them on return. She may offer regular sessions working with the child's class teacher for a few weeks, and then gradually decrease her involvement over a period of months.

It is important not to paint a picture of the special school system changing overnight. The numbers of children returning to the mainstream from Haug School, for example, are a fairly small proportion of the total intake. In the long term, however, we could hope to see statistical evidence of the changing use of special education resources in this way. Preliminary indications from 1977 to 1981 show some decline in pupils in separate special education in Norway (see below).

THE FUNDING OF SPECIAL EDUCATION

This is seen as the most important way of implementing the principle of supported integration for individual children in their local schools. As a general principle, finance is organised so that communes have refunded to them by central government extra costs of facilities for pupils with special needs. These costs must be *over and above* those incurred in the education of an 'ordinary' child. Thus the financial provisions require the identification and assessment of children with special needs in order for the extra resources to be provided.

A recent survey of progress in integration in Norway by Dahl *et al.* (1982) describes these provisions in detail. Resources for mainstream schools are in general allocated to the school unit as a fixed number of teaching hours. A fundamental concept is the '*frame–hour–number*' which is the total number of teaching hours allocated to each school. The 'frame–hour–number' is higher than the number of teaching hours. In 1979–80 this gave an extra 22–28 per cent of teaching hours at the primary level, and 58 per cent at the lower secondary level.

These extra teaching hours have various functions:

1. Contact work with parents.
2. Special education.
3. Secretarial work.
4. Hours for splitting-up classes.

The intention behind the 'frame–hour–number' system was primarily to help schools to adjust better to the individual needs of the pupils. Schools can use these hours as they wish, but are generally expected to use around 10 per cent of the total at primary level and five hours per class per week at secondary level for special education. It was expected that these hours would cover some special education for 10 per cent of pupils.

These resources are limited, though. The evaluation study showed that help was not intensive – 16,000 pupils in ordinary classes received 30,000 hours of special education in this way, i.e. just under two hours per pupil per week. In addition, the evaluation project showed that a quarter of the teaching time for special education was being used for splitting classes primarily for reasons *other* than the provision of special education.

A second fund, called 'B' hours, provides more intensive help from central government for individual children. This fund was originally established to compensate for the teaching of children for whom there were not sufficient places in special schools, but was later extended in order to facilitate integration. Between 2 and 3 per cent of the pupils get some teaching from 'B' funds.

'B' funds have increased from Nkr 7.4 million (£643,478) in 1977 to Nkr 56.6 million (£4,921,739). In order to receive 'B' funds for a specific child there must be a professional evaluation of the child's needs and a formal administrative procedure, which identifies the pupils as 'special'.

As might be expected applications for 'B' funds consistently exceed the money available. The system has a built-in tendency for expansion, irrespective of the objective situation of its clients (Eide 1978). This is specifically the case in the Norwegian system which largely puts the responsibility for assessment of special needs on the local commune while the resultant additional expenditure is the responsibility of central government.

LESSONS FROM THE NORWEGIAN SYSTEM

It is important to acknowledge the contribution made by the Scandinavian countries in general and Norway in particular, to international debate about the principle of integration and its practical implementation. As we have seen, Norway's method of financing the integration of individual children into their local school offers a clear example of how such a system can and does work. As such, it offers important lessons for administrators everywhere who wish to offer 'supported integration' for particular children. It provides clear evidence for parents that individual integration *is* possible. A child does *not* need to be part of a separate group in order to have appropriate teaching in the ordinary school. Norwegian education, therefore, shows us alternatives to the proliferation of 'integration' units at present mushrooming in ordinary schools in Britain.

It is also interesting that current debate in Norway centres around the process and details of resources allocation, rather than around controversy on advantages and disadvantages of integration *per se*. That latter argument has already been won in the favour of integration. This is in marked contrast to Britain where people at all levels in the education service, as well as parents and young people's

75

groups, are still intent on debate about both the principle of integration and whether integration is yet a practical possibility for children with various types of handicap.

It is important, however, to recognise the limitations in the Norwegian approach. The model still entails the need for extensive assessment of children in order to gain extra resources for them. Thus it inevitably emphasises the child's defects rather than abilities and assesses the child herself, rather than the whole school's provision of opportunities for all pupils. Tying resources to one child must inevitably militate against examining the whole school, and seeing how far the needs of *all* pupils can be met within available resources.

The type of resourcing used in Norway also makes children with special needs vulnerable to administrative and political expediency. 'B' funds could be at risk if the country's economic condition changed, or a new government had different political priorities. Could this lead to individual children again being segregated in special schools away from their local community? Under present legislation they remain part of it only because additional funds are provided.

What we are arguing here is that separate administrative and financing systems for children with special needs *always* leave them vulnerable. Far from offering resources protected from financial cut-backs, separate financing means that these children have in effect no *right* to be in their local school. If finance is withdrawn, the question will inevitably arise as to whether the child should also be withdrawn. The educational rights of the child with special needs will only be safeguarded when society accepts that *all* children have a right to be free from the discrimination implicit in segregated schooling.

If schools were resourced on the basis that they would cater for the needs of *all* children in their local area, then singling out particular children, and labelling them for administrative and financial convenience, would no longer be necessary. This point is explored further in our discussion of innovative schemes of integration in Britain. Our present argument is that the financing of integration in Norway militates against a more radical approach of this type. Norway's insistence on the identification of particular children so that adequate financing is provided in schools is an approach which closely resembles some of the provisions in the British 1981 Education Act. Nevertheless, Norway's central government has at least allocated a pool of money to be available for this purpose – in contrast to the total absence of resources from central government following the 1981 Act.

It is also important that we look at evidence on how the 1976 Act is being implemented in practice in Norway. One immediate effect has *not* been the closure of numerous special schools. The following table

Special education in Norway and the United States

shows a moderate downward trend in numbers of children in separate special schools in Norway in the years since the Act was implemented.

TABLE 4.1: Children attending special and mainstream schools in Norway

	Number of compulsory school-aged children taught in the basic school (B), special school (S) and social and medical institutions (SM) 1975–81			Total pupils in all schools	% of all pupils in S & SM schools
	B	S	SM		
1975	567,077	2,638	—	569,715	0.46
1977	579,496	2,520	2,242	584,258	0.82
1979	585,889	2,358	1,967	596,214	0.73
1981	578,413	2,301	2,041	582,755	0.74

Using figures in Table 4.1, the years 1977 to 1981 saw a fall of 420 pupils in separate special schools (combining special schools and social and medical institutions). This comprised a reduction of 9 per cent of the total special school population compared with a drop of just .26 per cent in the total school population over the same period. When we exclude children in social and medical institutions, the reduction of children in special schools is 8.7 per cent from 1977 to 1981, and 12.8 per cent between 1975 and 1981.

The decline of 437 pupils in special schools and schools in social and medical institutions between the years 1977 and 1979, when the overall school population rose by 11,956 pupils, may reflect an enthusiastic early response to the 1976 Act. The following period, however, 1979 to 1981, saw a reduction in the total school population of 13,459, but an increase of 74 children in social and medical institutions and a decrease of 57 pupils in special schools. Thus, the pace of change has slowed considerably although the numbers of segregated pupils have not clearly returned to 1977 levels.

We in Britain have no cause for complacency, though. Hegarty and Pocklington (1981) found that special schools or units were educating 1.55 per cent of pupils over Britain as a whole. This compares with around 0.7 per cent of the Norwegian school population. In Britain in 1980 we were sending proportionately about twice as many children into special schools as in Norway.

The Norwegian authorities have begun the task of reducing numbers of children in special schools, and have chosen a financial method to achieve this. Despite our reservations about the path chosen they have at least taken on board the need to restructure allocation of resources, and there is a clearly visible reduction in segregated provision. It would be an optimist indeed who forecast that Britain could make similar claims five years after the implementation of the 1981 Education Act.

THE UNITED STATES

BACKGROUND TO THE EDUCATIONAL SYSTEM

The development of the educational system in the US has been characterised by appeals to egalitariansim as an American ideal. James Coleman (1983) described four basic elements to this ideology:

1. Providing a *free* education up to a given level which constituted the principal point of entry to the labour force.
2. Providing a common curriculum for all children regardless of background.
3. Partly by design and partly because of low population density, in many areas providing that children from diverse backgrounds attend the same school.
4. Providing equality within a given locality since local taxes provided the source of support for schools.

James Carrier (1984) argues that these ideals have deep historical roots in the beginning of the nineteenth century. The divisions that have become obvious in American society since that time do not totally invalidate this historical perspective. The civil rights movement in particular appealed to American ideals of equality of opportunity and forced the American public to re-examine these ideals. Clear evidence of discrimination against black people was publicised precisely because it contradicted this egalitarianism, on which all American institutions were said to be founded.

SPECIAL EDUCATION IN THE US: HISTORICAL OVERVIEW

The US system of education aimed to allow children with 'ability' from all social classes to be educated to their full potential. This aim implicitly recognised a need to differentiate between children, but emphasised merit rather than social class as a criterion for selection. Education in the US came to rely heavily on intelligence and attainment testing as a way of reliably sorting children into groups.

There emerged, however, deep disagreements among educationalists and the general public alike about the use of IQ as a criterion for selection. Black groups in particular resented tests which discriminated consistently against members of ethnic minority groups leading to the over-representation of blacks in the lowest streams in education. Demands for equal opportunities in education came also from groups of disabled people who attributed both their own restricted opportunities and the prejudiced attitudes within American society to their earlier experiences of segregated education. Hence, dispute focused on how and where special education should be provided.

As in Britain, resources for special education have grown massively over the last twenty-five years.

In the school year 1957–58 2.4 per cent of primary and secondary pupils were receiving special education of some sort. In 1967–68 this had increased to 4.5 per cent, in 1970–71 to 7.4 per cent and in 1978 to 8.2 per cent (Chandler 1981). There has also been an increase in federal support (government funding) for the training of special educators in the United States. In 1960 the number of trainees was 177 costing the US government 1 million dollars. In 1972 this number had increased to 22,000 costing the government 35 million dollars.

Much of the expansion, particularly for the mildly retarded and the emotionally disturbed, came into being as an extensive tracking system (ability grouping) was developed in the US schools system. This occurrred at the same time as racially segregated schools were abolished, forcing black and white children into the same schools. A degree of differentiation and allocation of pupils within the same comprehensive school began to be seen as necessary. Hence, the inequalities that had previously existed between schools became increasingly evident *within* schools. The most famous case of this type of discrimination in education was the Washington DC school system which introduced IQ based tracking 'shortly after it was ordered to dismantle its dual school system' (Kirp 1974). The ending of racial segregation in schools then led to research for new and legitimate differentiation devices which would both explain blacks' poor school performance, and justify their allocation to special programmes.

This picture was complicated, however, by the greater community involvement in education in America compared with Britain. In the US it has always been much easier for pressure groups to exert an influence on policy and practice. Parents became more concerned with their children's education, and less tolerant of school programmes which did not give them what they wanted. According to Carrier (1984):

> This coupled with the realisation, springing from the history of the civil rights movement, that the schools were vulnerable to political and legal pressures, led to a host of legal actions, lobbying efforts, new legislation in the 1960s and 1970s as various public pressure groups sought to mould special education to suit their image of what it ought to be. (p. 56)

Not surprisingly, there was no consensus. Some parents wanted special education to expand within ordinary schools. Others wanted it to contract. Broadly speaking, parents of severely retarded children wanted an extension of education so that their children had a right to go to school. This was embodied in the consent decree in the case of the Pennsylvanian Association for Retarded Children versus the

The education of disturbing children

Commonwealth of Pennsylvania issued in 1972. This decree required the state to accept severely retarded children, a legal principle which was extended shortly afterwards in *Mills* v. *Board of Education* to include all handicapped children. Government legislation followed with the Public Law 93–113, and the Rehabilitation Act of 1973, which stated that no handicapped person could be discriminated against in any federally supported activity or programme. This included all public schooling. The parents of the severely mentally handicapped argued that these laws amounted to a recognition of the handicaps of their children and an offer of equal educational treatment.

Those parents who wanted a contraction of services were concerned primarily with the mildly retarded, and their argument was that existing practices stigmatised those so labelled, while failing to provide any educational benefits. They argued, furthermore, that the application of the label reflected bias against the poor and the black people and was in many respects arbitrary. These arguments blended easily with discussions about the integration of handicapped people, or mainstreaming, as it is called in the US. It was argued that labelling a child is stigmatising, and that segregation into special schools or buildings compounds the problem. As a result of these and other pressures, in 1975 the US Congress passed the Education for All Handicapped Children Act, Public Law 94–142.

THE ROLE OF LEGISLATION IN AMERICAN SPECIAL EDUCATION: PUBLIC LAW 94–142

This law became effective in September 1978, pre-dating implementation of the British Education Act by five years. It provides the basis for special education in *all* states in the USA, both in principles of organisation, and details of implementation.

The law required:

1. That school districts had to provide a plan of special education in their areas; if this plan was not approved, central government funding would be denied.
2. That the plan should have as a goal full educational opportunities for handicapped students.
3. That, in future, handicapped children be taught in the 'least restrictive environment' possible, given:
    (i) the needs of the child;
    (ii) the needs of other children in the class with whom the handicapped child might be placed;
    (iii) the competence of the teachers involved.
4. That all handicapped children should have Individual Education Programmes (IEPs); these included written assessments of each

child's attainments, and statements of annual and short-term educational objectives, the need for special education services, the duration of the special programme, and the criteria for evaluating the child's progress.
5. That procedures for testing, evaluation and placement of handicapped students were to be selected without racial or cultural discrimination.

In 1977, specific rules and regulations were published for the implementation of these new evaluation procedures. Nine aspects require mention here.

1. A 'full and individual evaluation' of a child's needs must be made prior to an initial placement of the child in a special educational programme.
2. Tests must be administered in the child's native language or present mode of communication.
3. Tests must have been validated for the specific purpose for which they are used.
4. Tests must be administered by 'trained personnel' in conformity with instructions by their producer.
5. Test and other evaluation materials must include those intended to assess specific areas of educational needs and not merely those designed to yield a single general IQ.
6. When tests are administered to students who have impaired sensory, manual or speaking skills, the results must reflect aptitude or achievement rather than the impairment.
7. No single criterion is to be the sole criterion on which special education placement is determined.
8. Evaluations for special educational placement must be made by a multi-disciplinary team, including at least one teacher or other specialist with knowledge in the area of the suspected disability.
9. Children must be assessed in all areas related to a suspected disability, including health, vision, hearing, social–emotional functioning, general intelligence, academic performance and communicative status.

The right to 'due process' was established in law, offering parents the right to appeal. Parents' rights are summarised by Ysseldyke and Algozzine (1982) in their penetrating account of special education issues in the USA.

> The provision for due process is clearly specified in Public Law 94–142. The law states that handicapped children's parents, guardians, or parent surrogates have the right to examine all pupil records and the right to secure independent evaluations of their children. Whenever a school proposes or refuses to initiate or change the identification, evaluation, or placement of a child, the parents must be given written prior notice. Such

notice must be in their native language 'unless it is clearly not feasible to do so.' Parents have a right to complain at the time they are notified, and those who complain have the right to an impartial due process hearing at which they may challenge the school's decision. Parents who are not satisfied with the findings of the due process hearing may (in most states) appeal the decision to the state education agency. Either party not satisfied with the actions taken by the state education agency may appeal the decision to the civil courts. When the due process hearings are held, parents have several rights: the right to be accompanied by counsel and/or experts in the education of handicapped students; the right to present evidence, cross-examine, and compel the attendance of witnesses; the right to an independent evaluation; and the right to a written or electronic verbatim recording of the hearing. (p. 224)

DEVELOPMENTS IN SPECIAL EDUCATION SINCE 94–142

Public Law 94–142 came about because of a combination of political pressures, from groups of handicapped people, from parents with handicapped children, from the black community and from professionals working within the education system. The interpretation of sections of the law is the subject of a great deal of discussion. In the USA, the ground for much of the ensuring dispute has been in the courtroom. Controversy has centred around issues such as whether a state is fulfilling its obligations under the law, whether the effect of the law is discriminatory against certain groups in the population and what constitutes an 'appropriate' education for children. The question of assessment procedures and testing instruments has also been the subject of heated debate, particularly between the school authorities and black groups.

In 1978 the case of *Laraz* v. *The New York City Board of Education* established that the Education Department had discriminated against black and Hispanic students in assessment procedures and placement. Furthermore, the court ruled that New York's monetary problems did not excuse this violation of the students' rights. Court rulings have, however, proved conflicting. In 1979, in the case of *Larry* v. *Riles*, the court ruled that IQ tests used to place black students in special classes were discriminatory, and should no longer be used. Yet one year later, the judge in the case of *PASE* v. *Hannon* ruled that two standard intelligence tests were *not* biased against black children. Clearly, until there is an agreed operational definition of terms such as 'bias', 'discrimination' and 'non-discrimination' it will remain problematic whether any test exhibits these characteristics.

These court cases displayed in public a debate which had continued in professional circles for many years. Our own contention would be that assessment instruments of all types are *designed* to discriminate.

Whether they do so fairly depends on the perspective of the beholder. This is particularly true about ideas of what constitutes intelligence in a person. As Sarason and Doris (1979) point out, the bewildering array of intelligence tests may well lead to the conclusion:

> That the concept of intelligence has all the characteristics of an ink blot on to which people have projected meanings on the basis of which they wish to urge other people to see what they see, to measure it in the same way as they do. In a society in which definitions of such conditions as mental retardation, learning disabilities, and emotional disturbance, are constantly changing, it makes little sense to seek after the most valid test to identify these disabilities, because the disabilities themselves reflect change in societal values and attitudes.

Some groups of parents clearly see the law as providing them with an instrument to force local states to provide what they regard as suitable education for their children. Frequently these are parents of children with severe learning or physical difficulties. They too have resorted to the courts for action. In the case of *Frederick* v. *Thomas* the judge ruled that Philadelphia school district had failed to provide appropriate education for learning-disabled students. The school district was therefore ordered by the court to engage in a massive screening task, and follow this up with individual psychological evaluations in order to identify learning-disabled students in its area.

Interested groups seem to be extracting every ounce of value from Public Law 94–142. As we have shown, sometimes the law is used to argue that children are being denied programmes for their special needs. At other times the law is used to remove children from programmes for 'special needs', on account of the allegedly discriminatory nature of such allocation.

Public Law 94–142 does not offer a charter either for parents or for integrationists. The law contains restrictive clauses which permit different interpretations by school authorities. It states that:

> All handicapped students, including those in public or private institutions or other care facilities, are educated with children who are not handicapped, and that special classes, separate schooling or other removal of handicapped children from the regular education environment occur only when the nature or severity of the handicap is such that an education in regular classes with the use of supplementary aids or services cannot be achieved satisfactorily (Section 612–5).

The question centres around what constitutes satisfactory education, and which modifications or aids would be necessary in the ordinary classroom to achieve it. This raises in turn the whole issue of what are the goals of education for any child. Once again discussion about children with special needs has highlighted issues which are in dispute within the education systems as a whole.

The question of Individual Educational Programmes (IEPs) exemplifies this clearly. What is a valid IEP for a student? Assessment may give an indication of *what* to teach, but rarely indicates *how* to teach. This is a decision usually left to professionals. One teacher may choose a method totally different from another teacher who has identical goals for the student. An IEP therefore is only capable of being justified in retrospect, when it has been carried out and demonstrated as effective. This is, of course, an issue relevant to curriculum choice for any child, not simply for those with special needs.

In our description of the impact of special education legislation in Norway, we looked at how far the 1976 law had been implemented throughout the country, and at its effects on various groups in the population. It is by no means clear that in America Public Law 94-142 has been taken up enthusiastically in all states by all school authorities. For example, when we look at the interpretation of the clause 'the least restrictive environment', some school districts take this to mean that all handicapped children, regardless of the severity of their handicap, are to be placed in regular classroom programmes. To others, the law means that all handicapped children are to be placed in separate special education classes. It may well be that the administrators of each state's education service interpret the clause in line with their own convenience, resources and policy direction.

Vaughan and Shearer (1986) quote studies which showed inconsistency between states in implementing Individual Education Plans, and confusion over which children should be eligible for special educational help, and thus for Federal funds. In addition, Federal evaluation of the performance of different states was inadequate. In 1982 the Federal Department of Education proposed amendments to Public Law 94-142. These might have eased the financial expenditure and administrative burden which it imposed. The proposed amendments resulted in 30,000 letters of protest and huge numbers of protesting witnesses at regional hearing. As a result, they were dropped.

The fate of the Federal Department of Education's proposed amendments illustrates the absolute necessity for well-orchestrated public pressure on special education legislators. We have already argued, however, that children with learning and adjustment difficulties attract less support from independent interests than any other group of children with special needs. Hence, it is instructive to see how they have fared under the American legislation. The state of Massachusetts provides a useful example. Not only is it often held up as a model of good practice within America, but its own special education law was enacted in 1972 and came into force in 1974. In its first year of operation the number of children identified as having special needs within ordinary classes fell from a third to a fifth. In the last few years it has remained fairly stable at around ten per cent.

Conversely, the proportion of students remaining in an ordinary class, but receiving special help outside it, has risen from 25 per cent to 50 per cent (Vaughan and Shearer, 1986).

The evidence suggests, then, that legislation both at state and at federal levels has resulted in an *increase* in the number of pupils in facilities separate from the ordinary class. Other evidence suggests that children from minority ethnic groups and children with adjustment difficulties are disproportionately represented. Carrier (1984), for example, points out that school districts frequently interpret the law in a conservative fashion, especially when parents or other interest groups are not actively campaigning for a more progressive interpretation. Greater use of withdrawal or resource rooms can result in increased segregation within ordinary schools. He quotes Weatherley and Lipsky's (1977) claim that the law may have resulted in:

> a wholesale shifting of responsibility for troublesome children from the regular class teacher to a specialist resource room teacher. (p. 183).

Certainly, the progressive philosophy of Public Law 94–142 emphasises in our view the individual rights of the child and parents. It aims to extend special education, in an integrated setting, to a larger group of children. The result of this may be more physical, functional and locational integration in the future for some handicapped children. Individual children may, through their IEPs, be given specialised, sometimes more restricted, curricula in the ordinary classes or in withdrawal groups. Whether this results in further integration, or increased segregation, greatly depends on the numbers of children remaining in separate special schools. As in England, if the numbers of children segregated from the system remain constant in future then the use of these new resources will lead to segregation of increasing numbers of children, albeit on a part-time basis and within ordinary schools. If numbers in special schools decline dramatically in future then the use of these resources may herald a move along the continuum of integration.

THE CONTRAST BETWEEN RECENT LEGISLATION IN BRITAIN AND THE USA

The American law has a stronger integrationist philosophy than the British 1981 Education Act. The former concentrates primarily on the needs of the child. While it does not insist that these are met only in the ordinary classroom, the onus is on demonstrating the need for special education provided elsewhere. By contrast, the 1981 Education Act considers also whether the LEA can use its resources more efficiently in segregated facilities. As we have seen this consideration has been specifically excluded by the American courts (Ysseldyke and Algozzine 1982). It would be unbelievably optimistic to suppose that financial considerations were not important to local authorities in America when considering the placement of a child. What they are theoretically not allowed to do by the Act, however, is give them public credence as an excuse for segregation. This is not the case in Britain where many education authorities are already arguing 'efficient use of resources' as the reason for being unable to satisfy the parents' wishes for a particular school placement.

A second major difference between the situation in America and in Britain is demonstrated by the expectations of parents in other campaigning groups. We would argue that in general parents in America have a stronger sense of their power in society than parents in Britain. They see education as a political area in a way that few British people do. The American civil rights movement has emphasised this by comparing segregated education with other discriminatory acts and institutions in American society. In Britain some black parents' groups are debating similar issues. However, their smaller representation in the total population and the absence of mass political protest such as occurred in the American civil rights movement offers them less publicity and consequently less public debate. As Kirp (1983) stresses, neither politics nor the law has effectively challenged professional power in special education in Britain. Little political attention has been paid to special education, leaving policy to administrators and professionals, at both local and national levels. The absence of public debate gives great power to professionals within the British education system.

We doubt whether the 1981 Education Act offers parents much hope for change. The Warnock Report avoided all use of the term 'rights', referring instead to 'partnership' and 'goodwill'. These remain charitable notions which assume that both parties agree on goals, and on the route to achieve them. The language used effectively muffles dispute. It refuses to recognise that people involved in the placement of a child have different views, based on the different positions they occupy.

Kirp concludes that the British approach has been to enable professionals through the exercise of their discretion to offer what they consider to be the highest level of service on the least stigmatising terms possible, given the available social resources. This model of social welfare does not recognise conflict, is silent concerning politics, and is actively antagonistic towards the law.

In contrast the American approach creates a dynamic tension among competing interests. In this framework, conflict is expected, as different groups in the process are *expected* to have different perceptions on the same problem. Structures therefore exist both within education and through use of the courts, to balance these tensions, allowing a more open and vigorous debate from a variety of different viewpoints. The British approach to education (and special education in particular) relies heavily on debate within professional circles leading to reform. Given the philanthropic history of special education, this means that legislation is interpreted cautiously in professional circles and public debate tends to be limited.

CONCLUSIONS

The American experience in special education has a great deal to offer us as a contrast to this approach. Special education has become a matter of political interest there. In this atmosphere, searching questions are likely to be debated in public. Many of these questions are bound to challenge professional judgements which, in this country, have been held sacred and unquestionable for many years. Our own view is that both children and professionals benefit enormously from challenges presented by consumers who have high expectations of public services. Open and public debate of issues surrounding special education and special schooling is long overdue in Britain. This is the vital lesson the American experience has to offer us.

The lessons to be learned from Norway are rather different. Here too there is a stronger legislative basis for special education than exists in Britain. The evidence suggests a modest increase in the number of children in ordinary schools who would formerly have attended separate special schools. Progress has been achieved, moreover, without the intense legal disputes that have characterised special education in the USA. The financial provision for meeting special needs in ordinary schools may be vulnerable to changes in government policy, but the same could be said to apply to separate special schools.

Neither Norway nor the USA offers a blueprint for development in Britain. In each case there is evidence that education authorities are able to interpret the law in ways which may be administratively convenient, but which effectively subvert its intentions. Precisely the same applies in Britain. Yet both in Norway and in the USA the intentions behind recent legislation are more coherent, less ambiguous than in Britain. Consequently progress is not so dependent on the initiative of individual teachers. Nor is it so vulnerable to administrative convenience. These points will become clearer in the next chapter, when we discuss some recent developments in Britain for children with moderate learning difficulties.

Chapter five
INNOVATIONS IN THE EDUCATION OF CHILDREN WITH LEARNING DIFFICULTIES

INTRODUCTION

In this chapter we describe some innovatory projects to integrate children with learning difficulties into the ordinary school. We describe, in some detail, three projects. One involves the integration of children with severe learning difficulties into special classes in infant schools in Bromley; the second is based in Banbury School in Oxfordshire; and the final one describes integrated provision within a well-known Leicestershire Upper School, Countesthorpe College.

We also consider how far these particular innovations are seen as trail-blazing experiments within the local authorities, and whether the authority encourages the development of similar initiatives in other schools. Were they set up by energetic and imaginative professionals working in isolation within particular schools? Did they arise from a policy at local authority level, or did their existence promote such policy development?

N. Jones (1983a) identifies three models to classify the development of policies for integrating children with special needs into ordinary schools. He labels them the 'limpet model', the 'persuasion model' and the 'whole school approach'. The limpet model occurs when a special unit is located on the campus of an ordinary school, in the hope that some 'waves of normality' will wash over the children so placed. The 'persuasion approach' involves persuading ordinary schools to take into mainstream classes a number of children with special needs, sometimes with the promise of extra resources. The 'whole school approach' involves an examination of how the school caters for the needs of *all* children, with children with special needs becoming integrated into the total school organisation.

In this chapter we describe the units in Bromley as an example of the 'limpet model' of integration. The special classes are attached to ordinary schools, but rarely involve functional integration of children in work situations. We examine how the units were first set up, how they have developed, and the depressing picture of Bromley's failure to encourage further integration schemes.

We have not described examples of the 'persuasion approach' to integration as case history material showing successful integration of individual children has been extensively published elsewhere (Booth and Statham 1982). We have concentrated instead on two examples of a 'whole school approach'.

INTEGRATION IN BROMLEY: AN ABOUT-TURN IN POLICY?

The London Borough of Bromley is a particularly interesting example of pragmatic decision making in a local authority, and illustrates the pitfalls excellently. This borough has been integrating children, aged three to eight, in special classes attached to primary schools since 1971. The children involved are children with severe learning difficulties, a group regarded by many as presenting difficult problems for integrationists. The success of the primary school scheme was expected by many national observers to lead to a natural expansion to junior and secondary age children. This has not happened. Segregation into large separate special schools remains the norm in Bromley.

A description of the integration scheme itself, how it came to be put into operation and an examination of subsequent changes in the authority will serve to illuminate this disappointing trend.

THE INTEGRATION SCHEME

The first special class for children with severe learning difficulties began in St Paul Woods School in 1973, and others followed later at Alexandra, Crofton and Poverest Schools (Chamberlain 1973). Ten children were educated in each school, the classes being staffed by one qualified teacher and two child-care assistants. An additional teacher was appointed for one day a week to allow for home visiting, and in order for the unit teacher to teach mainstream classes. Two dinner supervisors took care of the children during the lunch break.

Children were referred to the classes by the schools' psychological service. Some children requiring special care continued to be sent out of the borough. Taxi transport was provided daily, as the children came from a wide catchment area. The children were normally placed in the class nearest to their home community.

The physical location of the classes within the school building varied from school to school. In the new schools, the room was centrally situated near to the 'heart' of the school, whereas, in the older building, two rooms had been adapted in an annexe close to the school nursery, geographically separate from mainstream classes.

The amount of integration of the children varied from school to school, and from child to child. There was no central policy about this, and it seemed to depend on the wishes of the teacher running the separate classes, although the headteacher of the school may also have been instrumental in encouraging it. Thus in one school some of the children spent a short time each day in the reception class, accompanied by the welfare assistant. In another, the special and the reception classes joined together for music lessons. A similar picture was true of social integration. One school encouraged children to eat with the mainstream classes, whereas another provided lunch within the child's classroom, the children in the latter school also played in a separate yard.

There appear to have been few problems encountered by the schools from parents of local children. One headteacher wrote to all the parents of infant children, telling them about the new classes, and offering to deal with any queries. She noted that the general response from parents was favourable. So far as is known, the parents of the special class children found the scheme acceptable. One indication of the support of parents was the way in which parents of non-handicapped children raised £10,000 in order to rebuild a unit at one school when the administration had decided to move it to a different school, because the building had deteriorated (Booth 1982).

A POLICY INITIATIVE?

Clearly the setting up of the units in Bromley represented an important development for the borough's special education facilities. Did the initiative come from an authority-wide commitment to integration as a matter of policy, or arise as an isolated scheme from an interested professional? The practical relevance of this question becomes obvious when we examine changes in Bromley's policy since 1971.

No policy document arguing for the integration of children with special needs into mainstream schools seemed to have been accepted by the council before the units were set up. Instead what appears to have happened is that practical considerations forced the Assistant Education Officer for Special Education to consider the need for further provision for one particular group of children. In 1970 the Education (Handicapped Children) Act became law, requiring that local authorities provide for the education of children over the age of

Innovations in the education of children with learning difficulties

three who had previously been catered for by the Health Service. There was thus an urgent need for Bromley to find places for children who had previously been in training centres. In addition, no places were available for the under fives, now covered by the new law. There was also considerable pressure from the Bromley Society for Mentally Handicapped Children, a vociferous and well-organised group who pressed strongly for integrated provision.

The then Assistant Education Officer for Special Education was also influenced by Jack and Barbara Tizard, whose work in the Institute of Education suggested that children with severe learning difficulties could respond well in a good infant school.

At first the classes were attached to 'good' schools, in middle-class areas of the borough, although a unit was later placed in a working-class area. The problems of starting the units appeared to be no greater, whatever the catchment area of the school.

Booth (1982) described an interview with the retired Assistant Education Officer responsible for setting up the classes.

> He made it clear that it had been his proposals to the education committee which had established the classes, and that there had been little opposition to the plan. He thought that once administrators had reached a position of trust with their education committee, proposals were usually ratified without detailed discussion of philosophies. There had been little opposition from his colleagues either (Booth 1982).

Thus the Bromley scheme for integrating children with severe learning difficulties is a clear example of an enlightened professional initiating change. In this particular case, the administrator had pressing practical problems which forced him to provide resources for a 'new' group of children, when the 1970 Education Act (Handicapped Children) gave the Education Department responsibility for a whole group of children who had previously been catered for by Area Health.

While we would not wish to detract from the value of isolated 'experiments' of this type, we would argue that the Bromley scheme had limitations which should have been evident at the outset. The major limitation was that the Education Committee clearly failed to set up the units as part of an overall policy to promote integration. Indeed, it would appear that the scheme was ratified virtually 'on the nod', and certainly without extensive discussion of its implications (Chamberlain 1973). The authority therefore did not consider provision for *all* children in mainstream secondary and primary schools rather than in special schools; nor did it decide to adopt the principle of integration in future provision for pupils with special needs.

Had this happened, there would have been clear implications for ordinary schools whose curricula, organisation and management would have required examination in order to *include* more children.

Similarly, special school closures would have been seen as inevitable and desirable. This failed to happen even after the units were established and running well, as can be seen from an examination of developments in Bromley's provision over the last five years.

DEVELOPMENTS IN BROMLEY

Changes in special education in Bromley since the setting up of the classes show a clear move towards maintaining separate provision. No integrated classes for children with severe learning difficulties have been started in junior schools. One reason given for this by the Assistant Education Officer was that the junior schools in the area did not contain heads with the same interest in working with these children. A second, perhaps the most important reason, was that the demand for provision had been miscalculated.

The Education Committee had been led to expect that large numbers of children with severe learning difficulties would be coming into schools. It therefore set up the integrated units but in addition agreed to finance the building of a new school for these children. The special school, built for 100, opened with only 12 children. This was potentially embarrassing for the local authority, as the council was open to criticisms of poor planning and wastage of ratepayers' money. What the Education Department decided to do was to move into the new school the most profoundly handicapped pupils who had previously been educated in schools outside the authority. In these circumstances, over-provision in the special school meant that no extension of the integration project was likely to be contemplated.

The Assistant Education Officer felt that, with the benefit of hindsight (and retirement) a mistake had been made. He said that he had increasingly come to question the validity of special schooling, and thought that plans to relocate the resources within them to ordinary schools should be initiated as soon as possible (Booth 1983).

Instead, Bromley seems to have pursued a policy of keeping its special schools open. On 12 January 1984 the local paper carried as its front page lead the news that Bromley planned to close three schools for children with *moderate* learning difficulties, and bring all the pupils together on one site to create a new large special school. This report led to protests from parents who were keen to extend previous integrated provision, by implementing the spirit of the 1981 Education Act. It also led to protest from the special school children of secondary age, who were concerned to demonstrate their 'normality' to readers of the paper. One interesting point is that these children had to counteract prejudice from the press and public, which had been created in the first place by the children being grouped together into one special school.

The publicity arose because Bromley Council was considering a consultative paper on special education. This plan, prepared in 1983, went some way towards terminating the *ad hoc* policy pursued in the previous ten years. The framework was based on a four-fold philosophy:

1. That a total concept of special services should be adopted which, in line with the 1981 Education Act, would abolish the distinction between 'normal' and 'special' provision.
2. That links needed to be established and maintained between services.
3. That provision should be based on the needs of individuals.
4. That services should be based on the principle of integration, achievement and 'quality of life'.

Despite these lofty-sounding ideals, the details of the plan reflect no charter for integration. Instead, what appears to have been envisaged is a rationalising of existing resources and a clarification of the role of the support services. Thus:

> It is not the aim to reduce Special School provision – rather to identify the best areas of expertise and to provide this sort of resource for mainstream provision . . . The intent is to make current special provision more effective, . . . (Bromley Education Committee 1983).

The proposals contained some curious inconsistencies. Thus, it was proposed that children with *moderate* learning difficulties should be taught within units attached to ordinary junior schools. At secondary level, however, these children were to be placed in the new large, reorganised secondary special school. No rationale was given for this apparently arbitrary switch at secondary age.

With regard to the children with severe learning difficulties, the framework proposed to link the integrated units more closely with the special schools structure. Although this may seem at first sight like sensible coordination, experience in other authorities has shown how this move can weaken the unit's identity as an integral part of the school, and links it into the network of segregated provision. There were in addition no proposals to extend the units to children of junior school age. At the post-sixteen level, one centre was proposed for children with all types of special need. It was not seen as essential that this centre should be an integral part of an ordinary college. One of the most serious omissions of the paper, however, is that it continued to see special provision as a grafting process. Nowhere was the question addressed of changing ordinary schools to make them more inclusive. Nor was an integrated administrative system for special education proposed. It is interesting to note that parents in the Bromley Society for Mentally Handicapped Children had been instrumental in setting up the integrated units. There appears to have been parental support for their continuation. Yet parental pressure, in the final analysis, took second place to the necessity for using existing (separate) resources. The muddled scheme outlined above seems a poor successor to the pioneering projects set up by Bromley in the early 1970s.

DEVELOPMENTS IN OXFORDSHIRE

The period 1970–85 saw the growth of several interesting projects in schools in Oxfordshire. Many of the earlier examples, such as the Bicester unit (Garnett 1976), reflect the 'limpit' approach to special needs. Later developments, however, such as the Banbury Sector scheme, were clearly designed to adopt a whole school approach to catering for children with special needs.

In all instances these projects appear to have arisen as initiatives stemming from headteachers of ordinary and local special schools. There seems so far to have been no overall policy in Oxfordshire for special education, whether in ordinary or special schools. The county is currently reviewing aspects of special education, and a number of working groups will report to the Director of Education in 1986. These groups will cover:

1. The integration of children with moderate or severe learning difficulties.
2. Sixteen to nineteen provision for pupils with special needs.
3. The future role of a school for physically handicapped children, some of whom are integrated into local ordinary schools.
4. The future of nursery assessment units attached to special schools.
5. Provision for children with behavioural problems.
6. The implications of integration and demography for the future role of special schools.

At present, though, provision is undoubtedly patchy. A child from one home may only have access to segregated schooling, whereas a child with exactly the same special needs from a different home may have access to integrated provision. Nevertheless, it remains true that some interesting and widely publicised initiatives have already taken place in Oxfordshire.

We describe below examples of different types of development in the region.

INITIATIVES IN OXFORDSHIRE

Five types of integration have been, and continue to be, developed in Oxfordshire:

1. Joining up different types of special schools.
2. Developing links between special and ordinary schools.
3. Special units attached to ordinary schools.
4. Resources centres or withdrawal rooms within ordinary schools.
5. A whole school approach to provision for children with special needs.

One example of the rationalisation of links between special and ordinary schools came about when, in 1978, the head of a newly built special school arranged for a complete class of children with severe learning difficulties to move to a nearby primary school. This in turn led to similar provision being made in the local comprehensive – a marked progression which as we have seen was not made under similar circumstances in Bromley. Similar moves took place in developing the resources for physically handicapped children in 1981.

In addition there was a growth in special units attached to ordinary schools, catering for children with behaviour or learning difficulties. As Neville Jones (1983c) points out in his description of policy-making in Oxfordshire during this period:

> In Oxfordshire the setting up of units reflected the national trend but the planning was *ad hoc*, and nowhere was there explicitly a policy, written or by practice, to move towards integration. . . . Three special units for the mildly retarded were set up on the campus of three comprehensive schools. But at the same time segregated provision was also increased through the opening of two special schools for severely mentally retarded children.

In 1969 an early innovation was the attachment of a unit for children with moderate learning difficulties to the Bicester comprehensive school. As Garnett (1976) describes, the Bicester scheme was at first an attempt to graft a unit for children with moderate learning difficulties on to a comprehensive school. This led, at one stage, to a situation in which there were remedial groups in the school which worked parallel to, but remained separate from, the new unit. Separate staffing and finance existed – an unsatisfactory model which provided a valuable lesson in past mistakes when the new high school opened in 1971. The Progress Unit in the Cooper School was specifically designed to be more open and less separate than the one in the Upper School. Children with both moderate and severe learning difficulties (aged eleven to thirteen) were individually timetabled to work in the two rooms of the units, and spent varying amounts of time in the mixed ability classes. Integration with remedial work in the school became commonplace. The role of the Progress Unit staff also extended to supporting children within the ordinary classroom, and providing modified materials to help the class teacher (Garnett 1975).

It is interesting to note that the identities of the unit staff, and of the remedial staff in the school persisted, despite the obvious anachronism. One reason may have been the labelling of the unit staff as 'special' by the administration outside the school, and the enhanced capitation given to children in the school who were identified as having moderate learning difficulties.

The provision in the Cooper School later became known as the 'Resources Model' of catering for children with special needs. A resources department based at Carterton School came to be seen as a model for this type of development. The need for attitude change and awareness of handicap was recognised in an in-service training programme for teachers which started in 1980. An additional recommendation from experience at Carterton School was that a group of schools, together with their support and advisory services, should be nominated specifically to investigate the management and organisational problems which result when the LEA promotes a policy of integration. The Banbury Special Needs Project was set up for this purpose.

The brief of this group was to look at the implementation of the Warnock proposals, to examine national initiatives on integration, to evaluate the 'Resources Model' and to explore what changes would be required in mainstream education if a school or group of schools decided to respond to all the children within the catchment area who had special educational needs. This latter part, which involved examining the management and organisation of the schools within the context of the communities they served, came to be seen as the hallmark of the Banbury Sector.

Elizabeth Jones (1980) describes the resources approach adopted by schools within the Banbury pyramid. She defines resources as 'a room or rooms having specialist teachers and auxiliary helpers', and 'approach' meaning individual programming to meet one child's needs, rather than a grouping system for children. She outlines the guiding principles of this resources approach as:

> all children's educational needs should be met as far as possible within an ordinary school and as far as possible within an ordinary class. The resource programme is developed as an integral element in the total curriculum and organisation of the school. The 'special education' provided is conceived of primarily as an instrument for the facilitation of change and the development of better ways of meeting the learning needs of all children, not only of those who are deemed to be different.
> (Quoted by N. Jones, 1983a)

Innovations in the education of children with learning difficulties

This model questions whether special educational needs should exist as a separate administrative system. Moreover it highlights what may yet be the fundamental issue of the debate, namely, the problems confronting both special education and ordinary schools are those which are intrinsic to education in general – one of the major problems being how to educate those who are difficult to teach.

John Sayer, the headteacher of the comprehensive school involved, became a national advocate of this 'resource or whole school approach'. He stressed that the problems posed for the teaching of children with special needs were only a manifestation of teaching problems for the school as a whole. What the children with special needs did was to expose gaps in the organisation for all children. Thus he was vehemently opposed to the assessment procedure laid down by the 1981 Act, as these statementing procedures single out individual children as having problems *within themselves*, rather than looking at how a child interacts with, and relates to, the situation in which she finds herself. He argues instead for a whole school approach to assessment in which *all* children should have their strengths and weaknesses regularly reviewed, in order that the school system can be responsive to their changing needs (Sayer 1983).

The logic of this approach was that management training for headteachers and senior staff became a top priority for in-service training. In addition, the whole school approach required a flexible use of financial resources. Rather than resources for teaching children with special needs becoming attached to particular children (as is the case with 'B' funds in Norway), this approach argues for adequate funding for schools, assuming that they will be catering for all children from their catchment area. No screening or assessment procedures should be necessary to identify individual children if the sector as a whole has been adequately financed.

The implications of this approach run directly counter to some of the detailed provisions of the 1981 Education Act, despite the close initial similarity in philosophy. The distinction made between children with and without special needs, becomes meaningless on the Banbury Model. This is because the Act, as we showed in Chapter 1, defines special children as those for whom the ordinary school does not normally cater. This definition is totally obscured if schools begin to cater for the needs of all the children in their catchment area. Discussion begins to focus on resources and support provided, rather than on the strengths or weaknesses of the child. An interactive approach, altering the environment to cater for the needs of any child, becomes the norm.

As Neville Jones (1983c) makes clear in his account, the assessment of the children's needs was not a problem, as this could easily be done by surveys:

The question of resources was a greater problem. The County's earlier practice of allocating resources to individual schools, often with unsatisfactory methods of determining needs, had brought an imbalance in extra staffing to ordinary schools for special needs. Furthermore, high priority had been placed in staffing establishments for children in segregated provision, namely, a special school, a small unit for the maladjusted and a hostel. The locking-up of resources, in the form of teachers, in the segregated area reduced the flexibility for their deployment in a Resource Style of management.

The development of two systems, one related to children in segregated provision (special schools) and the other to having children with special needs integrated in mainstream education raises a major policy decision for an LEA. To date (1983) integration has been achieved by taking up any slack in the resources, but this has been done without in any way reducing the numbers of special schools. The effect of this is to create a dual system of management, with competition from each system, and duplication, for the limited resources of the LEA (p. 247).

Elsewhere, Jones (1983b) describes the parallelism endemic in the administrative structures of most LEAs.

Parallelism comes in many forms and guises. It affects such minor details as who draws up the advertisement for new special needs staff, who shortlists, who is on the interview panels, and where the authority for the final choice of candidate is posited. Of more major importance, it poses the question of who is accountable at advisory level for the new teachers in the sectors who will be specialized in areas of learning difficulty: the county primary adviser who has responsibility for the peripatetic remedial services or the special needs adviser under whose auspices the new staff are appointed according to one interpretation of the Warnock recommendation that 'remedial' should not be separated from 'special'? (pp. 70–71).

In times of cut-backs in education which are taking place in Oxfordshire, as elsewhere, inadequate resources management severely limits the scope for extending the Banbury scheme to other areas. Without adequate resources, children will continue to receive radically different types of special education, depending on where they happen to live. This may be justified if the projects are promoted on an experimental basis, and evaluated as example of 'good practice', but that hardly seems to be the case for a project begun in 1980!

To increase integrated provision without a concomitant reduction in special school provision is clearly not going to be possible for administrators, irrespective of central government cut-backs. In addition, as Swann (1985) argues, the extension of special facilities, particularly units, in the ordinary sector, without closing special schools will lead to more children, not fewer, being segregated in some way.

The Banbury scheme raises the question of the need for a radical reorganisation in financing for integration schemes. At present, if children in an ordinary school are Statemented, this fact is recorded on Section 6 of Schools Form 7 which forms the basis for calculations about the group size of the school, and 'points' allocation for teachers' salaries. As Oxfordshire adopts a policy of refusing to single out particular children in ordinary schools by Statementing them under the 1981 Act, the entry under this section is generally zero. At present the number of children entered under Section 6 does not affect staffing or capitation; they are simply regarded as 'ordinary' children. If, however, the Banbury Model is more widely adopted, it will clearly be necessary to find a way to ensure that schools receive the staffing and other resources to cater for their integrated pupils.

One logical step was taken in Oxfordshire to service an integrated model, a step which is frequently missed by other education authorities in England and Wales. This involved a reorganisation of the county administrative staff, so that all area education officers, as part of their normal duties, now cover also many administrative aspects of special education which would have been previously covered by an area officer with special responsibility for special education. However, the elaborate bureaucracy entailed in the assessment process under the 1981 Act required the appointment of an Assistant Education Officer to look after individual children during the Statementing procedure. Thus, the Act involved a move away from integration at County Hall level.

We turn now to an example of one school which set out to examine the assumptions on which all children are educated. A description of Countesthorpe College in Leicestershire shows how one school can, on its own initiative, make great strides by making provision for all children within its community.

COUNTESTHORPE COLLEGE, LEICESTERSHIRE

So far we have considered the fate of one LEA's initiative in integration. We have also discussed initiatives in Oxfordshire where the general impression is of interesting developments taking place with the LEA's blessing, though not necessarily at its instigation. We now turn to a well-known Leicestershire school which well illustrates the evolution of a whole school approach to special needs.

Countesthorpe College is an upper school in Leicestershire, for pupils aged fourteen to nineteen. When it opened in 1970 it catered for pupils aged eleven to nineteen. It is situated about eight miles south of Leicester, and takes children whose homes are in three villages, and one large urban council estate. Children come from three main feeder high schools (eleven to fourteen age range). One of the feeder schools, which now shares the campus with Countesthorpe College, was housed in the college building from 1970–74. The feeder schools differ considerably in organisation, in teaching style and curriculum design. None shares a teaching approach which is closely related to the style adopted by the college.

When pupils come to Countesthorpe College they are usually faced with a period of adjustment to a different system of organisation. The college has had an explicitly innovative approach to education. Makins (1975a, b) notes that the college provided, from the outset, an opportunity for radical re-thinking of the total learning process, the only constraints being those imposed by availability of resources and by outside bodies such as universities, examination boards and parents. It was not expected that the college would necessarily adopt new and different policies, but that procedures established in other secondary schools would not be repeated without good reason.

Within this re-examination, the education of children with special needs was seen as an integral part. Throughout the years since Countesthorpe first opened, provision for children with special needs was closely tied to the overall school organisation and curriculum.

The school was purpose built with an unusual design – a central courtyard, large areas suitable for team teaching and open-plan specialist areas for art, craft and design work. Two separate rooms were initially designated for withdrawal work, one for younger pupils and the second for fourth and fifth years.

Any description of support work for children with special needs requires detailed information about facilities for the education of all children in the school. In the early years when the college catered for the full age range from eleven to nineteen, each child was placed in a mixed ability tutor group, based on friendship groups from feeder schools. Students followed a core curriculum for about half of each week. This core generally comprised social studies, English and maths. Sometimes a class was taught by different teachers for each core subject. For the remainder of the week pupils could choose from a wide variety of options. Some of these would be self-selected and negotiated between the child, her parents and the class tutor. Work within core subjects was individualised as far as possible, although some younger children would work together on a particular topic. Some specialist subjects, which involved cumulative learning and oral communication (such as language work) were taught in tutor groups.

Within this organisation, mixed ability teaching was supported by the remedial department. Three teachers, each given a free timetable, worked with children aged eleven to fourteen, and two

Innovations in the education of children with learning difficulties

teachers worked with fourth and fifth years. Each 'remedial' teacher was attached to a year group, and stayed with it for two or three years, until the children left the high school section at fourteen years; or left the upper college at sixteen years.

The main aims of this remedial department were:

1. To withdraw some children for extra help in reading, writing and spelling.
2. To provide support for slow-learning students in their 'classrooms'.
3. To provide suitably modified materials, for children with reading problems, within subjects areas across the curriculum (Goodwin 1974).

Each remedial teacher decided on the allocation of time to each of the roles described above.

The organisation of withdrawal groups for work on basic skills proved difficult to arrange because of the complexities of timetabling within the whole school. These sessions were often seen as separate from the student's work in other areas of the school, and were stigmatised accordingly by students. The remedial rooms were seen as offering easier work for slower children, despite the best efforts of staff to disguise the reality. In working relationships between staff in subject areas and staff in the remedial department, integration was limited.

Provision of support for students within ordinary lessons attempted to surmount this isolation. It succeeded, to some extent in allowing class teachers and remedial staff to work alongside each other. In practice, however, support provided for class teachers in ordinary lessons was very limited. Children with reading difficulties were often spread across six or eight groups. Sometimes the remedial teacher would bring the students together, thereby creating a 'remedial sub-group'. At other times she would move around six or eight lessons, without being able to offer a reasonable amount of time to any student.

Modification of subject materials also posed problems. For the remedial staff a great deal of work was involved in modifying materials across the curriculum – in humanities, science and maths. It proved impossible to pitch modified materials at a level suitable for the whole range of children with reading difficulties. Also, much of the material could not easily be simplified without losing its conceptual structure. The problem faced by subject teachers was that they were then given materials to work with which they had not been involved in designing. In addition behavioural difficulties arose when the curriculum or organisation was unsuitable for the student.

It was acknowledged, therefore, that the organisation described above was in need of modification. Some children were faced with a large number of teachers in their working week, and the need for security of a small number of pupil–teacher relationships became an issue that was widely discussed in the school. These problems were not confined to children with special needs, but their difficulties highlighted problems that were facing all students.

Following the departure of students aged eleven to fourteen into their own building, an alternative model of organisation for the whole school was agreed (Chisholm 1977). Students were divided into 'teams' on entry. At present there are three teams in each of the fourth and fifth years, and a sixth form team. Students in the fourth and fifth years cover maths, social studies, English, science and art work in their team lessons. Each team was staffed by a group of teachers who taught the children for a majority of their teaching time. A good deal of work was done on the primary model of tutor-to-group, but specialists were also available. The work was individualised and project-based, with far less emphasis on the worksheets, than in earlier years. The tutors had pastoral responsibility for all students in the group. This involved agreeing individual timetables with the student and parents. Students varied in the amount of time spent in the 'team'. Many students with special needs opted to have 'extra team time', under the supervision of a team teacher. Most students, however, spent up to 50 per cent of the week in options with specialist teachers. These options were intended to be mixed ability, but the guided choice system resulted in a degree of selectivity. During option times some children with special needs chose to work in the Book Room (see below), to get help in basic skills.

The remedial staff offered time to students on a withdrawal basis, but also spent half their time supporting the year teams within their working areas. The withdrawal room became known as the Book Room. It was staffed to allow it to be open most of the week. It was open to any student who had permission from her tutor to work there. This 'open access' policy was established to remove the stigma attached to students using remedial department facilities. Some children were timetabled to have option lessons in the Book Room. Others used it as a quiet study area, away from the hurly-burly of their team base. At present the staff feel that 'open access' has been a vital fact of encouraging some children to use the facilities offered. The Book Room remains popular with students, with or without learning difficulties.

The Book Room provides a range of books and teaching resources which have been modified in reading level. Specific literacy and numeracy resources are available to help students who wish to improve basic skills. Much of the material is topic-based, to help students who need material for a particular project in team time.

Subject specialists now prepare materials for children with limited reading skills, and submit it to the remedial staff for comment. This has led to closer working relationships, and to the responsibility for all students being seen to reside within subject areas, with specialist staff. It has also led to specialist teachers becoming more involved with, and knowledgeable about, the needs of all children – and using the remedial staff to help them rethink their approach.

Remedial teachers spend time working with students in the team base. This work is sometimes additional to work with a student in the Book Room. But on occasion it replaces withdrawal work, at the student's request. In team bases remedial teachers work with any student who requests help. Many students see them therefore as an additional English teacher and do not appear to realise their more specific role. The remedial teachers see their work in team time as supporting the student's normal curriculum, and teaching additional skills through that work.

Naturally, problems remain in the provision of support for students with special needs. For example, most adolescents find it difficult to read aloud when other students can overhear. They are sensitive to any situation which highlights their reading problems, so privacy is essential. A team area is therefore unsuitable for oral work with some students, and withdrawal to the Book Room is itself not ideal. It is expensive of staff time, and the open access policy may mean that the Book Room is used by several students already. The problem of space and privacy may be eased by a small room which is being modified next to the Book Room. Individual oral work will be more private, but the questions of staffing efficiency remain.

The facilities provided for support work in Countesthorpe are teacher-intensive for all students. Adequate staffing for this type of work must be seen by the headteacher and staff as a high priority within the school. This is particularly true at the present time with falling rolls and government restrictions on spending in education.

It is apparent from the above description that the work of special needs staff in the school, and the work of tutors and specialist teachers is inextricably linked. The support structure can only function in this way because of the general ethos in the school. The way in which education is conceived of and organised for all students – particularly the idea of individual timetabling – makes it easier to provide for the needs of each individual child. The question of labelling individual students with 'special needs' is minimised. Nor does the school have to identify the nature of a student's problem or disability in order to cater for her education. The accent in individual timetabling is on what a student *can* do, and wishes to achieve. Comings and goings from class groups are a routine part of life in school. In this context students do not 'miss' part of a lesson if they attend withdrawal groups; nor is their absence noted. Everyone expects to move around the school campus on an individual timetable.

The above account also emphasises the importance of staff commitment. Some tutors, as team teachers, are encouraged to attend courses with teachers from the remedial department. Specific in-service courses on readability or spelling have also been run within the school for tutors. In general, however, the tutors appointed to the school have a strong commitment to working with students across the range of ability. They see the remedial teachers providing them with support for students in their group, but not as taking responsibility from them. As one teacher put it:

> One of the most important things about our department is that it has high status in the school. In some schools remedial teachers are as stigmatised by the staff as the children they work with.

CONCLUSIONS

Booth (1982) has distinguished between two types of local authority policy making, passive and active. He characterises the former with the word 'drift', when the LEA fails to spell out the direction in which it hopes to develop. In contrast, active policy making involves a deliberate attempt to control the course of events, bringing a rational, coherent philosophy to bear in the area of special education. At national level this has been attempted in Norway and in the USA, though as we saw in the last chapter the process has not been smooth.

It is interesting, and rather depressing, that none of the projects described in this chapter resulted from active policy making at LEA level. The Bromley units stemmed from an administrator's far-sighted thinking, but must now be seen as an essentially short-term response to the 1970 Education Act under which the LEA assumed responsibility for children with severe learning difficulties. Faced with the prospect of an embarrassingly empty special school the LEA's commitment to integrated provision weakened. Bromley Education Committee (1983) paid lip service to the idea of integration but in fact seemed far more likely to consolidate existing separate provision than to lead to its termination. This is an excellent example of policy 'drift'.

Both at Banbury School in Oxfordshire and at Countesthorpe College in Leicestershire provision for pupils with special needs resulted from the energy and vision of the headteachers concerned. In each case the LEA administration and support services were generally supportive, but there was no pretence at an authority-wide strategy. This led to major differences in provision from one school to another and from one part of the county to another. Such differences could be justified on the grounds that the LEA wished to experiment

Innovations in the education of children with learning difficulties

with different models, in order to plan future policy in a more informed way. On the other hand it seems both surprising and diappointing that few, if any, LEAs have grasped the opportunity offered by the 1981 Education Act to consider how to cater for all pupils, including those with learning and adjustment difficulties, in ordinary schools. In accepting the Fish Report, ILEA has taken a step in this direction, but has yet to decide how to carry out Fish's recommendations.

Booth (1982) argues that a major barrier to active policy making is the changing political and economic climate:

> Periods of economic and political stability favour coherent policy making. The cuts in public expenditure in the UK and the drive to reduce taxation in the US are both likely to contribute to arbitrary disorder in education. (pp. 42–43).

While we accept that the political and economic climate since the implementation of the 1981 Education Act has made policy making more difficult, we do not think that this is the whole story. We argue in the next chapter that failure of policy development at LEA level results largely from failure to recognise the conflicting needs of all the interested parties involved in identifying and meeting special educational needs.

Chapter six
A STUDY OF CONFLICTING NEEDS

INTRODUCTION

Much has been written about children's needs, but less about those of teachers. The contention of this chapter is:
1. That no attempts to integrate children with serious learning or behaviour problems into ordinary schools are likely to succeed unless the needs of their teachers are recognised and met.
2. That teachers' needs have implications for LEA policy, and that many well-meaning attempts to encourage integration have been unsuccessful because of failure to recognise these implications.
3. That teachers' needs also have implications for policy within the school.

We shall support and illustrate our argument by describing the development of special education in Sheffield, a city with a long tradition of commitment to the education of children with special needs. Since 1976 the Education Committee has expressed a commitment to a policy of integration. Support for special education has consistently been generous in terms both of resources and of personnel. Most educational psychologists and most members of other support services described below share their employing council's commitment to the general principle of integration. Yet children in Sheffield with learning or behavioural problems – a high proportion of those considered by the Warnock Committee to have special educational needs – were no more likely to be integrated into ordinary schools in 1985 than in 1975. Why?

BACKGROUND

THE COMMITMENT

In January 1976 a Special Education Working Party consisting of teachers and officers of the LEA submitted a report to the Schools' Subcommittee of the Education Committee. They hoped that this report would 'offer a sound basis for development for at least the next decade or so' (Sheffield Education Department 1976a). The report was concerned with the integration of handicapped, and particularly of ESN(M), children into the city's ordinary schools.

A strength of the report was its clear recognition of the implications for successful integration of the social and educational climate in the host schools. It endorsed a memorandum by David Blunkett, written with personal experience of disability, which argued:

> If, as some would suggest, the handicapped child needs shielding from the unkind and often spiteful actions of non-handicapped children, is this not a reflection on the educational process and the society as a whole which tolerates and perpetuates this antisocial and tragic situation. Is it not to be hoped that familiarity with disability will remove both fear and prejudice and will thereby decrease the kind of hurtful actions which are not just a fact of life but which have explanations in the system itself (p. 4).

The working party's report proposed that only schools which could respond positively to the individual needs of handicapped children should be encouraged to integrate. It also stated that educational opportunities in ordinary schools should be at least as good as those in special schools. In view of the research reported in Chapter 3, it might have been more appropriate to urge the reverse: that special schools should offer opportunities at least as good as ordinary schools. That, however, would have been seen as unnecessarily provocative. Elaborating on the conditions for successful integration, the report continued:

> We should like to see in each ordinary school with ESN children at least one teacher appointed to coordinate the work of those teaching and caring for its ESN pupils: these appointments will affect the organisation of staff and teaching methods in the school. . . .
>
> We believe therefore that the most important criterion in deciding where to integrate is the attitude, awareness and collective expertise of head and staff, and that ideally this should be associated with an existing commitment to mixed ability teaching (p. 3).

The report argued strongly against units for ESN(M) children in ordinary schools. It endorsed a view of the Joint Council for the Education of Handicapped Children that units in ordinary schools 'hold the danger of the worst solution of all – isolation in a large community, far worse than the loneliness of the small community'. A continuing role for special schools was envisaged, with ESN schools having 'an important role as training agencies and resource centres'.

The Schools Subcommittee accepted the working party's report and passed a resolution to 'support in principle the recommendations regarding the integration of handicapped children in ordinary schools' (Sheffield Education Department 1976b). This was subsequently accepted by the Education Committee on 19 February 1976 and approved by the full council on 19 March. The committee did not commit itself to any timetable for integration, nor did it specify in precise terms how it should take place or which schools should be involved. The broad commitment was nevertheless quite clear, and has become an acknowledged part of the Education Committee's policy.

DEVELOPMENT OF SPECIAL EDUCATION UNTIL 1976

The resolution of 1976 needs to be seen in the light of consistently generous allocation of resources to the special education sector. It was emphatically not a penny-pinching attempt to save money by closing special schools. Rather it reflected a responsible view that changes in educational thinking about the needs of handicapped children should be reflected in the committee's formally expressed policies. Indeed Sheffield could legitimately claim to be one of the first LEAs to attempt to move towards integration.

In 1976 the LEA had two full-time day special schools for maladjusted children, seven catering mainly for ESN(M) children, one for children considered to be ESN(M) *and* maladjusted, and two for delicate children. One of these possessed boarding facilities. In practice both the schools for delicate children accepted a high proportion of children with learning or behavioural problems. A further facility was a full-time centre for severely disruptive pupils in their last two years of compulsory education. In addition there was a comprehensive range of schools for children with physical or sensory disabilities and two day schools for children with mild learning difficulties. This category has never been recognised by the DES. In practice schools for children with mild learning difficulties were classified by the DES prior to the 1981 Act as ESN(M) and subsequently as catering for moderate learning difficulties. Although Sheffield adheres to the distinction, it is very imprecise with many children who could quite easily fall into either group. It is, however, noteworthy that the schools for children with mild learning difficulties tended to admit children for a limited period, usually two years, after which many of the pupils returned to the mainstream. For an LEA with a school population of roughly 109,000, the authority's provision of special school places for children with serious learning or behavioural problems was not ungenerous.

Nor had the support services been overlooked. The city council had established a child guidance service in 1936. Since 1940 this had been directed by an educational psychologist in an attempt to make its service relevant to educational rather than purely psychiatric needs. Unfortunately this was only partially successful. At national level both Plowden (DES 1967) and Seebohm Reports (DHSS 1968) criticised the service provided by educational psychologists for being unnecessarily isolated and remote from the needs of the clients. Hence, in 1972 the service was reorganised to enable educational psychologists to develop the LEA's psychological service on matters related to education, while the child psychiatrists continued their diagnostic and treatment service as part of the school health service. By 1976 the LEA had about thirteen educational psychologists, or just under one per 8,500 children of school age. In 1976 this was quite a generous provision by comparison with many other LEAs, even though the Underwood Report had recommended this ratio some twenty years earlier (Ministry of Education 1955).

DEVELOPMENTS SINCE 1976

Changes in special school provision since 1976 reflect demographic factors, notably a drop in the school population by nearly one-quarter, as well as the Education Committee's integration policy. Following the 1981 Education Act, ESN(M) schools became schools for children with moderate learning difficulties, schools for maladjusted children were designated schools for children with adjustment problems, and one former school for the delicate became a school for secondary age children with (unspecified) learning difficulties.

Since the 1976 resolution two of the former ESN(M) schools, one of the schools for the delicate and one school for children with mild learning difficulties have closed. In addition, there are currently plans to close three further schools for children with moderate learning difficulties. Against this the authority has opened a residential school for children with adjustment difficulties and a school for children with mild learning difficulties and is planning an annexe to the centre for severely disruptive adolescents. In addition six further initiatives require mention.

1. Full-time units for children with moderate learning difficulties have been established in one primary and one secondary school as a replacement for the former ESN(M) schools.

Two further units have replaced the school for children with mild learning difficulties and these continue to admit pupils for a two year period. One of them provides a considerable measure of integration. Closure of the three schools for children with moderate learning difficulties is intended to coincide with opening of further units in ordinary schools. The existing units act as a long term alternative to separate special schooling. The children are not, on the whole, integrated into ordinary classes. This, of course, is what the 1976 Special Education Working Party considered potentially 'the worst solution of all'. It represents a curious U-turn in policy. At the time of writing there are plans to encourage more integration in future units for pupils with moderate learning difficulties. It will be interesting to see whether these plans come to fruition.

2. Two schools for children with mild learning difficulties and one for moderate learning difficulties have started to admit children on temporary one- or two-term placements. There are currently plans to extend this innovation to one school for children with adjustment problems. The aim here is to prevent the need for long-term special education by providing more help than is available in an ordinary school at a relatively early age. These children are *not* formally assessed under the 1981 Education Act.

3. Nursery school placement was offered to young children recognised as having special needs. These special nursery placements were in units attached to three schools with existing mainstream nursery provision. They opened in 1979–80, and aimed to cater for children with general development and/or communication problems. Each unit was staffed with one teacher and one child care assistant, and accepted twelve children full-time or an equivalent number part-time. Ages on admission ranged from two to four and a half, with the possibility of remaining in the unit after the child's fifth birthday. The physical location of the units varied. Originally two were in separate rooms, along the corridor from the main nursery, but one of these is now integrated on an 'open-plan' basis. The third was fully integrated into the main nursery from the outset.

4. 'Integrated resources' were established at six ordinary primary schools. These were originally known as 'Centres of Integration'. These schools served the whole city, with transport provided from home to school. One teacher and one child care assistant were attached to each school to support ten children with special needs, aged five to twelve, in ordinary classes. A separate teaching room was provided, but this was intended for withdrawal work only. Children placed in these schools are Statemented under the 1981 Education Act. Admission criteria are extremely vague. However, it was intended that:

A study of conflicting needs

... children with a range of different special educational needs should attend ordinary classes in the school and not be provided for in a separate class or unit. Their educational needs in curriculum terms will be as for other children in an ordinary class, that is a mainstream focused curriculum. They will not be children with moderate learning difficulties who require a modified curriculum variant as defined and recognised by the Department of Education and Science (Sheffield Education Department 1984: 1).

It is not yet clear how these admission criteria will be interpreted. Early indications are that most centres are admitting children with a range of less severe physical and sensory disabilities though one centre in a voluntary aided school has admitted a few severely disabled children. The decision, as a general principle, to exclude children with moderate learning difficulties from the integrated resources is a most unfortunate missed opportunity. It may in part represent anxiety about the social problems thought to be associated with the presence in ordinary classes of children with moderate learning difficulties.

5. The home tuition service extended its operation. Traditionally this service had catered for children who, for one reason or another, could not attend school. Many of the pupils, however, were not prevented from attending school by physical disability, but rather by some adjustment problem. In the absence of more satisfactory alternatives, members of the 'home' tuition service started to see some of these pupils in small groups, at a unit opened for the purpose.

6. A new service of 'support teachers' was set up to extend the LEA's existing advisory and support services. Support teachers were based in special schools but worked in ordinary schools for most of the week. They were experienced in special education and aimed to help class teachers in ordinary schools to work effectively with their pupils with special educational needs. The local council undoubtedly saw this as a practical and positive step towards implementing its policy of integration. It still sees the service in this way. The initial aims of the service have been summarised as follows:

  (i) To deploy, as effectively as possible, special education expertise and teaching skills to teachers in mainstream schools who have children with special educational needs in their classes.

  (ii) To provide (if requested to do so) information and help for the head of the mainstream school about special education provision and procedures, or the services offered by another support teacher or supportive agency.

  (iii) To nofity the Assistant Education Officer for special education of children who might possibly be 'at risk' in the future.

(iv) To fulfil a preventative function, by intervening and offering prescriptive support for children with special needs.
(v) To fulfil a curative function when necessary to prevent a 'failure syndrome'.
(vi) To facilitate the 'transition' of children from special to mainstream schools.
(vii) To be available in the base special school for at least half a day per week to undertake some work within the school.
(viii) To liaise with other support teachers and supportive agencies (from Mullins 1982).

Unfortunately these aims seem quite remarkably muddled. To start with, every child in every school might possibly be 'at risk' in the future. Presumably they were not all to be reported to the Assistant Education Officer. A 'curative function' was proposed, as was facilitating the transition from special to mainstream schools. On the other hand support teachers were to give heads 'information and help about special education provision and procedures' which at the time were almost entirely based in separate special schools. The job description failed to specify whether support teachers should aim gradually to empty special schools, or to identify a *new* group of children in the mainstream and work with them. In practice support teachers do follow children's progress on return to the mainstream, but the great majority of their work is with a completely new group of children identified within ordinary schools.

Initially three teachers were appointed to work with children with mild or moderate learning difficulties, and three with adjustment problems. By 1985 the numbers had grown to six and six respectively. This growth may to some extent have reflected the welcome the service received from headteachers in ordinary schools. In its first year, over 100 children were seen, even though the new service had received minimal publicity in the city.

OVERVIEW

The picture, then, is a mixed one, with gradual development of a range of provision in and outside the ordinary school system. The service of support teachers was intended to help class teachers in ordinary schools to cater effectively for their pupils with special needs. The short-term placements in special schools were set up to avoid the need for long-term special school placement with its associated educational and social problems. The designated units and the 'integrated resources' were both attempts to cater for children in ordinary schools, and in the latter case in ordinary classes, on a long-

A study of conflicting needs

term basis. Even the obvious anomalies could possibly be seen as broadly consistent with a policy of integration. The residential school for maladjusted children, the centre for disruptive pupils and the so-called home tuition unit all opened with the stated intention of returning pupils to the mainstream, though in reality this was seldom achieved. The special nursery places were also seen in the same light, and two thirds of the first thirty eight children leaving the nurseries entered the mainstream (Lindsay and Desforges, 1986).

It is worth pointing out that these developments took place in a decade of fairly consistent contraction in the education services. As we have somewhat cynically noted elsewhere, the problem children industry was one of the very few sectors of education to escape this contraction (Galloway *et al.* 1982). Nor is there any suggestion that Sheffield was less committed to special education than other LEAs. The reverse is the case. Average *per capita* spending on special education in Sheffield continues to exceed the average for metropolitan authorities. Indeed Sheffield is also above average in expenditure on the nursery, primary and secondary sectors of education.

Thus, it seems clear that the city council has maintained its generous support for special education. In 1976, when the authority first committed itself to integration, the number and range of special *schools* bore testimony to a long tradition of generous support for disadvantaged children and for children with special educational needs. The diversification in the next ten years showed the authority's continuing support, coupled with a willingness to explore new approaches. There is no suggestion that counsellors encouraged special education for children with learning and adjustment difficulties as a cynical exercise in removing misfits from the mainstream. At least until the end of 1985, Sheffield's record illustrates the liberal ideology in special education as accurately as any LEA in the country. Yet as we have argued before, this liberal ideology can be viewed from different, less charitable perspectives. We are not justified, however, in doing so unless we have evidence on the effectiveness of the policy to promote integration.

THEORY INTO PRACTICE?

We are concerned here simply with the question whether integration is actually taking place for children with learning and adjustment difficulties. We reviewed evidence in Chapter 2 that this is not the case nationally. In Sheffield the council's commitment to integration dates back to 1976 and has been generously supported. Is the picture in Sheffield any different from the national one?

The answer, briefly, is that it is not. The number of children in *all*

The education of disturbing children

special schools or units recognised by the DES, including physical and sensory handicaps, increased from 2.03 per cent of the total on roll in May 1976 to 2.05 per cent in April 1985. Table 6.1 shows the number of children attending schools for pupils with learning difficulties and with adjustment problems in the years 1976, 1981 and 1985. The right-hand column shows the total as a per cent of the total school population in each year. From these figures there is evidence of a moderate overall reduction in the number of pupils placed full-time and indefinitely in special schools or units. However, this is largely accounted for by the drop in the school population. Sheffield children were almost as likely to be placed in separate special schools or in special units, with all the associated educational and social restrictions, in 1985 as in 1976. This becomes clearer when we consider which children are *not* included in Table 6.1.

TABLE 6.1: Number of children attending schools or full-time units for pupils with learning and adjustment problems over a ten year period

	Number of full-time pupils on roll			
	Learning difficulties*	Adjustment difficulties†	Total	Percent of total school population
1976(May)	669	276	945	0.87
1979(September)‡	526	251	777	0.77
1982(April)	595	247	842	0.88
1985(April)	487§	205	692	0.82

* Schools for children with moderate or mild learning difficulties
† Includes one former school designated for 'delicate' children, one school for children with moderate learning difficulties *and* adjustment difficulties and pupils receiving home tuition following exclusion or suspension from school
‡ Figures were only available for September 1979. As this was the start of the school year, several schools had vacancies which would have been filled during the year
§ Includes 32 pupils in full-time units attached to ordinary schools in 1982 and 52 in 1985.

The figures in Table 6.1 do not include pupils attending a full-time centre for disruptive teenagers, children on temporary placement in special schools, children attending the 'integrated resources' attached to ordinary schools, or the special nursery placements mentioned earlier. Nor do they include children attending schools attached to social services institutions or a hospital psychiatric unit. Nor, of course, are disruptive pupils attending special groups in ordinary schools included, even though these pupils are likely to follow a severely restricted curriculum, often for a prolonged period (Galloway *et al*, 1982). Thus, it could be argued that recent initiatives have increased the number of children in forms of separate special education.

One thing, however, cannot seriously be disputed. Whatever else happened in the decade since the Education Committee expressed its support for integration, there is little evidence of any reduction in the relative numbers of pupils being placed long-term in special schools separate from the mainstream or in units where they are generally taught separately and follow a separate curriculum. This apparent total lack of progress has occurred in the face of: (a) an expensive and generously staffed service established largely to facilitate integration; (b) the firm commitment to integration of the overwhelming majority of educational psychologists. We have, therefore, a situation in which a group of professionals responsible for assessments under the 1981 Education Act believe in theory that children's special educational needs can be met more effectively in ordinary schools, yet continue to write reports which result in them being placed in special schools.

There is no evidence that educational psychologists, or indeed any of the other professionals responsible for assessments, are deliberately trying to subvert their employer's policy. Another possibility is that they recommend special schooling on the grounds that the education of the majority of children in the class is being harmed by the presence of one or two particularly disturbing children, even though they do not consider special school placement in the best interests of the children themselves. This certainly does happen, but as an explanation for the continuing segregation of children with learning and adjustment problems it is too simplistic. Our contention is that much more complex issues of policy are involved, at national, LEA and school levels. The behaviour and decision of individual professionals, or of professional groups, cannot be understood except in the light of the political and social pressures imposed on them by the situations in which they find themselves. It is to these pressures that we must now turn.

NATIONAL AND LOCAL POLICIES: A CRITIQUE

OVERVIEW

A recurring theme in this book is that special schools or classes for children with learning or adjustment problems exist rather more for the benefit of pupils and teachers in the mainstream than of pupils selected to attend them. The fact that parents are almost invariably told that special education is recommended in their child's interest in no way invalidates this claim. Nor does it impugn the integrity of ordinary school teachers, doctors or psychologists. To tell parents that their child needs special schooling, is not necessarily inconsistent with a view that *other* children will benefit from his removal, especially when teachers in the mainstream school seem unable or unwilling to cater for his needs.

Nevertheless, the question *whose* needs special schools and units are designed to serve is not answered by this kind of verbal sleight of hand. The question is seen most starkly in the aims of centres or units for disruptive pupils. The first centre in Sheffield set out to cater for pupils who could not be contained in ordinary schools, and for whom all other possibilities had been exhausted. Here at least the aim of providing a service for ordinary *schools* was fairly explicit. Yet the offer of a place, almost inevitably, had to be 'sold' to parents on the grounds of benefits for their adolescent child.

This kind of double-talk becomes more complex in the case of designated special schools. We know of pupils who have been refused admission to a school for children with adjustment problems following assessment under the 1981 Education Act. In principle, at least, children are admitted to a special school on the basis that the school may be able to help them. This is not always the case in practice, but professional reports almost invariably recommend special schooling on the grounds that this is the most appropriate way to meet the child's needs. Following the special school's refusal to offer a place, education officers have felt obliged to consider placement in the centre for disruptive pupils, perhaps because the child has been suspended from school. On the surface this simply implies that LEA officers are exploring an alternative way of meeting the child's needs. It can be argued, though, that it also requires a re-definition of needs in two important ways: (a) the pupil's needs must be defined in such a way that education in a centre for disruptive teenagers appears more suitable than in a school for pupils with adjustment problems; (b) the needs of the referring school suddenly assume much greater prominence, if, indeed, they were mentioned at all in the original reports. Thus, while the child's needs may not necessarily be said to have changed, they may at least be described differently, in the light of available resources.

ASSESSMENTS UNDER THE 1981 EDUCATION ACT

In theory the 1981 Act was designed to overcome this sort of anomaly. Quite explicitly, the DES (1983) guidelines on assessment stated that professional reports should describe the child's current needs. The question of placement was to be logically and administratively independent of the reports. In practice, however, any assessment is influenced by the context in which it takes place. A headteacher who says he cannot contain the child in the school any longer is part of that context. So is an education officer who says that all the local special schools have several vacancies (or, for that matter, that none of them have). Schools vary in their willingness and their ability to cater effectively for children with special needs. Within each school teachers vary in a similar way. The apparent belief of the DES that educational psychologists can carry out assessments without taking these factors into account is, at best, extraordinarily naive.

The problem, however, goes much deeper than this. The Act's lukewarm commitment to integration cannot conceal its emphasis on assessing the child's cognitive and educational skills rather than the classroom or school context in which those skills are evident. Teachers and educational psychologists may not be able to ignore this wider context, but it seems to be regarded as relatively unproblematic in the DES (1983) guidelines. The obvious answer to this argument is that extra provision is defined in the guidelines in relation to the school. Thus, a child might be deemed 'worthy' of a statement at school X, but not if he attended school Y. This is true, but conveniently overlooks the fact that once an assessment has been requested, virtually all the information specified by the DES (1983) guidelines focuses on cognitive, perceptual and psycho-social factors. It is therefore easy for professionals to individualise the problem, and relatively difficult for them to see it as the product of the child's interaction with teachers and peers.

Since the DES encourages this individualistic focus on special educational needs we should not be surprised if teachers do likewise. In other words we should expect teachers to see the origin of learning and adjustment difficulties in the children they find disturbing rather than in the ways they have been teaching these children. Further, if the DES establishes elaborate procedures for identifying children with special needs, we should not be surprised if teachers use these procedures. Indeed it would be surprising if the number of pupils referred for assessment did not increase as a result of the introduction of the new procedures. This is in fact exactly what has happened in Sheffield.

The city implemented the 1981 Act on 1 April 1983. In the six months up to this date 160 children were referred for assessment for special education. In the next two comparable six-month periods the number referred for formal assessment under the new procedures increased to 180 and 220 respectively. Thus, from 1 September 1984 until 1 April 1985 the number of children referred for assessment showed an increase of 37.5 per cent over the comparable period immediately prior to introduction of the new procedures. This was to some extent due to the district Health Authority notifying the LEA of young children who might have special educational needs. The number of 'notifications' has dropped since the first year of implementation of the Act.

Unfortunately figures on final placement are not available. Again, it is quite possible in principle that the new procedures have led to more frequent recommendations for additional help within the ordinary classroom. This, however, seems improbable for four reasons.

1. The per cent of children placed indefinitely in special schools or units has shown no noteworthy decrease.
2. In general, children are referred for formal assessment *after* teachers have sought preliminary advice from the educational support services. In other words, formal referral occurs after teachers have decided that the child still has special educational needs which are not being met within the school in spite of advice or assistance from a support teacher and an educational psychologist.
3. The number of temporary placements in separate special schools for one or two terms has increased steadily since the introduction of this scheme. In theory, formal assessment is not required for these pupils. Certainly, many have been admitted on an informal basis, but others have been accepted on the basis of recommendations made during or subsequent to formal assessment.
4. The way special education is organised makes it difficult to provide additional help within the ordinary school on either a flexible or a generous basis. Overall, as we have made quite clear, the city's financial support for children with special educational needs is irreproachable. The problem lies in how this support is allocated. When both the referring school and the support teachers say there is nothing further they can do with their existing resources, long- or short-term special school or unit placement becomes inevitable by a process of eliminating all other options. Having placed its faith, and its money, in special schools and units and in the support services, the authority often lacks the flexibility to provide the additional staffing or material resources which might enable an ordinary school to integrate a child successfully.

LOCAL PLANNING

The architects of the 1981 Education Act almost certainly intended to encourage ordinary schools to identify and cater for pupils with special educational needs. Unfortunately their conceptual muddles about the nature and origin of these needs has done little to help LEAs to achieve this intention. In Sheffield the Education Committee shared the same ideal. Yet the distribution both of resources and of responsibility for special education ensured that the ideal would not become reality.

The Assistant Education Officer for Special Education had two broad areas of responsibility: (a) to ensure that the authority met its legal responsibilities towards children with special needs; (b) to implement the committee's policy. The first was largely bureaucratic. Education law in Britain is broadly enabling rather than narrowly prescriptive. To set up a system which conforms at least to the letter of the law is essentially an administrative task. The second responsibility was both political and professional. Irrespective of his own views, the Education Officer's freedom of action was limited by three major constraints.

1. His first responsibility was widely seen as the administration of the existing network of special schools and special units. The 1981 Act imposed the further burden of responsibility for the labyrinthine complexity of formal assessment, appeal and placement procedures. This massive workload of day-to-day responsibilities can have left little time for long-term planning to implement integration policy.
2. The Special Education Officer's *administrative* responsibilities were confined almost exclusively to designated special schools, centres or classes. Responsibility for ordinary schools remained firmly with the Assistant Education Officers for primary and secondary schools respectively. Yet as the 1976 working party's report recognised, an effective policy of integration has implications for organisation, curriculum and teaching methods in ordinary schools. In practice these were as remote from the responsibility of the Assistant Education Officer (special) as were the organisation, curriculum and teaching methods in special schools from his colleagues responsible for the primary and secondary sectors. Certainly, schools in which to base units or centres of integration were carefully selected for their favourable climate, but that was quite another matter from responsibility for helping to create such a climate in ordinary schools.

The problem cannot have been helped by the vested interests involved. Managers and senior staff of special schools expected the Special Education Officer to maintain the existing network. This was predictable. If you think you are offering something worth while you fight to maintain it, especially if you anticipate the alternative, at best, as loss of status, and at worst as redundancy. For the Primary and Secondary Education Officers the pressure was different. They were at the receiving end of demands for extra resources or, more frequently, of complaints at reduction in existing resources. At a time of economic recession, combined with falling school rolls, the part-time 'remedial' teachers appointed to many medium sized and smaller primary schools were among the first to go. Transferring pupils to special schools or units then became one of the few practical forms of support to

hard-pressed teachers in ordinary schools. Thus, for different reasons, Primary, Secondary and Special Education Officers all had a vested interest in maintaining the *status quo*, irrespective of their employers' stated policy.
3. The limitations to the Special Education Officer's field of responsibility were seen most starkly in the administration of the Centre for Disruptive Pupils. Whereas admission to schools for pupils with adjustment difficulties was the Special Education Officer's task, the Centre for Disruptive Pupils remained firmly under the administrative control of the Secondary Education Officer. There can be few more explicit acknowledgements that special education is concerned with special schools, and should not infiltrate ordinary schools. Far from integrating special schools into the mainstream, the administrative structure at education officer level perpetuated parallel systems.

Headteachers are entitled to feel cynical when they see obvious inconsistency between policy and practice. Lacking a clear lead from their employing authority, their own policies towards children with special educational needs inevitably remained uncoordinated and idiosyncratic. Any LEA plan to implement an integration policy would, however, have had to take account of pressures on teachers, many of them quite unrelated to special education. The reason is that the way teachers react to children with special needs is influenced to a considerable extent by how they feel about other aspects of their work.

PRESSURES ON TEACHERS

BACKGROUND

The impact of new demands on any group of workers, whether they be teachers, factory workers, or doctors, probably depends less on the demands themselves than on the context in which they are introduced. For thirty years from 1945, virtually all sectors of education were expanding. Free and compulsory education was part of the liberal dream of equality of opportunity within an expanding economy. The main debate in 1971–72 did not centre on the usefulness of raising the school leaving age to sixteen, but on the cost and the possibility of providing the necessary extra resources. Teachers enjoyed a high level of professional autonomy. For those with moderate energy and ambition, promotion could be rapid.

This picture faded in the late 1970s, and in the first half of the 1980s it became virtually unrecognisable. The reasons lie in demographic, economic and political factors. We have already referred to the first two. The falling birth rate resulted in a sharp drop in school rolls. Economic recession provided a convenient excuse for not taking the opportunity to reduce the pupil : teacher ratio and improve buildings, other resources and support services.

The political reasons are more complex. They cannot be explained solely in terms of an ideology which saw no reason to allow education to join the police, the prisons, the armed services and the nuclear weapons industry as exceptions, to be spared the rigours of strict monetary policy. In general both academics and politicians reflect rather than create trends in public opinion. Certainly, they both helped to reflect a climate of scepticism about the achievements of schools. There seems, in retrospect to have been an unconscious and unholy alliance between unwavering opponents. While politically right wing educationists were attacking teachers for supposedly declining standards (e.g. Cox and Boyson 1977), Marxist sociologists were claiming that schools, far from promoting equality of opportunity, were merely reproducing the inequalities in society (e.g. Willis 1977). As an ironic tribute to the changing climate, a major report on secondary education commissioned by the largest and politically most radical LEA in the country concluded that many schools were catering inadequately for the majority of below average pupils (ILEA 1984).

ACCOUNTABILITY

Historically teachers in Britain have had greater control over the curriculum than their colleagues in most, if not all, other developed countries. This has given them a high level of autonomy within the classroom which in turn has restricted parents' opportunities to participate actively in their children's education. Recent years, though, have seen a change in the balance of power. Teachers now are not only more openly accountable to parents for their pupils' progress, but also to their employers.

The Warnock Report devoted a chapter to the topic 'parents as partners' (DES 1978a). The committee advocated a relationship in which teachers and parents could work together to meet a child's special needs. The 1981 Education Act went a stage further by giving parents the right and responsibility to participate in the assessment process, as well as to appeal against decisions to which they objected. Teachers and other professionals were no longer able to write confidential reports recommending special schooling to which parents would have no access.

On a wider front, the 1980 Education Act gave parents greater freedom in their choice of school. It also required schools to publish information, including examination results, which might help parents to make informed choices. In addition HMI reports on schools became available free of charge to any member of the public. DES (1984) proposals for a majority of parents on all school governing bodies met with little favour, but increased parental representation remains a certainty. Similarly, the DES's original suggestion of financial incentives, or penalties, based on the results of an annual teacher appraisal scheme may have foundered on both practical and professional grounds. Nevertheless some kind of formal appraisal is clearly on the horizon.

CONDITIONS OF SERVICE

Greater accountability, with the obvious implications of more open criticism, is *potentially* beneficial both to teachers and to their pupils. After all, one characteristic of a profession is a willingness to review its own standards. Yet here too new demands have to be seen in a wider context. What teachers see as the erosion of their salaries *vis-à-vis* other government employees such as the police and the nurses is part of that context. So is the gradual deterioration of school buildings due to inadequate maintenance, and the similarly gradual deterioration in the quality of teaching due to inadequate resources. That this deterioration has occurred is well documented by the inspectorate, and is not controversial (e.g. HMI 1985a, b).

At the same time central government was adopting a much more active role in the curriculum. HMI's increasingly directive function was seen in a series of curriculum reports (e.g. DES 1979; HMI 1983). Further, funding for the new Technical and Vocational Education Initiative for the fourteen to nineteen age group was conditional on the Manpower Services Commission approving detailed curriculum proposals. By placing responsibility for this new development with the MSC the government was not only bypassing the existing channels for curriculum development, with their heavy representations of practising teachers, but also passing a vote of no confidence in them.

We would emphasise that some of the recent developments are overdue, and may lead to long-term benefits for teachers and for their pupils. Change, however, is stressful. The circumstances in which teachers were expected to adapt to change in the period 1975–85 made it potentially even more stressful. Integration of children with special educational needs is merely one of many developments that have been proposed. Against this background, we need to consider the main sources of stress from day-to-day classroom teaching. These will indicate some of the practical difficulties in implementing an integration policy. They will also suggest how they may be overcome.

SOURCES OF STRESS IN TEACHING

Teachers experience stress when they feel that demands are being made on them which threaten their self-esteem or their general welfare, and when they feel uncertain of their ability to cope with these demands (see Kyriacou and Sutcliffe 1978a). In Britain between 20 and 30 per cent of teachers have reported finding their work very stressful or extremely stressful (Kyriacou and Sutcliffe 1977, 1978b).

One common response to stress is that teachers become increasingly susceptible to symptoms such as colds, migraines, minor infections, sleeplessness, irritability and so on. Pratt (1978) used Goldberg's (1972) General Health Questionnaire to investigate the prevalence of such symptoms in a sample of primary school teachers in Sheffield. Using Goldberg's criteria he found that 25 per cent reported a range and severity of symptoms indicating mild psychiatric disorders. We used the same questionnaire in New Zealand, and found no fewer than 44 per cent of primary teachers reporting a similar range and severity of symptoms (Galloway et al. 1984a). This does not mean that all these teachers, either in Sheffield or in New Zealand, were in need of psychiatric help. It does mean that their symptoms could be seen by a GP or by a psychiatrist as evidence of *minor* psychiatric problems, of the type that are frequently associated with feelings of stress.

In our New Zealand study we were able to compare teachers' reports on their own health with those of a survey carried out twenty years previously (Borland 1962). Both surveys used identical wording, and asked teachers to say which of five statements best described their current state of health. The results showed that 26 per cent of teachers were reporting generally poor health in 1981 compared with 13 per cent in 1961. Both surveys relied on postal questionnaires and both were funded by the primary teachers' professional association. It is unrealistic to conclude that the physical health of New Zealand teachers has fallen sharply over the last twenty years. Although other possibilities have been discussed (Galloway et al. 1984a) it seems probable that the responses reflected a general fall in morale throughout the profession. As in Britain this resulted from demographic, economic and political factors. The background of insecurity included falling rolls, with a very real threat of unemployment for young teachers in urban areas, declining funds for resources and increasing public criticism of teachers' achievements. It is unrealistic to regard this background as irrelevant to the main sources of stress in the classroom.

Both in Britain and in New Zealand these have been shown to be associated with children's behaviour and with their educational progress (Pratt 1978; Galloway et al. 1984b). Conversely, these are among the main sources of satisfaction at work reported by the same sample of teachers in New Zealand (Galloway *et al.* 1985a). Looking at the evidence as a whole, it appeared:

1. That job satisfaction results from intrinsic aspects of the teacher's work, which obviously include relationships with children and seeing them make progress.
2. That stress is felt when a child's poor progress or behaviour reduces the teacher's scope for satisfaction from the job.
3. That a teacher may feel satisfied with the behaviour and progress of the majority of pupils, yet feel acute stress from one or two individuals.

This becomes clearer when we consider some of the other sources of stress: 28 per cent of teachers reported extreme stress or quite a lot of stress from interviews with parents, and 30 per cent from taking children on class trips. In contrast the key curriculum areas of reading and maths were seen as stressful by fewer than 18 per cent of teachers. Interestingly, these are all areas in which support should, in principle, be available from senior colleagues. Yet they are also areas in which teachers are frequently left to sink or swim without any kind of support. Few schools, for example, routinely include interviews with parents as part of their in-service induction programme for all recently appointed teachers.

Consequently it came as little surprise that relationships with colleagues were seen as an important source of stress by many teachers. Other studies have reached similar conclusions, especially for beginning teachers (Coates and Thoresen 1976; Rudd and Wiseman 1962). Nor did it come as a surprise that relationships with colleagues were also among the main sources of satisfaction at work.

For our present purposes the principal issues are:

1. That children with learning and adjustment difficulties, whose behaviour and progress cause their teachers concern, are probably the main source of stress from day-to-day classroom events.
2. That the stress teachers feel from this and from other sources may be increased or reduced by the quality of support from senior colleagues in the school; too frequently, teaching is a lonely profession (e.g. Hargreaves 1978).
3. That wider issues of national policy and LEA policy may affect the way teachers respond to potentially, though not necessarily, stressful incidents in the course of their work.

Whether a teacher sees a child with special educational needs negatively, as an additional burden, or positively as a challenge with the possibility of enhanced satisfaction from her work, does not depend solely on the child. It will also depend on the amount and quality of help available within the school and from the education

A study of conflicting needs

support services. We now need to consider the contribution of these services and the pressures which their members face.

PRESSURES ON THE SUPPORT SERVICES

'HIDDEN AGENDA' IN REFERRAL

Even among staff with responsibility for special needs, only a small minority has received any training in work with these children. It might therefore be thought that the relationship between mainstream teachers and members of the support services should be a symbiotic one. Without support and guidance, teachers who lack specialist training cannot hope to contain their pupils with special needs, let alone to teach them effectively. At the same time the 'support' services would lose their entire *raison d'être* if teachers did not need support.

The relationship is not, however, quite so straightforward. The support services may not be able to survive without teachers to support, but teachers often feel they could get along quite nicely without the support services. From the teacher's perspective there may be three problems.

1. The advice offered by members of the support services may be seen as unrealistic and/or impractical. Alternatively it may appear inconsistent with the teacher's overall approach to teaching or classroom management. A highly structured behaviour modification programme, for example, will probably not appeal to a teacher who favours an integrated day in which children have considerable freedom to choose when to carry out each activity.
2. The teacher may feel, perhaps rightly, that she already knows what Johnny's needs are, and how they can be met. At best, the support services may then be seen as an unnecessary layer of bureaucracy, delaying decisions which could otherwise be taken more quickly.
3. From past experience, the teacher may feel that members of the support services have insufficient time, if not knowledge, to provide sufficiently regular and practical help to enable her to meet a child's needs successfully. Hence, a request for 'help' is seen essentially as the first stage of an exercise in bureaucracy.

One or all of these scenarios usually lie behind the 'hidden agenda' which leads teachers and members of the support services to talk at cross purposes. The latter usually *accept* referrals on the basis that the teacher wants help in identifying a child's special needs and planning a suitable programme to meet them. Yet teachers often *refer* children only when they have already decided that they cannot meet the child's needs. The real reason for referral is to initiate a process which will culminate in the child's removal from the school. The referral, in other words, is to the Special School Removals Service, not to the School Psychological Service.

THE PARADOX OF ACCEPTANCE: OR WHO'S THE CLIENT?

When members of the support services have successfully established that the real, as opposed to nominal, reason for referral is to help the class teacher meet the child's needs, their problems are just starting. School and classroom organisation as well as methods of classroom teaching have a profound influence on children's behaviour and progress. Moreover, this influence is probably greatest with those vulnerable children who may be thought to have special needs. It follows, then, that members of the support services cannot operate effectively without considering school and classroom organisation and management.

It is one thing for an educational psychologist, or in Sheffield for a support teacher, to identify cognitive, personality, perceptual or family factors which contribute to the child's special educational needs. It is quite another to identify weaknesses in teaching method and classroom or school organisation or management. This could imply that the teacher, or headteacher, has special educational needs, not the child! More than one educational psychologist has found him and herself *persona non grata* in a school for doing just this.

Most members of the support services learn fairly rapidly that their advice will not be taken seriously unless they are accepted as individuals. The problem is that they will not be taken seriously as individuals unless they are sensitive to what teachers see as their needs. This requires them to formulate suggestions in terms which are consistent with the nominal reasons for referral. In practice this means that they are under powerful pressures to individualise the problem, locating it within the child or family, even though they may feel that it lies in the school or classroom. Thus, they find themselves in a 'catch 22'. To work effectively they have to be accepted as individuals, since otherwise their advice will almost certainly be ignored. Yet to be accepted as individuals they have to work ineffectively, by individualising the problem, and playing down the school's contribution.

Some educational psychologists have found a way out of this vicious circle (e.g. Gregory 1980; Rabinowitz 1981). To do so requires them to move beyond the model of assessment and teaching proposed in the 1981 Education Act, to consider wider aspects of school and classroom management. This requires a high level of personal and professional trust between the psychologist and the school's teachers. Such trust is seldom achieved before the psychologist has demonstrated her ability to work with members of the staff, helping them with problems they have identified in ways they find useful. *That* is seldom achieved without some of the professional compromises we have described.

'DE-SKILLING' TEACHERS

Both educational psychologists and support teachers in Sheffield have experienced the pressures described above. Both groups may also, unwittingly, have reduced rather than increased the teachers' feelings of competence to deal with problems themselves. This is seen most strikingly in the early experience of support teachers.

In their first year of operation, seven teachers saw 135 children (Mullins 1982), in spite of an LEA policy to give the service minimal publicity. Case-loads were unevenly distributed, but by their second year in the job support teachers working with children with learning difficulties each had a case-load of between thirty and fifty pupils. Waiting lists had already developed, and few cases were regarded as closed.

The trouble was that support teachers and class teachers defined the role of the service in different ways. Mullins found that 65 per cent of class teachers wanted the support teachers to act as peripatetic specialist teachers. None of the support teachers saw their role in this way. They saw themselves as specialists enabling class teachers to work effectively with children who had special needs. In other words, they expected to work on a consultancy model.

What actually happened illustrates how professionals can be socialised into accepting group norms. With a confused brief and little coordination, either of their activities or of their methods, individual support teachers necessarily developed their own idiosyncratic approaches. Some removed individuals or groups of children from the class and taught them separately. Others taught children within the class. Others devised learning and behaviour programmes for individual pupils with the class teacher. This third group was the only one to approach a partnership with class teachers. Rarely were they given any encouragement to consider aspects within the school that could have contributed to the child's difficulty. Even more rarely were they invited to provide in-service training.

The central points are:

1. That the great majority adopted the model of peripatetic specialist teachers which in theory they considered inappropriate.

2. Even when they moved beyond this model they confined their activities to planning learning and behaviour programmes for individual pupils rather than wider issues of classroom management.
3. The roles they found themselves were generally acceptable to class teachers, since any role that was *not* acceptable would have made their position in the school untenable.

This initial process of socialisation continued as the support teacher service became more established. Teachers' expectations when referring children to the service were often high. As the support teachers became better known, they were increasingly expected to take over responsibility for dealing with the child's problem. This not only legitimised their presence in the school but also gave them status. Unfortunately there were two side-effects.

1. The limited amount of support that the service could give individual pupils often seemed to produce relatively little change. Given their previous years of failure this was scarcely surprising. The children's lack of progress, though, resulted almost inevitably in a call for placement in a special school. Moreover, the support teacher frequently endorsed this call, feeling that more time was needed in small groups than could be provided in the ordinary school.
2. The process of transferring responsibility from the class teacher to the support teacher could involve a change in the child's status *and* in that of the class teacher. For the child this could mean a gradual change from 'ordinary' to 'special' in the eyes of his peers and of his teachers. For the latter the change involved a subtle process of 'de-skilling'; in other words their perceived competence to teach the child could actually be reduced. When a child becomes 'special', then 'special' skills are needed and 'special' resources required. These, clearly, were the province of support teachers.

Far from 'giving away' their expertise, using their experience to help class teachers identify and meet the child's needs, the service inadvertently contributed to the mystique surrounding special education in the eyes of many teachers in ordinary schools. Indeed it could easily be seen as a funnel into special schools or units rather than a preventive measure to obviate the need for special schooling. Here, though, a further socialisation process must be mentioned.

Most support teachers were based in special schools and had previously worked in them. Many special school teachers were anxious about the possible effects of integration on their school's future and their own. Given the large number of ordinary schools they served, it was inevitable that members of the service should turn for professional support to special school staff. Yet their position here would have been highly ambiguous if they had seriously been seen to be reducing special school rolls by supporting children who would otherwise have been referred in the mainstream. From the perspective of a full-time teacher in these schools, someone who does you out of a job is hardly likely to be a respected colleague and friend. Given this background, together with their own limited scope for helping their child clients in ordinary schools, it is scarcely surprising that support teachers quite frequently concluded that special schooling was the only answer.

In an attempt to reduce the ambiguity in their role, support teachers were instrumental in setting up the temporary special school placements mentioned earlier. The theory was that intensive help for one or two terms would equip children with the educational and social skills to cope successfully in the mainstream. The theory was, quite simply, wrong both for theoretical and for practical reasons.

On theoretical grounds there is no reason for thinking that improvements in a child's behaviour, established in one context, will transfer to another. Children's behaviour varies widely according to the context. Temporary special school placement implies a naive belief, unjustified by research evidence, that this is not the case. With learning difficulties the problem is slightly different. Research in remedial reading shows that children can indeed make rapid progress in small 'remedial' groups. Yet this progress is rapidly lost on return to the mainstream unless: (a) fairly intensive support is maintained; and/or (b) the remedial programme is directly related to the child's curriculum in the ordinary class (see Ch. 3). Neither condition applied in the case of the temporary special school placements discussed here.

The placements were, however, popular with class teachers and headteachers in ordinary schools. Disturbing children could be removed temporarily from the mainstream, with the possibility of permanent removal if they did not 'respond' to a term or two of special education or if they continued to present problems on return. Once again, the support teachers were providing a funnel into special schools. The gap between the original intention and the actual practice could hardly have been wider.

CONCLUSIONS

Sheffield Education Committee's policy to integrate children with special needs into ordinary schools has been perfectly clear since 1976. The committee's generous financial support for special education is not in dispute. Its commitment to the welfare of children living in socially disadvantaged circumstances is equally clear. The committee's abolition 'at a stroke' in 1983 of corporal punishment and school uniform reflected, at least in part, its concern that working-class children were more likely to receive corporal punishment and to suffer from school uniform requirements than middle-class children.

Nor are there legitimate grounds for discussion regarding the long-, or even medium-term benefits of separate special schooling. Overwhelmingly, the research evidence we reviewed in Chapter 3 suggests that these seldom exist. The curriculum is frequently limited. Children's educational progress is *less* likely to improve than if they remained in ordinary schools. Their chances of successful return to the mainstream are small, (with the exception, in Sheffield, of schools for children with 'mild' learning difficulties).

Yet in the decade after this humanitarian, politically radical council committed itself to integration, there was no noteworthy drop in the proportion of children, predominantly from working-class backgrounds, placed in long-term special schools or units. If we take into account the short-term special school placements, the unit for disruptive pupils, the 'home' tuition units and the school attached to a hospital child psychiatry unit the proportion of children receiving separate special schooling for at least some of their education may even have increased.

The apparent failure of Sheffield's policy resulted from the lack of any coherent plan to implement it. Any such plan has to start in the administrative structure at education officer level. The distribution of responsibilities here served to perpetuate a special education network operating in parallel with the mainstream. Yet the logical implication of the council's policy was that special education should become an integral part of the mainstream.

Lacking any clear, firm, direction from the administration, teachers in ordinary schools and members of the support services had to evolve their own solutions to the day-to-day problems they encountered. Inevitably these solutions reflected the special education network that actually existed, not the network that might have existed if the council had recognised the implications of its own policy. Consequently, many of the developments in special education services for children with learning and adjustment difficulties merely extended the existing network. The effect was to strengthen the identity of this network as separate from the mainstream, effectively deepening the divisions between mainstream and special education rather than integrating them. 'Integrated resources' constitute the one possible exception, but even they regarded children with moderate learning difficulties as beyond their remit.

It is striking that the period since 1976 has seen considerable advances in Sheffield, as nationally, in the integration of children with sensory, and to a lesser extent physical handicaps. The only

A study of conflicting needs

groups for whom there has been no evidence of integration, either in Sheffield or nationally, are children with adjustment difficulties and moderate learning difficulties. The relocation of some children with mild or moderate learning difficulties from special schools to special units attached to ordinary schools cannot on present evidence be regarded as effective integration. The indications are that the 1976 working party's cautions about unit provision may have been justified. Almost all these children come from working-class homes. Few articulate pressure groups demand better facilities in mainstream schools on their behalf. Their treatment can only be described as discriminatory, an unhappy irony for a LEA which prides itself, with some justification, for its progressive policy making, and for its commitment to the education of under-privileged children.

The most probable explanation is that the plan to implement Sheffield's integration policy was not based on any clear analysis of the class, race and sex implications of the special education facilities for pupils with learning or adjustment difficulties. Such an analysis would have shown that nationally schools for children with learning or adjustment problems:

1. Catered almost exclusively for the working class.
2. Catered disproportionately for children from ethnic minority groups and for boys.
3. Lacked the confidence of many parents, especially those from ethnic minorities (ILEA 1985a).

Sheffield Council was explicit in its analysis and outspoken in its rejection of government initiatives which seemed to discriminate on class lines, for example the scheme to provide assisted places in independent schools. Yet it did not seem to recognise the relevance of these same issues in its own provision of special education for children with learning and adjustment difficulties. Many councillors seemed to retain a 'liberal' philosophy which saw the task of special education as catering for the poor in mind and providing separate services for the unfortunate – an outmoded and patronising philanthropy which they would have been quick to condemn if it had been applied to the city's housing or social services. This need not be the case. In the next chapter we consider how an integration policy might be implemented, for the benefit of children *and* of their teachers in ordinary schools.

Chapter seven

DISTURBING CHILDREN IN THE ORDINARY SCHOOL: PROBLEMS AND POSSIBILITIES

INTRODUCTION

One of the questions in evaluating provision for disturbing pupils in ordinary schools is: whose progress should we evaluate? The problem pupils may be seen to make excellent progress on a wide range of criteria, but teachers and researchers may still ask whether their presence exerts a harmful effect on the progress or the behaviour of other pupils in the school. Integration of maladjusted or disruptive pupils cannot be justified solely by the progress of integrated pupils. It also requires, at the very least, that their presence should not harm other pupils.

In this chapter we review evidence which suggests consistently that:

1. Schools exert an enormous influence on their pupils. Whether a pupil is considered disruptive or maladjusted depends at least as much on factors within the school as on factors within the pupil or the family.
2. In general, schools which cater successfully for their most disturbing pupils *also* cater successfully for the rest of their pupils.

We look at the implication of the research evidence for policy and practice in ordinary schools, and consider a number of popular responses to disturbing behaviour in the light of these implications. More specifically, we argue that on-site units, behavioural approaches and a well-developed pastoral network can all make an important contribution, but only when seen as part of an overall school policy towards all pupils. Finally, we discuss the paradox that the most effective ways to help disturbing or potentially disturbing pupils are often a by-product of procedures aiming to improve the quality of education for all pupils in the school.

SCHOOL EFFECTIVENESS AND SPECIAL EDUCATIONAL NEEDS

COMPARISONS BETWEEN SCHOOLS

Few teachers would wish to claim that school can exert a greater influence than home on children's adjustment, but not even the most pessimistic would be happy about the idea that school is of negligible influence. They would be supported by the growing body of research in the last ten years which shows that a school does in fact exert a substantial influence on the lives and futures of its pupils.

The first people to provide statistical evidence that schools have an influence on whether or not their pupils become delinquent were Michael Power and his colleagues (1967, 1972; Phillipson 1971). Power claimed to find large differences between secondary schools in delinquency rates. These he could not attribute solely to differences in delinquency rates in the schools' catchment areas. He argued that some of the schools whose delinquency rates he studied might have helped to prevent delinquency while others might have actually contributed to its development. What features *within* the 'delinquogenic' school might contribute to delinquency *outside* it, Power did not know, and ILEA refused permission for further related research in its schools. In fact, Power's conclusions were attacked by Baldwin (1972) on the grounds that he did not adequately control for differences in catchment area, and research in other London schools by the Cambridge Institute of Criminology (Farrington 1972; West and Farrington 1973) indicated that high delinquency schools tended to admit more children who might reasonably be regarded as 'at risk' on the basis of evidence about their home district. On the other hand Gath *et al.* (1972, 1977) found major differences both in delinquency rates and in the numbers of children referred to child guidance clinics from London schools with broadly similar catchment areas.

Other work in London was also starting to confirm the influence of schools over their pupils' behaviour. Rutter (1977) used statistical techniques to predict the number of ten-year-olds whose teachers would report deviant behaviour at the age of fourteen. He found that the number of 'deviant' pupils as reported by teachers was much higher than predicted at some schools, and much lower at others. In other words, whether pupils were regarded by teachers as deviant depended to a considerable extent on their experiences at school since the age of ten, not just on personal or family characteristics.

These results led to the most influential study of school effectiveness in recent years. Rutter *et al.* (1979) studied twelve Inner London secondary schools in detail. After controlling for pupil intake, the authors found significant differences between the schools in their pupils' examination results, delinquency rates and behaviour within the school. There was clear evidence that pupils' behaviour within the school was not associated with their background, behaviour or attainments on entering the school. In other words, the children's behaviour at school depended largely on factors within the school, not on their social backgrounds.

Rutter's work has received a great deal of critical attention. The statistics have been challenged, and the limited number of measures of the pupil's backgrounds, behaviour and attainments on entering their secondary schools have been criticised. Probably the most reasonable conclusion is that the use of more rigorous statistical techniques might have reduced the differences between the twelve schools, though some would still have remained (e.g. Radical Statistics Education Group 1982).

Rutter's evidence for a school's influence on pupils' behaviour is supported by studies in South Wales (Reynolds 1976; Reynolds *et al.* 1980), and by a series of studies in Sheffield. A study of persistent absenteeism from school showed a marked relationship between absence rates and poverty in the catchment area, as measured by the number of pupils receiving free school meals. This association was not evident in the case of pupils suspended from school for disciplinary reasons (Galloway 1976). Over the following four-year period we continued to find very large differences between secondary schools in suspension rates. In a study of the pupils, their schools and their families, five out of thirty-seven schools accounted for roughly 50 per cent of all suspensions (Galloway 1982).

We therefore collected all the available information about each school's catchment area, using census data and LEA records, and about its curriculum, buildings and general organisation. This gave us twenty-two catchment area variables and thirty-six school variables (Galloway *et al.* 1985b). Virtually all of the catchment area variables were strongly related to persistent absentee rates, but *not* to exclusion or suspension. The implication was that although the pupils' social backgrounds might have some effect on their attendance, this was almost certainly not the case on their behaviour within the school. The obvious objection to this argument is that suspension rates may not accurately reflect the overall prevalence or severity of disruptive behaviour within schools. Perhaps some schools are simply more tolerant than others. This is certainly true, but our observations suggested that most schools with high suspension rates also had very high rates of disruptive behaviour. More important, the differences between schools in pupils' behaviour were just as striking as the differences in suspension rates.

Our conclusions in Sheffield were supported by evidence from an anonymous LEA (Grunsell 1979, 1980) which also found major differences between schools in suspension rates. In addition Grunsell reported a disproportionate number of children of Afro-Caribbean origin among suspended pupils. The consistency with which behaviour at school has been found to be relatively independent of the pupils' families and social backgrounds could be seen as extraordinarily encouraging for teachers. It suggests that teachers can exert a powerful and beneficial influence on their pupils' adjustment. The evidence also suggests, however, that the reverse can be the case. On both practical and logical grounds it is very hard to find evidence of success without also finding evidence of problems. 'Success' here implies that the school inhibits the patterns of behaviour which could be taken as evidence of special educational needs by promoting other, more constructive patterns. The opposite side of this coin is that schools may also encourage, if not create, the behaviours which teachers see as evidence of special needs. The question is how.

THE PROCESS OF SCHOOLING AND PUPILS' BEHAVIOUR

In one of our Sheffield studies we found no relationship between any of the thirty-six school variables and either persistent absentee rates or suspension rates. These variables, however, all described aspects of the school's formal organisation and structure (Galloway *et al.* 1985b). This is consistent with other evidence which shows that structural variables such as a school's size and buildings have relatively little influence on pupils' attendance, behaviour or educational progress (e.g. Reynolds 1976; Rutter *et al.* 1979). In contrast, variables that contribute to school ethos or climate seem much more important.

By school climate we refer to the network of relationships between pupils, between teachers and between pupils and teachers that determines what they expect of each other and what kinds of work or behaviour they regard as acceptable. It is a nebulous concept, but one which is central to the experience of every individual in the school, teachers as well as pupils. Research on the process of schooling aims to identify aspects of pupils' and of teachers' experience which may contribute to school climate.

A study carried out in one secondary modern school, as a participant observer, convinced Hargreaves (1967) that the school's policy of streaming led to the formation of two opposed subcultures. The higher stream boys not only took external examinations but were disproportionately represented in the school's sporting activities and shared attitudes compatible with those of their teachers; in contrast lower stream boys were prevented from taking external examinations and by the third year were adopting a self-protective and unified wall of opposition to the system which they felt had condemned them to failure. Hargreaves argued that the two opposing subcultures within the school resulted from the streaming system; the teachers at the school would presumably have argued the reverse case – that the existence of an anti-school subculture necessitated streaming for the benefit of the brighter and more cooperative children, but this view overlooked the uncomfortable fact that low stream boys in the first two years were not on the whole united in their opposition to the school's value system; this opposition arose from the recognition that they had been 'written off' as examination prospects. Hargreaves comments laconically: 'If the examination is the carrot by which we entice the horse to run, we should not be surprised if the horse stands still when we take the carrot away.' Other research (Douglas 1964) had shown that high stream pupils improve their IQ test scores at each IQ level between the ages of eight and eleven, while lower stream children deteriorate in the same period; Hargreaves found an analogous polarisation into social and antisocial attitudes as boys in high and low streams progressed up the schools.

Participant observer studies have the strength of allowing a detailed investigation of the social relationships in one school. The picture which emerges achieves a degree of realism, impossible in a numerical survey. In a later book Hargreaves *et al.* (1975) describe in more detail the social interaction between pupils and teachers which results in certain children being labelled as difficult and consequently forming *themselves* into a deviant, anti-school subgroup. By its very detail, though, participant observer research cannot look closely at the progress of a large number of children in different schools. Hargreaves demonstrated some of the policies and attitudes contributing to problem behaviour in one school. On the other hand a detailed study of one school can no more justify extending the conclusions to all schools than a detailed study on one child can justify conclusions about the whole class; comparison of statistical evidence from several different schools can yield evidence that some appear to have striking success in certain areas.

Reynolds (1976) adopted a comparative approach in his study of secondary modern schools in a Welsh mining valley. Like Rutter *et al.* (1979) he found that schools which did well on one outcome measure, for example attendance rates, tended also to do well on others. He argued that an important characteristic of the successful schools was a 'truce' between older pupils and teachers in which teachers' expectations were not inflexible, and pupils generally felt able to compromise when confronted with authority. In the younger age-groups at these schools, rules were clear and were enforced. As pupils got older, they found their teachers willing to negotiate on matters such as uniform and the amount and quality of work. This contrasted with the situation in the less successful schools where relationships were characterised by lack of flexibility on both sides.

A different perspective on a similar point was provided by

Finlayson and Loughran (1976) in their study of pupils' perceptions of teachers at schools with high and low delinquency rates. Children in the high delinquency schools considered their teachers to be as caring towards them as *individuals* as teachers in the schools with low delinquency rates. There was, however, an important difference in how the pupils assessed the teachers' interaction with the class as a whole. Here the teachers in the high delinquency schools were more likely to be seen as defensive and authoritarian in their relationships with their classes. An obvious implication is that extensive guidance or counselling services with an essentially individualistic focus are unlikely to compensate for weaknesses or tensions in teaching styles and classroom management techniques.

In London Rutter *et al.* (1979) regarded a large number of measurable variables as contributing to school climate. Thus their most successful schools were characterised by a prompt start to lessons, well-presented pupils' work on the walls, clear and generally high expectations on completion of work, generally low rates of punishment and relatively high rates of positive recognition for good work or behaviour. These schools also had little evidence of graffiti or vandalism. Perhaps as a result they appeared well cared for and attractive, frequently with pot plants contributing to the overall impression. It is said that one result of the publicity this research attracted was a sharp increase in the number of pot plants in secondary schools, and a similar increase in pupils' work being pinned up on walls!

SOME IMPLICATIONS

To state the obvious, school climate will not be changed simply by buying a few pot plants. Indeed it seems more likely that the survival rate of pot plants may reflect school climate. In some schools powerful social pressures prevent vandalism. In others the reverse applies. Nor should it be assumed that the school's buildings are unimportant, even though the research has found no systematic link with pupils' progress or behaviour. Work in New Zealand has suggested that the quality of a school's buildings exerts a significant effect both on the stress teachers experience at work (Panckhurst *et al.* 1982) and on their satisfaction at work (Galloway *et al.* 1985a).

There is little evidence from the research that schools reduce inequality between pupils. The gap between the highest and lowest attaining pupils in the most successful of Rutter's twelve schools was as great as in the least successful. The successful schools seemed to raise the standards of all their pupils. This raises an interesting question about the identification of special needs. If *all* schools reached the standards of the most successful in Rutter's study we would still have the disturbing minority of 10, 20 or 30 per cent of pupils, depending on the preferred criteria, at the bottom of the academic continuum. This will almost certainly always be the case, but the position is not as straightforward as it seems.

Rutter *et al.* (1979) checked the influence of schools on their less able pupils by analysing the Certificate of Secondary Education grade four and five passes. These were the lowest possible grades in public examinations, and had been excluded from previous analyses. The results again showed significant variation between schools, indicating the importance of a school's influence on the progress of its least able pupils as well as on the majority.

Some earlier research in America strengthens this view. A massive research programme had attributed virtually all the variation between pupils to individual or family factors (Coleman *et al.* 1966). Re-analysis of this work suggested that schools might in fact have exerted a considerable influence on *some* of their pupils, mainly those of low ability, of low social class and from ethnic minority groups (Dyer 1968). Grosin (1985), too, in a review of American and Swedish studies argued that:

> . . . the space for improvement of the pedagogical and social climates should be greatest in schools which recruit children from socially and economically less fortunate families. In a similar way the schools in high status areas are even now characterised to a greater degree by pedagogical and social climates which are favourable to pupils' results and social adjustment. Improvement of the climate in schools should in other words mean that the gap between different social groups within a generation would be narrowed (p. 14).

The important point for our present discussion is the suggestion that those most influenced, for better or worse, by the process of schooling, are the least privileged and most vulnerable pupils in the school. These, of course, are the pupils whose teachers are most likely to regard them as having special educational needs because of their poor progress or behaviour.

There appears so far to be *no* evidence from the school effectiveness research that this group is helped by provision of special units and a curriculum separate from the mainstream. In explaining differences between schools, including differences in the progress and behaviour of the least able and most disadvantaged groups, the evidence points overwhelmingly to the importance of factors contributing to overall school climate. It is in the light of this conclusion that we need to consider the range of existing provision for disturbing pupils in ordinary schools, and to consider the actual and potential effectiveness of this provision.

ON-SITE UNITS

OVERVIEW

These started as an attempt by educational psychologists and child guidance clinic staff to extend their expertise to provide a more direct and practical service to schools (see Chs. 1 and 2). Their growth in numbers was rapid and unplanned. Her Majesty's Inspectorate of Schools (HMI) has expressed concern about the quality of education revealed in reports on a national survey (HMI 1978) and on a series of inspection visits in Inner London (HMI 1980b). Many of the units in both reports were off-site, admitting pupils from several schools, but there is evidence that similar problems exist in on-site units (e.g. Galloway et al. 1982).

The idea that a spin-off of units would be to benefit the classes from which difficult children had been removed, and their teachers, was recognised both by the early therapeutically oriented projects and by later ones with an explicitly custodial orientation. Similarly, virtually all schools establishing units have expected that the majority of pupils would come from stressful, unsatisfactory home backgrounds. David Davies, the teacher in charge of the unit at Brislington School in Bristol for five years, took this a step forward by arguing that a unit's existence should teach the rest of the staff to work in a different way, to become more receptive to the advice of psychiatrists and educational psychologists, and to become 'readier to deal sensitively with regressive behaviour as the unit's members are fed back into normal classes' (Rowan 1976).

Yet even this progressive and sensitive view skirts round the critical points: (a) that disturbing behaviour can only result from an interaction between the child and other people with whom he comes into contact; and (b) that many of the children who present problems at school do not do so at home (Rutter et al. 1970). There is nothing inherently illogical or contradictory in holding the view that a child's difficult behaviour in school is precipitated by family circumstances even though it is not evident at home and his parents deny other problems, but before taking this position we must be absolutely certain that he is not reacting, logically or otherwise, against something he finds stressful or unpleasant at school. Similarly, there is nothing inherently illogical in trying to provide a therapeutic educational milieu to alleviate problems which arise at home (especially when, as in the Brislington project and some at least of the ILEA nurture groups, there is a simultaneous attempt to work with the parents), but before doing so we should ask not only whether the treatment is appropriate to the 'illness' but also whether the illness is such as to alter the child's basic educational needs, since placing him in a full-time unit will necessarily restrict his curriculum.

Inevitably there will be a lot of compromise; some children may be considered unable to benefit from an ordinary curriculum because of their anxiety, self-consciousness or lack of confidence; the more restricted curriculum of a special unit will be a small price to pay if the alternative is at best to sit apathetically at the back of the room or at worst to refuse to attend school at all. On the other hand, other children are able to benefit educationally from ordinary classes but present so many problems that they have to be removed for the benefit of their teachers and the rest of the class. To argue that the first group of children need to attend a special unit for their own benefit, while the second group need to be removed for the benefit of teachers and other children is to miss the more basic point that in both cases the children's behaviour is the product of the way they react to the ordinary classroom situation, and this poses the question: What is it about that situation which elicits this reaction? In some cases the answer may simply be, nothing, as the child's behaviour can clearly be seen as a direct response to stress outside school, though, as we argued earlier, this is by no means always the case. In theory, units might help children cope with the things they find difficult in ordinary classes, for example by developing the confidence of the timid, withdrawn child or by teaching the aggressive extrovert to redirect his energy into more socially acceptable channels. However, the success of various forms of treatment for disturbing children was discussed in Chapter 3 and does not need repeating.

The main point here is that this conceptual model – one of treating the child – implies dual standards for children and teachers: 'they' are the ones with problems and 'we' are the ones who provide treatment. Both the therapeutic unit and the 'sin-bin' tend to suffer from the same conceptual limitation, imposed by their individualistic orientation. Neither focuses explicitly on meeting the needs of *teachers* in ordinary classes, nor on dealing with *curriculum* problems in the mainstream which may have contributed to, if not caused, educational failure and associated disruption. There is no reason, though, why these problems should not be overcome, given sufficient coherence in the aims of the unit and sufficient back-up from senior staff.

USING AN ON-SITE UNIT EFFECTIVELY

In the course of a research programme on recent provision for disruptive pupils in New Zealand, we worked in four schools which had made conscious attempts to cater for the needs of their most difficult pupils without additional funding from the government (Galloway and Barrett 1984). Only two of the schools were currently operating on-site units. A third had opened a unit some years previously. This unit had been closed because it attracted all the school's most difficult pupils, and provided little incentive for return to the mainstream. A similar situation was reported by the head of a school in our Sheffield study (Galloway *et al.* 1982).

There was, however, one school in which the unit appeared to play an important and useful role (Galloway 1985a). Pupils could be referred without prior notice by the principal or deputy. They would not, however, normally attend the unit full-time for more than two or three days, certainly not more than a week. They could continue to attend for a longer period, perhaps two to three weeks, on a part-time basis, withdrawn from lessons with which they had been having particular difficulty.

The unit's aims were:

1. To provide a 'cooling off' period for pupil and referring teacher alike, or rather to prevent the entrenched confrontation that might eventually require a prolonged cooling off period.
2. To enhance the pupils' self-esteem by giving them an experience of success in the subjects in which they had been failing or presenting behavioural problems.
3. To provide an opportunity for special education staff to plan the pupils' future work with the relevant teachers, in order to prevent history repeating itself on their return to ordinary classes.

Thus, it was understood by pupils and by teachers that the unit's function was not to provide a long-term alternative to ordinary lessons. Rather it aimed to provide short-term help directly related to the pupils' current difficulty, and to enable teachers to plan for an early return to the mainstream. This model assumed the teacher's willingness and ability to adapt the curriculum to the needs of the pupil. In contrast many other units, both in Britain and New Zealand, were based on the assumption that pupils should be removed if they were unable or unwilling to adapt to the needs of the curriculum.

Teachers, though, cannot be expected to adapt the curriculum in the light of their pupils' special needs without the active support and help of colleagues with acknowledged expertise in this area. Expertise in working with individual children may be necessary for teachers in special needs departments, but it is certainly not sufficient. The achievement of this unit did not lie principally in the excellence of the work carried out in the unit, but rather in the opportunity provided by the unit's existence for special education staff to work with teachers of classes in which the pupils had been presenting problems.

Two further points should be made here. First the unit was merely one aspect of the school's network for children with special needs. The teacher in charge of the unit was also head of the special needs department. Hence, the split between the unit and the special needs department, so evident in many other on-site units, did not arise. The second point is related to this. No distinction was acknowledged between learning difficulties and behaviour problems. The underlying assumption was rather that behaviour problems arose from problems in the curriculum or teaching method. The problem was not individualised, implicitly attributing responsibility to the pupil or the family background. Rather, it was seen as evidence of a need to review future ways of working with the pupil. In Chapter 8 we look in more detail at the range of provision for children with special needs at this school. First, though, we need to consider the usefulness of approaches which have received enormous publicity in recent years, with corresponding controversy.

INTERACTION ANALYSIS AND BEHAVIOUR MODIFICATION

OVERVIEW

Until the late 1960s most therapeutic work with children and families was derived from the work of Freud and other early psychoanalysts. Today a much wider range of approaches is practised in child guidance clinics and hospital child psychiatry out-patient departments. Many children with severe adjustment problems at school are referred to these services. A frequent limitation to the help they can offer is that assessment and treatment are based in the clinic when the problem may lie in the child's interaction with teachers and peers at school. A different approach involves assessment and treatment in the classroom, or wherever the problem actually occurs.

Behavioural work makes the assumption that behaviour is learned, and consequently that it can be changed with appropriate teaching. Behaviour modification in the classroom first made a notable impact in the 1960s when experimental psychologists started to demonstrate that the principles used to describe the behaviour of animals in the laboratory could also be used to describe, and change, the interaction between children and teachers in the classroom. Throughout the 1960s and early 1970s behavioural work increased rapidly in popularity, with an explosion of articles in specialist journals and of books and training materials for teachers (e.g. O'Leary and O'Leary 1979; Harrop 1983; Wheldall *et al.* 1983).

Almost as a matter of definition behavioural work aims to help teachers to teach more effectively and/or pupils to learn more effectively. Some programmes have aimed to improve academic and learning strategies, others to reduce aspects of disruptive behaviour, for example 'out of seat behaviour', to use a not untypical piece of behaviourist jargon. They have been used both with individuals and with the class as a whole. Before looking at some of the problems in behavioural work, we need to summarise the stages of a typical project.

First, the teacher has to identify in specific terms the aspects of the child's behaviour which she wishes to modify or which she wishes the child to develop. This is followed by a stage in which the frequency of the target behaviour is recorded, thus providing a 'baseline' against which subsequent progress may be measured. Third, the teacher, or the psychologist acting as consultant, analyses the 'antecedents', i.e. events preceding the target behaviour, and 'consequences', or events following it. The aim here is to describe in precise terms what elicits the problem behaviour, and what reinforces it. For example, one child may find the teacher's attention when being told off highly reinforcing; another may find the laughter of other children reinforcing. The fourth stage is to use this analysis to plan a programme to achieve the desired goal, and the fifth to implement the programme and maintain records on its effectiveness to compare with the baseline measures. The final stage is to review progress, and revise, extend or change the programme as necessary.

ANALYSING BEHAVIOUR: POSSIBILITIES AND PROBLEMS

Many of the techniques behaviourists use in analysing classroom behaviour are derived from research on classroom interaction (e.g. Flanders 1970). They use time-sampling and event-sampling techniques to record the frequency of specific aspects of behaviour. It is not, of course, only behaviourists who can use these techniques. One important study set out to investigate how teaching styles might affect the progress and behaviour of maladjusted children in ordinary American primary schools (Kounin *et al.* 1966).

Using video recordings, they showed that the teachers who were most successful in managing ordinary children were also the most successful with emotionally disturbed pupils. Moreover, the effect of a disturbed child on the rest of the class was closely related to the teacher's control over the rest of the class. Of special interest, though was the discovery that techniques of handling bad behaviour had no observable effect on its incidence. (In contrast, Hall *et al.* (1968) found that the more times children were told to sit down, the more they spent standing up!) With only one teacher out of thirty in Kounin's study was there any close association between her technique for checking bad behaviour and the immediate success of her efforts. In contrast what Kounin awkwardly called 'teacher with-it-ness' *was* closely associated with good behaviour from both the emotionally disturbed and the normal pupils. By 'teacher with-it-ness' he meant variety in learning activities, recognising what was happening at a given moment, techniques for handling group movement around the classroom and so on.

Kounin's study had at least three important implications for an attempt to understand the needs of maladjusted children. First, he confirmed that even successful experienced teachers have little theoretical understanding of the principles of classroom control (shown by the lack of success of all but one teacher in their explicit efforts to control the children). Second, and more important, he showed the importance of the teacher's expertise in her subject; common sense would suggest that the teacher who is not competent in her subject, or has inadequate materials with which to teach it, will have discipline problems, yet this rather obvious fact is overlooked in much of the literature. Finally, and perhaps most important of all as far as this book is concerned, he provided further evidence that 'emotionally disturbed' (his term) and normal children do not form separate populations; the teaching styles which worked with the normal children also worked with the emotionally disturbed pupils. This hardly supports the all too prevalent idea among special school teachers that different, and special, qualities are required for their sort of work.

Moreover, if it can be shown that the same sort of teaching skills and personal qualities are needed, a policy of segregating the most disturbing children into special schools of their own is hardly logical, especially as common sense is supported by research findings that children influence each other's behaviour. This is implicitly recognised in the widespread and sometimes justified concern about the effect of a maladjusted child on the rest of his class; the teacher's concern is partly that the difficult child demands an undue proportion of her time, and partly that other children may start to copy his behaviour. In fact, children copy 'good' as well as 'bad' behaviour, and if one unsettled and disruptive child has an undue influence on the others it may be that they feel there is a greater pay-off for disruptive behaviour, than for cooperation. This becomes not probable but inevitable where the teacher lacks confidence in her subject, or where she fails to notice and approve of effort and success.

Although Kounin's work was essentially descriptive, it does suggest how a detailed analysis of pupil–teacher interaction may be used to plan subsequent intervention. Unfortunately, however, the explicit emphasis on *observed* behaviour has led to a number of theoretical and practical problems. These have limited the usefulness of much behavioural work in schools.

The practical problem can be described briefly. The obvious applications of behavioural principles in classroom management have led to enthusiastic, and often uncritical use of the techniques derived

Disturbing children in the ordinary school

from these principles. At least three eminent British psychologists with a behavioural orientation have warned against their inappropriate use.

Wheldall (1982) talks of 'behavioural overkill', referring to the treatment of quite minor problems with unnecessarily 'heavy' techniques such as sending a child out of the room for a period ('time-out'), or a systematic reinforcement system involving the use of tokens ('token economy'). Earlier Berger (1979) had written of the dangers of a 'mindless technology' in which behaviour modification techniques are used without an adequate understanding of the practical and theoretical issues on which their successful use depends. Harrop (1980) describes major practical difficulties in obtaining reliable baseline observations. To obtain reliable information, two observers need to record independently over a period of time. This luxury is open to virtually no one outside well-funded research projects, certainly not to practising teachers or educational psychologists.

A more theoretical problem is that the applied behavioural analysis paradigm focuses explicitly on *observed* behaviour. This is a useful, even necessary, starting point, but it is plainly wrong to ignore other influences on teachers' and children's behaviour. The point is that the classroom behaviour of teachers may be influenced by factors outside the classroom. These may include staffroom pressure to adopt particular teaching or management techniques, lack of suitable resources, or fear of criticism from an influential head of department or deputy head. Pupils' classroom behaviour, too, is affected by factors outside the classroom. Family problems may affect concentration ('on-task behaviour' in the jargon). Alternatively, membership of an anti-school subculture in which social approval depends on opposition to the school's *mores* may provide a strong disincentive to respond to conventional methods of reinforcement from teachers.

None of these problems negates the potential value of behavioural work with children with special needs. As Berger (1982) argues, social learning theory provides a valid alternative to the exclusive focus on observed behaviour in applied behavioural analysis. What we are suggesting, though, is:

1. That pupils' behaviour is influenced very strongly by school climate.
2. That school climate is dependent on a wide range of factors that extend beyond any single classroom.
3. That the usefulness of many classroom behaviour modification projects is limited by their failure, if not inability, to take account of factors outside the classroom.
4. That if behavioural approaches are to make a more extensive contribution to the education of children with special needs they will need to address themselves to wider aspects of school curriculum, organisation and climate than the classroom behaviour of teachers and children.

Analysis of classroom interaction, then, gives us a necessary starting point. Yet in order to plan an effective programme we may also need information both about the pupil's own cognitive abilities and family background, and about social pressures in and out of the classroom that may affect either the teacher's or the child's behaviour. The usefulness of behaviour modification is too often restricted by a piecemeal approach which fails to recognise the range and complexity of social pressures on children and teachers. Thus, while the strength of much behavioural work results from the clarity of its objectives, its weakness results from their limitations. Regrettably, clarity of objectives has not always been an attribute of pastoral care and counselling. It is to this that we must now turn.

PASTORAL CARE AND COUNSELLING

CATCHING RED HERRINGS

Any discussion of the role of pastoral care and counselling in meeting the special educational needs of children who present behaviour problems needs to catch two red herrings and put them in permanent deep freeze. The first of these concerns the appointment of specialist counsellors in all schools. The second concerns the principal aim and orientation of pastoral care.

The first British training course for school counsellors opened in 1965. The years 1969–78 witnessed a rapid growth both in the number of training courses and in the number of counsellors appointed to secondary schools (Bolger 1983). Since then there has been a steady decline (Murgatroyd 1983). There is now virtually no prospect of Britain following the path of other developed and developing countries (for example, the United States, Canada, New Zealand, Nigeria, Malaysia, South Korea), by encouraging the appointment of a counsellor to every secondary school.

Part of the reason lies in the financial pressures both on schools and on universities. The de-centralised education system in Britain is also relevant, since a requirement to use a post to appoint a counsellor could be seen as an attack on the headteacher's and school governors' autonomy in employing and deploying staff. There are, however, also several sound educational reasons for not choosing to employ counsellors, and these are of particular importance to the education of disruptive and disturbing pupils.

Probably no school would appoint a counsellor in the hope that the counsellor would solve all the problems created by disturbing pupils. Nevertheless, it is quite clear that teachers refer disruptive pupils to counsellors in larger numbers than any other group. This is the one absolutely consistent point to emerge from discussions with school

Disturbing children in the ordinary school

counsellors and with teachers in at least six countries. Yet this is precisely the group whose behaviour is least likely to change as a result of individual or group counselling (see p. 61).

Other problems can arise from a counsellor's appointment. Teachers often feel that if a counsellor is trained and paid to deal with problems: (a) he had better get on and deal with them; and (b) they ought to help him by referring all their problem pupils! Hence the counsellor's appointment may act as an active disincentive to teachers to find their own solutions in their own classes. A similar problem arises when considering the pastoral responsibilities of form tutors; there is frequently a sense of reluctance to undertake tasks that might be dealt with by the counsellor. There is a legitimate argument that counsellors should act as leaders, or coordinators of a pastoral team involving all teachers in the school. The difficulty with this idea, though, is that neither their training nor their status within the school equips them to fill this role.

Needless to say all these problems result either from unrealistic expectations of what a counsellor can offer, or from failure to appreciate how he can best contribute as a member of the wider pastoral team. It is clear that in some schools counsellors have played an important part in this team (e.g. A. Jones 1980). Our argument is not that a specialist counsellor has no role to play, but that individual or group counselling is unlikely to meet the special needs of difficult and disturbing pupils. That requires attention to much wider issues of the school's policy, curriculum, teaching methods and climate.

This leads us to our second red herring, namely the 'negative net' model of pastoral care. This model sees the principal function of pastoral care as dealing with problem pupils. Year tutors with pastoral responsibilities are often appointed not for their ability to coordinate work of a team of form tutors, but rather for their perceived ability in working with difficult pupils. Year tutors operate as trouble-shooters, or as untrained counsellors (in practice, the difference is not always very great). As a result they have low status compared with heads of the main subject departments. This low status is not altered by their responsibility for interviews with parents. They frequently act as a 'buffer' to prevent parents discussing matters directly with the form tutors or subject teachers with first-hand knowledge of their child.

Ironically this 'negative net' model involves year tutors in spending a disproportionate amount of time working with pupils with special educational needs, particularly pupils whose behaviour disturbs their teachers. The usefulness of their work is limited by the same factors which limit the usefulness of counsellors' work with these pupils. Individualising the problem, locating it in the pupil or the family, does not solve it. Individual pupils may need attention and help in their own right, but this cannot be divorced from attention to wider issues of policy and practice throughout the school.

SCOPE AND FUNCTIONS OF THE PASTORAL TEAM

If the aims of pastoral care often seem vague and ill-defined, this is partly due to failure to define the term. Essentially it refers to the school's procedures for catering for the welfare of its pupils. If we want to go further than this we have to consider what Marland (1980) has termed the pastoral curriculum. This may be defined as the facts, skills, attitudes and concepts which children need to acquire in order:

1. To make the most effective possible use of the school.
2. To promote their own personal and social education.
3. To make informed choices on subject options and ultimately on their future careers in work or further education.

It is clear from this that the pastoral curriculum should have a clearly defined *content*, which must be *taught*. Moreover, this teaching takes place in groups. As Marland (1983) notes succinctly, the aim is to: 'help individuals without giving individual help' (p. 26). Every curriculum, whether pastoral or academic, is implemented through a clearly defined programme. Hence, the pastoral programme refers to the school's arrangements for implementing the pastoral curriculum. Some of this will be taught in subject departments. For example, study skills might be taught by members of the English department or by a specialist librarian. Similarly aspects of health education could be taught in PE lessons, home economics or biology lessons. Much of the pastoral curriculum, however, will be taught in the tutorial programme, which refers simply to those aspects of the pastoral programme which are taught by form tutors in their tutorial periods.

It is clear that the pastoral curriculum aims to cater for all pupils in the school, and is concerned with all aspects of the school's work. It also involves the great majority of teachers, either as form tutors or as heads of year coordinating the work of a tutorial team. It involves careful planning if tutorial time is to be used effectively. It complements and supports the academic curriculum, but goes further than this, aiming to *teach* children how to make the best use of their time at school. This will not be achieved solely through the pastoral programme, however excellent and comprehensive that may be. It also requires what could loosely be termed a pastoral ethos, in which the aims of the pastoral curriculum are reflected not only in the content of the academic curriculum, but also in how it is taught.

THE PASTORAL TASK

The pastoral task as described here will do little or nothing to mitigate the special educational needs of some children. What it can do, however, is to ensure:

Disturbing children in the ordinary school

1. As far as possible that these needs are not aggravated, or created by tensions in school organisation and teaching practice.
2. That a framework exists in the tutorial system for early recognition of special needs, reflected in educational progress and/or behaviour.
3. That there are well-recognised procedures for meeting the personal and educational needs that are identified.
4. That conscious attempts are made to develop in pupils an attitude which accepts and respects exceptionality.

The role of pastoral care in the early recognition of special needs requires further discussion. It is not really controversial that every pupil should be known well by at least one teacher. Nor is it controversial that some members of staff should have a general oversight of each pupil's progress across the curriculum. Indeed these two points are related. The only conceivable justification for making such banal and obvious points is that they appear not to be recognised in a considerable number of schools.

The member of staff responsible for knowing pupils well and for maintaining oversight of their progress across the curriculum cannot be the head of year. He cannot possibly know all pupils in the year group well. Nor, for the same reason, can it be a more senior teacher such as deputy head. Purely for logistic and pragmatic reasons, responsibility must rest with form tutors. Yet the form tutors' contact with their tutorial groups in some schools is still confined to ten-minute registration periods daily. It takes about five minutes to complete the attendance register and give out notices. The remaining five minutes are insufficient to do anything useful, but quite adequate for pupils to start to become restless.

We are emphatically not saying that this is the case in all, or even in most schools. Nor do we think that a tutorial programme, however carefully planned, will in itself do much to ensure that special educational needs are recognised at an early stage. Nevertheless there are several ways in which this can become much more likely. We consider five here.

1. Form tutors can have responsibility for ensuring that homework is completed and handed to the appropriate teachers. This need not be a time-consuming exercise, and can give the form tutor oversight of a child's progress and attainment across the curriculum. As important, reasons for failure to complete homework can be extremely varied, for example dislike of a particular teacher or subject, incipient disaffection from school or deteriorating circumstances at home. At the most basic level, someone needs to know whether the problem is confined to a particular subject, or reflects wider problems in home circumstances or in attitude towards school. In addition, if a particular teacher is consistently lax about

setting or marking homework, some systematic procedure is needed to alert senior members of the school's staff.
2. Virtually all schools aim to establish close, cooperative links with their pupils' parents, but by no means all achieve this aim (Woods 1984). Form tutors are well placed to establish *regular, informal* links with parents. A procedure which has been found successful in some schools we have visited is to require pupils to keep a homework diary, and to ask their parents to sign this each week as confirmation that the homework has at least been attempted. The diary can contain space for informal queries or observations both from teachers and from parents, thus providing an ideal opportunity for an informal exchange with no necessity for the typed letter from a senior member of staff which so frequently intimidates or antagonises the very parents whose support the school claims to need most.
3. One of the most basic pastoral tasks is to give pupils opportunity and encouragement to reflect on their experiences at school. This is merely a slightly pretentious way of saying that we want pupils to consider their responsibilities, and rights, as members of the school. Part of this involves awareness of what they should reasonably expect from their teachers. Probably no teacher would deny that schools should aim to enhance the self-esteem of all their pupils. Nor is there much controversy that pupils with special needs frequently suffer from a very low self-esteem. This must be seen in the light of other evidence that secondary schools often cater inadequately for pupils of below average ability, for example the Hargreaves Report on London secondary schools (ILEA 1984). Tutorial periods can provide an opportunity to discuss with pupils what they can obtain from the school, and what they are contributing to it. This is one aspect of the first function of the pastoral curriculum, namely to help pupils make the most effective use of the school. Many pupils with special needs see little point in school attendance. The teacher's task is to involve them in their own learning. That, however, can be achieved only if teachers are willing: (a) to discuss the purpose and nature of their work at school with them; and (b) to use the conclusions from these discussions in future planning.
4. Children with more acute special needs may in some schools need to be withdrawn from certain ordinary classes for special help. The tutorial group provides an excellent opportunity: (a) to maintain contact with the mainstream; (b) to provide an introduction back into the mainstream. The assumption here is that all pupils will have a base as participating members of a tutorial group. The child's overall programme will probably be planned and coordinated by teachers in the special needs department, but the form tutor will have an active part to play in that programme. This leads to our final point.

5. The tutorial programme can help to create an ethos throughout the school in which staff and pupils alike expect to work with pupils who have special educational needs. In other words, as we implied earlier, it can help to promote awareness of and respect for individual differences. It is important to emphasise that this kind of awareness and respect can be taught, and is unlikely to be acquired without conscious planning. The range of activities and subject matter suitable for tutorial periods is virtually endless, but can include: (a) a survey of facilities for disabled people in the community and/or in the school itself; (b) recognition of special needs within the class (for example, regular medication, reading difficulties) and how the school caters for them; (c) the treatment of disabled people in the major world religions, for example the Bible or the Koran; (d) changing attitudes to people with special needs from medieval times to the present day; (e) the way that disabled people are portrayed in literature.

CONCLUSIONS

This chapter has reviewed research which consistently reveals significant differences between schools in their pupils' behaviour. Moreover these differences cannot readily be attributed to the catchment areas which the schools serve. The implication is that the number of pupils regarded as having special educational needs on the basis of their difficult behaviour depends more on the school they happen to be attending than on the pupils themselves or their families.

Just as consistently, the research has identified aspects of social and educational climate as the critical variables in a school's effectiveness in promoting high standards of work, behaviour and attendance. The most successful schools do not appear to be promoting behaviour modification techniques enthusiastically, nor do they seem to be regarding on-site units as the solution to the problems created by disturbing behaviour. The most effective procedures for preventing, rather than treating, disturbing or maladjusted behaviour are a by-product of processes which aim to raise the overall quality of education for *all* pupils in the school.

Thus, a pastoral programme which overlooks the personal and social development of the majority of pupils will also fail to cater adequately for the 15 to 20 per cent with special needs. However excellent it may be, no pastoral or academic programme is likely to meet pupils' special needs effectively unless planned so as to complement what A. Jones (1980) refers to as the 'solid core' of the school. It is this 'solid core' which not only influences the quality of provision for children with special needs, but also determines how that provision is perceived, whether as providing or as restricting opportunities, by the pupils for whom it is designed.

The integrated provision that we have been advocating in this chapter and in Chapters 5 and 6 places considerable demands both on teachers and on LEAs. At a time of economic recession, when many teachers feel that not only their employers but also their pupils' parents are unreasonably expecting them to achieve more and more with less and less, it would be surprising if such demands went unchallenged. Hence, we must now consider how school and LEA policies may facilitate the developments we have been discussing.

Chapter eight
SCHOOL AND LEA POLICIES

INTRODUCTION

Whatever the intentions of the 1981 Education Act, there is little evidence that mainstream primary and secondary schools have become more able or willing to cater for pupils with learning and adjustment difficulties. These children are still just as likely to be placed in special classes or units as in the years leading up to the Warnock Report. Whether they are placed in separate special schools or in designated units attached to an ordinary school their chances of return to ordinary classes are slender.

The overwhelming majority comes from socially disadvantaged working-class backgrounds, with a disproportionate representation of boys and of children from ethnic minorities (e.g. Ford *et al.* 1982; Tomlinson 1982). At least in the case of children with moderate learning difficulties the research evidence suggests consistently that they would make better educational progress in the mainstream. The philanthropic, humanitarian ideals of special educational provision should not obscure the clear evidence that its primary function is to provide a service for teachers in ordinary schools by removing disturbing children from their classes.

Nor, however, can we overlook the needs of teachers in ordinary schools in formulating special education policy. To quote from the report of the Sheffield Working Party on Special Education:

> We believe that handicapped children above all need education that is responsive to their needs, and that only those schools which can so respond should be encouraged to integrate . . . These schools need to become expert as well as willing to tackle their new role (Sheffield Education Department 1976b).

The point is simply that effective integration requires not only the active support of teachers in the mainstream, but also a high level of expertise. It cannot be achieved merely by political or administrative *diktat*.

The dangers can be seen in the burgeoning departments of special needs which are replacing the former remedial departments, especially in secondary schools. Ostensibly the curriculum may be designed to cater for the needs of each individual. In practice pupils often follow a separate curriculum. Hargreaves (1983) has shown how curricula for less able pupils are likely to be regarded both by the pupils concerned *and* by pupils in examination bands as a covert way of helping the more able pupils. The point is that 'academic' work is seen as having high status, and must therefore not be affected by the presence of less able pupils. More provocatively Tomlinson (1982) argues that increasing numbers of less able or disruptive pupils are likely to be regarded as having special needs and that:

> ... in terms of the normal goals of the school that they attend they will be offered a 'non-education', which will fit them only for low-status employment or non-employment (p. 177).

An interesting implication is that legislation and administrative pressure may be counter-productive. It is still too early to discern clear trends in the effects of the 1981 Act on education for the 20 per cent of children Warnock regarded as having special needs. Most of these children will not receive the doubtful 'protection' of a Statement. With or without such protection, there is already cause for concern that the special 'help' they receive may limit, rather than extend, their educational opportunities.

Yet this depressing picture is not inevitable. In our research in Sheffield and in New Zealand we worked in schools which appeared to cater successfully for their most vulnerable pupils. This chapter is concerned with two questions. First, what lessons can be learnt from policy and practice in these schools? Second, how may LEAs facilitate a climate in schools which is responsive to individual needs?

THE RESEARCH PROGRAMMES

In Sheffield ten secondary schools were involved, seven of which had established a special group for their disturbing pupils, while the remaining three had decided as a matter of policy not to do so. The New Zealand study included four secondary schools, selected for their reputation in work with pupils with adjustment difficulties. Most of the fourteen schools had allocated substantial resources to their special needs and pastoral care networks. Unfortunately these efforts were often a source of frustration to staff and pupils alike. We have already touched on some of the reasons, but will summarise them here.

Nine schools had established special groups for their disruptive pupils (seven in Sheffield and two in New Zealand). Yet only two of these groups successfully integrated the curriculum in the group with the curriculum to which pupils would return in the mainstream. For this and other reasons, return to the mainstream was fraught with tension. Moreover the groups did not enable schools to reduce the number of pupils excluded for disciplinary reasons. Similarly, several schools had established withdrawal groups to provide 'remedial' help. Yet here too the curriculum in the withdrawal group was seldom related to the curriculum in the mainstream. Research on remedial reading shows consistently that substantial progress is possible in withdrawal groups, but is seldom maintained without continuing support (e.g. Tobin and Pumfrey 1976). Another approach, adopted by several schools, was a separate curriculum for less able pupils, including a disproportionate number of disruptives. Our observations on the divisive nature of these separate curricula were consistent with those of Hargreaves (1983).

The common elements in all these approaches were:

1. That they served to 'protect' teachers and pupils in the mainstream from pupils with special needs.
2. That they aimed, unsuccessfully, to treat pupils with special needs in isolation from the mainstream.
3. That they gave mainstream teachers neither encouragement nor opportunity to review aspects of the school's organisation, guidance network, curriculum and methods of teaching or classroom management which might have contributed to the pupils' difficulties in the first place.

There were, however, four schools with remarkably low rates of disruptive behaviour (Galloway 1983) and one of these had also adopted a 'whole school' approach to special educational needs (Galloway 1985a). We shall describe six elements of this school's policy which seem relevant to its success. We shall then turn to the guidance and pastoral networks of the four schools in which teachers apparently experienced few problems from disruptive pupils. Finally we shall consider the implications for LEA policy.

A WHOLE SCHOOL APPROACH TO SPECIAL EDUCATIONAL NEEDS

BACKGROUND

The school served a mixed catchment area in which 30 per cent of pupils came from ethnic minorities. There was a firm commitment to mixed ability teaching, except in the older age-groups when the system of option choices led to some informal selection by ability.

Not many pupils with special needs, for example, were likely to take Latin and Greek. The head believed that any formal system of ability banding or streaming led to disproportionate representation in lower streams of pupils from ethnic minorities and from disadvantaged home backgrounds. This was socially divisive. In addition it transmitted a message through the hidden curriculum which was inconsistent with what schools should be trying to achieve in a multi-cultural society.

The school had referred no pupil for special schooling or special class placement for at least two years prior to our study, nor had there been any long-term exclusions for disruptive behaviour. Attendance was good. Examination results were above the national average, particularly for pupils from ethnic minorities. Perhaps the most pervasive characteristic of the school, though, was the scope of each teacher's responsibilities.

LOCUS OF RESPONSIBILITY AND CONTROL

Each teacher was held responsible for the progress and behaviour of all pupils in his or her class. The head and senior staff, as a matter of principle, did not remove responsibility from the teacher by imposing labels such as 'remedial' or 'disruptive' on pupils. Indeed the term 'remedial' had been consciously rejected for implying that the problem lay, in some quasi-medical way, with the child. If children were well taught according to their particular needs, the argument went, the question of remediation would not arise.

LEARNING AND ADJUSTMENT DIFFICULTIES: A SPURIOUS DISTINCTION

Disruptive behaviour was seen as the product of the pupil's lack of success in the curriculum, or as lack of motivation to act as a contributing member of the school community. Hence the solution lay in providing experiences of success in the curriculum, and in reviewing aspects of school or classroom management which might affect the pupil's motivation. Some of the other schools, in contrast, based special education provision on the psychologically and educationally false assumption that children could be divided tidily into two categories. 'Disruptives' were placed in a special unit while 'remedials' remained the responsibility of the remedial teachers. While the overlap between the two groups was acknowledged in theory, it was not reflected in the curriculum or in the school's organisational structure.

DECENTRALISED RESOURCES

It is one thing to hold subject teachers responsible for all their pupils' progress and behaviour, but quite another to give them the training and support to teach their most difficult pupils effectively. To make special education resources accessible, they were located in the relevant subject departments. The maths department's resource room, for example, contained materials suitable for pupils with a very wide range of ability. Some of the materials designed for pupils with special needs might have been prepared by members of the special needs department in discussion with members of the maths department. Others would have been prepared by maths specialists with cooperation from special needs staff. In this way specialist materials were immediately accessible, and expertise in special education could be shared throughout the school.

Again, the situation in several of the other schools is instructive. Resources were located firmly in the 'remedial' department and were available only to remedial staff. The notion that 'ordinary' and 'remedial' children were two separate breeds, requiring quite different teaching methods, was effectively communicated to teachers *and* pupils throughout the school.

SUPPORT IN THE ORDINARY CLASS

Teachers in this school expected to work in teams and were used to seeing each other teach. Members of the special education department, therefore, had no difficulty in going into ordinary classes either to observe or to give subject teachers practical help with particular pupils. Catering for these pupils thus became a partnership in which mainstream teachers could receive support and guidance in adapting the curriculum to these children's needs without removing responsibility from them. If a teaching programme established in discussion with a specialist proved unsuccessful, this would not be taken as evidence of personal or professional failure on the teacher's part. Rather it would indicate a need for a joint review of what had happened in order to plan an alternative programme in the light of this experience.

The idea of special needs teachers working alongside their mainstream colleagues would have been totally unacceptable in many other schools. Even within a subject department it would have been considered revolutionary for the head of department to observe colleagues teaching or vice versa – as offensive as intrusion into private grief. As a result teachers in these schools had very limited scope either to learn from each other or to support each other.

TEMPORARY REMOVAL FROM THE CLASS

Conflict can occur in any classroom. One aspect of work with children with adjustment difficulties is to prevent conflict escalating into a confrontation in which the pupils and/or the teacher lose control of the situation. Teachers at this school were given a list indicating where senior colleagues were teaching in each period. If a pupil started to present problems they could simply send the pupil, with a note and possibly an escort, to one of these colleagues. The receiving teacher would occupy the pupil for the rest of the lesson, and then send him back to the original teacher, without making detailed inquiries. This system enabled teachers to prevent potential conflicts from escalating, or from disrupting the work of the rest of the class. Yet at the same time, responsibility remained firmly with them, since the pupil would return at the end of the lesson. They might decide at that stage to seek more active help from a senior colleage, but the decision would be theirs.

TEMPORARY, SHORT-TERM WITHDRAWAL

To cater for more acute or more intransigent situations the head of the special education department was also responsible for a centre to which pupils could be sent with the agreement of a senior member of staff. We have already described the principal features of this centre (Ch. 7, pp. 140–2). We need only repeat here that its function was not to remove pupils from the mainstream but rather to give them and their teachers the support and guidance which would facilitate a successful return.

A WHOLE SCHOOL APPROACH TO PASTORAL CARE

BACKGROUND

It is difficult to envisage an integrated approach to special needs which does not also offer pupils throughout the school a high quality of personal, educational and vocational guidance. We described the scope and functions of pastoral care in Chapter 7 (pp. 148–51). Our purpose here is to outline characteristics of pastoral care at four secondary schools in which disruptive behaviour seldom appeared to be a problem. One of these schools had also established the 'whole school' approach to special needs which we have just described. Of the remaining three, one served a predominantly working-class housing estate built in the 1930s. The second had a considerably more affluent catchment area. The third was a denominational school with a very mixed pupil intake.

In terms of its formal organisation, pastoral care in these four schools was unexceptional. In each case there was a horizontal system with a year tutor responsible for all pupils in each annual intake and form tutors responsible for groups of around thirty pupils. The same applied in most of the other schools in the two surveys. The ways in which pastoral care in these four schools stood out were not immediately apparent, but nevertheless seemed to us to play an important part in the success of each school. As with the special needs network, we will briefly describe each characteristic.

UNDERLYING PHILOSOPHY

In each school the head was quite clear that the aim of pastoral care was to promote the pupil's progress and adjustment at school. The 'negative net' model which sees pastoral care catering primarily for pupils with personal or social problems was explicitly rejected. In contrast, there were other schools in which the time and energy of pastoral care staff was almost exclusively monopolised by problem pupils.

DISCIPLINE AND PASTORAL CARE: A SPURIOUS DISTINCTION

Senior staff were clear that pupils with problems could not be divided into 'discipline' and 'pastoral' categories. This, of course, is consistent with the insistence noted earlier that learning and behavioural problems could not meaningfully be distinguished. In other schools guidelines for teachers required them to refer discipline problems to the head of department and pastoral problems to the head of year. Yet the teacher responsible for making the distinction might see the child only once a week. Predictably, it caused confusion and inconsistency, leading to frustration and resentment for pupils and for teachers.

HELP AND SUPPORT FROM COLLEAGUES

As in the case of special needs, teachers were expected to take responsibility for all pupils in their classes or tutorial groups. This implied that referral of problems to senior staff was discouraged. On the other hand, senior pastoral staff were available to help teachers work out their own solutions. One headteacher explained that criticism was never directed at teachers who needed help, only at those who refused to ask for it.

THE FORM TUTOR'S RESPONSIBILITIES AND STATUS

We have already discussed the importance of the form tutor in the pastoral team (Ch. 7, pp. 149–51). With one possible exception the form tutor's role carried status and responsibility in these four schools. Form tutors had clearly defined functions, and were expected to contribute to any discussions about pupils presenting particular problems. Headteachers of other schools also acknowledged the importance of the form tutor. The reality, however, was often that they had no scope for anything more constructive than completing the attendance register and giving out notices in a ten-minute registration session at the start of each day.

COOPERATION WITH PARENTS

The heads of all fourteen schools claimed to encourage close cooperation with pupils' parents. In the case of these four schools this actually happened. Contact with parents was frequent, and often informal. Sensitive efforts were made to communicate in a way that would enlist parents' cooperation as partners, and to ensure that contact included positive feedback as well as discussion of possible problems. At other schools parents were sometimes antagonised by a 'hidden agenda' in which they felt teachers were blaming them for the problems their children were causing. On other occasions, the formality of a typed letter intimidated the very parents whose support the school claimed to need most.

COMMENT

Perhaps the single most pervasive characteristic of special educational policy in the school whose provision we have described was the insistence that responsibility could not be shifted on to specialists. The special education department was well staffed. Its members, though, saw their task as helping mainstream teachers to adapt their curriculum and teaching methods in the light of their pupils' needs. Similarly the guidance networks in each of the four schools aimed to enhance the quality of the pupils' experiences in the mainstream of the school. The difference in underlying philosophy from some of the other schools in which we worked was striking.

To take this argument a stage further, responses to learning and adjustment problems in some of the other schools were essentially reactive. At the crudest level, a remedial or special needs department

School and LEA policies

was established because some children had learning difficulties. Similarly, pastoral care networks were extended in the light of some children's adjustment problems, and when pastoral care or conventional punishment proved ineffective a special unit was set up. In each case the extra provision was superimposed on the existing system which itself remained unchanged. By the existing system we mean not only the formal organisation of teaching and guidance but also the interpersonal relationships within the school, including the staffroom, and teaching methods and techniques.

Tensions in these areas contribute to many children's learning and adjustment difficulties, even if they do not actually cause them. At best, responses which simply superimpose some new form of provision, whether it be a special unit, a withdrawal group or a tutorial programme are palliative. At worst they are counter-productive. Dealing with the *pupils* concerned, often by removing them from the situation in which problems arose, effectively removes any incentive to deal with the tensions which contributed to these problems.

The schools we have described moved beyond this essentially negative model. The aim was not so much to respond to events as to influence them. Learning and behavioural difficulties were seen as the product of the pupils' experiences at school. Hence, the social and academic climate which had provided these experiences must also stand in need of constant review.

This required a rigorous analysis of school organisation, the curriculum, pastoral care, teaching methods and classroom management. The analysis, moreover, was not a one-off event but a continuing process. This was not always explicitly identified as part of the headteacher's educational ideals, but it was nevertheless evident in the management of each school. It could not, however, have been successful without the support of the majority of teachers throughout the school. In other words critical evaluation became part of the ethos of the school. *That*, however, could not have happened unless most teachers felt that the school was meeting their needs for professional development, and for job satisfaction through their work with pupils and their relationships with colleagues.

THE LEA'S CONTRIBUTION

What we have been discussing so far is policy and practice at four excellent schools. The head and senior staff in each of these schools would have been the first to admit that practice often fell short of theory. That, however, was inevitable given the constructively self-critical ethos of each school.

The question for the administration and support services of LEAs is how to encourage the sort of good practice which we have been describing. These schools were prepared to adapt their curriculum and organisation to cater for their pupils' needs. The model in some of the other schools we visited appeared to be based on provision of extra services aiming either to 'help' the pupil adjust to the school's needs, or to contain the pupil so that no wider changes would be needed.

The position for LEA administration is very similar. The traditional response to children with learning and adjustment difficulties has been to remove them from the mainstream by setting up special schools or units. The 1981 Education Act has done nothing to alter this tradition. A more constructive response is to consider what policies and what forms of support might most effectively encourage and assist ordinary schools to create an educational and social climate that is responsive to special needs.

PARALLELISM

A useful starting point might be a commitment to a unified education system. Currently special schools and units operate in parallel with the mainstream (see Ch. 5, p. 98). N. Jones (1983b) points out that these parallel systems create divisions which affect the drawing up of advertisements for new staff, the appointment procedures, and accountability at advisory level within the educational offices. Thus, in some LEAs peripatetic remedial staff come under the general aegis of the primary adviser, while the special education adviser is responsible for other special needs staff. More important, parallelism fosters the view that ordinary schools ought not to expect to cope with a minority of their pupils. The damaging result is the LEAs continue to use their resources to help schools by removing pupils with learning or adjustment difficulties. The alternative is to use resources to help schools cater for these pupils themselves.

A commitment to a unified education system implies that the special and mainstream system should cease to operate in parallel. It does not necessarily imply the closure, or even the phasing out of all existing special schools or units. It does, however, imply the need for a major re- orientation in their emphasis. Instead of serving the mainstream by removing misfits, their function would be to serve the mainstream through a partnership in which mainstream teachers develop the expertise to work effectively with their disturbing pupils.

POLITICAL WILL

This kind of re-orientation would require an act of political will. Both in special schools and in the mainstream vested interests in most LEAs are too deeply entrenched to do more than tinker with the existing system. Neither the importance of an act of political will nor the need for it should be under-estimated. Criticising the Warnock Report recommendations on research Tizard (1978) pointed out that research will never 'prove' that integration is desirable. The decision to adopt an integration policy, like any other major educational policy decision, is essentially political. Comprehensive schools were not adopted in favour of the tripartite selective system simply because research showed the latter to discriminate against particular groups of children. By the early 1960s the idea that children could be divided tidily into categories at the age of eleven was no longer acceptable. The economic and political climate had changed radically since 1944. Research legitimised, but did not create, dissatisfaction with selection at eleven and with the second-class status of secondary modern schools.

In special education it is instructive to consider reasons for the increasing integration of children with physical and sensory handicaps. Research certainly shows that such children usually make good social and educational progress when integrated into ordinary classes (e.g. Anderson 1973). Yet it is doubtful whether parents and voluntary associations are pressing for integration because they have been convinced by research results. Rather they want their handicapped child to have the best possible opportunities, including the opportunity to learn to live and work with ordinary children.

It is even more doubtful whether LEAs would have consented to increasing integration of children with physical and sensory handicaps without well-orchestrated pressure from parents and from voluntary groups. Integration required an act of political will as well as cooperation from teachers in the mainstream. The pressure, though, came from outside the LEA.

For children with learning and adjustment difficulties the position is different. In the past their parents have seldom been articulate or well informed enough to demand better facilities and opportunities in the mainstream, nor are their interests looked after by many well-organised voluntary organisations. Indeed they have appeared virtually unique in the whole education system in that policy decisions about their educational needs have seldom attracted political debate. Politicians who would insist on intensive critical analysis of proposals for developments in primary, secondary and tertiary education have often been quite happy to be guided by professionals when it comes to the branch of special education concerned with learning and adjustment difficulties. This is now changing, at least in some inner city areas, for example London and Sheffield. Groups of Afro-Caribbean parents now recognise that special education may discriminate against their children. Pressure from these groups is requiring assessment teams and LEA administrators to look much more critically at their basic assumptions about special education.

In Sheffield the Education Committee abolished corporal punishment in all schools at least in part because this punishment was used disproportionately on working-class children. It also abolished school uniform in part because working-class parents were caused difficulties by uniform requirements. Yet the committee was apparently unable to grapple with the implications of its special education policy (see Ch. 6). The most probable explanation is that members' attitudes towards special education were still imbued with nineteenth-century notions of charitableness and philanthropy. In consequence they had hardly started to consider the possibility that their facilities for children they regarded as mentally or emotionally handicapped might actually be a way of discriminating against working-class children. In this connection it will be interesting to see the committee's reaction to a recent survey which showed that black children in Sheffield were twice as likely as white to be excluded or suspended from school in 1982–85.

DEVELOPING AN INTEGRATION POLICY

SPECIAL SCHOOLS

What role, then, could special schools or units play in a LEA with a unified education system in which special education resources were committed to helping schools to improve the quality of education for their most vulnerable pupils? In Sheffield the report of the special education working party envisaged a role as 'training agencies and resource centres' (Sheffield Educational Committee 1976a). These roles imply an active partnership with ordinary schools. They also imply an important element of accountability. If special schools are to provide a service to ordinary schools they have to convince teachers in ordinary schools that they have something useful to offer.

This will not be easy. In New Zealand the Department of Education hoped that secondary schools would benefit from the experience of off-site units (Galloway and Barrett 1984). These units appeared to contain successfully pupils who the referring schools had previously considered unmanageable. In reality, though, contact between the referring schools and the units was minimal.

The problem was partly that units were seen as a resource only in the sense that problem pupils could be off-loaded on to them. More important, any success the units achieved in containing their pupils was seen as having little, if any, relevance for the referring schools. Their reaction was almost always a variation on the theme: 'Ah, but you've got small classes and can give them the attention they need. We could do that if only we had the resources!' The *coup de grace* usually followed quickly: 'And anyway your methods wouldn't be suitable in a large secondary school!'

To be accepted as resource centres, then, special school staff will need to demonstrate that they can offer something of practical value *within* an ordinary school. Demonstrations of success in a different context will be of little value. This also has implications for their possible training role. Teachers in the mainstream will not want in-service courses that urge them to adopt the classroom organisation, curriculum and teaching methods of a special school. Quite rightly, they will demand something which helps them adapt their existing methods to become more responsive to individual needs.

All this is asking a great deal of special school staff. It requires not only the ability to work with children in the necessarily sheltered setting of the special school or unit. In addition it requires the ability to carry out in-service education with colleagues in a quite different context. While there are some notable exceptions, there is little evidence that special school staff are equipped to fill both of these roles.

The role of special schools in their immediate work with children in a unified education system is no less challenging. Abandoning the parallel system of special and ordinary schools implies that indefinite admissions to special schools will gradually be phased out. At present children with Statements under the 1981 Education Act are admitted indefinitely subject to annual review and reassessment at thirteen. In a unified system they would be admitted on a short-term basis, and remain on the role of the referring school. We suggest three possible reasons for admission.

1. Some children may benefit from a period of intensive assessment and diagnostic teaching in order to formulate a detailed programme for meeting their educational needs. The assessment would be carried out in close cooperation with teachers from the referring school, though the child would not necessarily return to this school. Another ordinary school with more extensive resources and/or a different social and educational climate might be considered more appropriate.
2. A period of short-term intensive help with some specific problem may be appropriate for some children. There are two dangers here, though. First, care could be needed to ensure that the school did not become filled with children who had failed to make the anticipated progress in the original admission period. There is

no reason to think that such children would respond better with indefinite special schooling than with return to an experienced teacher in the mainstream. The second danger is that progress achieved during the short-term special school period might be lost on return. This is also a problem with withdrawal groups in the mainstream. It can be overcome only by relating the 'remedial' lessons to the mainstream curriculum and by providing follow-up support (see Ch. 3). In either case close liaison between the special school staff and the mainstream would be essential.
3. Following a crisis, some children with adjustment difficulties require a 'cooling off period'. So do their teachers. Experience with pupils who have been suspended from school suggests that time can be a great healer. Following a confrontation, pupils and teachers may insist that future cooperation is out of the question. After three or four weeks both parties often see the problem in a different light. The special school's role, though, could not be the passive one of containing the pupil for a short period. The aim would be to contribute to a detailed plan for an early return to the original school or to another mainstream school. Admission would be based on the clear understanding that this was the aim, and that long-term placement could not be considered.

Each of these possible roles for existing special schools implies the need for a contractual relationship with referring schools in the mainstream, with parents and, when at all practical, with the pupils themselves. The reason for admission is thus clearly identified and recognised by all concerned. Hence, both special school and ordinary school may be seen as entering into a contract with each other and with parents in which each party will play a part in the child's future teaching. As in any teaching, the children's motivation will be critical. Hence, they too should be involved in the contract, understanding the reasons and objectives for their temporary transfer to a special school. Intensive remediation in a special school will be of little value without follow-up on return to the ordinary school. Similarly, acceptance by an ordinary school of a detailed programme of future work implies a commitment to implement that programme. Special schools would thus be operating in partnership with the mainstream, as an integral part of a unified system. They would lose their isolation, and their methods and achievements would be open to critical scrutiny of colleagues in the mainstream. This is a challenging role but, we believe, a necessary one if they are to justify their survival into the 1990s.

School and LEA policies

THE SUPPORT SERVICES

Our proposals imply a changing role for the education support services, and particularly for educational psychologists. In theory, one of their main aims has always been to help schools to identify and meet the child's needs. In practice they have often been regarded as special school gatekeepers and recently their time has been monopolised by the formal assessments required under the 1981 Education Act. In a unified system they would need to work more closely in partnership with teachers in the mainstream. As they would no longer be able to help teachers by recommending indefinite transfer to special education, they would also become more accountable to teachers for the advice they offer. Knowing that they were likely to retain responsibility for the child, headteachers and class teachers might take a closer interest in the practical usefulness of the psychologist's advice. Planning would involve a partnership with contractual obligations on each side similar to those we proposed for the relationship between special schools and ordinary schools.

Planning would not only require work with individual pupils but also it would involve recognition of the teachers' needs in areas such as assessment, diagnostic teaching and classroom management. Provision of in-service training in the light of the school's particular needs would therefore occupy an increasing amount of their time. A good example is the Disruption in Schools Scheme (Grunsell 1985). This aims to help teachers acquire greater understanding of the nature and reasons for disruptive behaviour and of what they themselves can do about it.

Our argument is that the support services should share responsibilities with teachers. To be successful this requires definition of the scope of each person's responsibilities. Teachers are fully justified in demanding specialist help in their work with pupils with learning and adjustment difficulties. The relationship we envisage is described by Galloway (1985b).

> A teacher may say to an educational psychologist: Can you suggest some activities I can use to help Helen learn to read? The teacher here is making clear that he retains responsibility for Helen's teaching. He is asking the psychologist to share in responsibility for choice of activities. By implication, if the suggestions do not prove successful the teacher and the psychologist can together work out some other approach. This is quite different from saying: We've already done everything possible for Helen in this school, so now we're referring her to you. Here, the teacher is explicitly passing responsibility for the child to the psychologist, effectively absolving himself from further involvement (p. 64).

CONCLUSIONS: FLEXIBLE USE OF RESOURCES?

BEYOND THE LAW?

Welton *et al.* (1982) have pointed out that some LEAs effectively evaded many of the intentions of the DES (1975) circular on the identification and assessment of children with special needs. There is already evidence that the intentions of the 1981 Education Act may also be evaded. Given the broadly enabling rather than narrowly prescriptive nature of education law in Britain this is perhaps inevitable, and not necessarily undesirable. It is worth repeating, though, that the Statement issued following a formal assessment is required only when children are placed in 'designated' special schools or classes (i.e. recognised by the DES). Parents may request a formal assessment, and may appeal against any decision not to issue a Statement. In practice, though, the great majority of assessments are carried out at the request of teachers or other professionals. Formal assessments and Statements are optional in respect of children with special needs remaining in ordinary schools. Some LEAs have adopted a policy of issuing Statements only in respect of children placed in designated schools or classes. So far this policy has not attracted criticism from HMI or from the Secretary of State.

The unified education system we have proposed involves phasing out special schools or classes in parallel with the mainstream system. Closure of existing special schools requires the Secretary of State's consent, but for three reasons that need not deter an LEA.

1. While it may be impractical for children already attending special schools to return to the mainstream, this does not mean that the same arrangements have to be made for similar children who have not yet been placed.
2. The LEAs' obligations are to identify and to meet the child's special educational needs. At least in theory, the Act encourages LEAs to do this in the mainstream, provided they can make adequate resources available.
3. It is not at all certain that formal DES approval would be required to use existing special schools in the way we have described. Nor is it likely that formal assessment and Statements would be required for children attending such schools on a temporary basis. If objections were raised, there is little to stop an LEA from using spare classrooms in a special school to open a reading centre or unit for disruptive pupils. The point is that pupils attending these facilities are specifically exempted from the assessment and Statementing requirements of the Act.

This last point raises an interesting possibility. Under our proposals there would be no need for formal assessments and Statements carried out under the Act except when requested by parents. The present machinery is unhelpfully cumbersome, involving a bureaucratic process more likely to intimidate or confuse parents than to involve them as partners. In addition it is based on an outmoded model of special educational needs which sees the problem as lying mainly, if not solely, in the child rather than in the context in which the child has experienced problems.

It could be argued that LEAs which bypass these procedures need to decide what to put in their place. This question, though, assumes that some children can and should be picked out for some kind of 'special' identification and assessment. John Sayer (1983), principal of Banbury Secondary School in Oxfordshire eloquently argues the opposite case:

> The individual Statements of the 1981 Act would not be needed if a school were committed to providing for all children and a local authority were committed to resourcing the school to do so. There may be two objections to this proposition. First, it may be said, and indeed has been said, that every child with special educational needs has a 'right' to a Statement, and that the Act provides a form of protection. It does nothing of the sort. It could well be argued that all children have a right *not* to have a special Statement made about them and instead to have the resources to receive an appropriate education in the ordinary school. Secondly, it is true that parents have the right to demand a Statement; but they would not normally do so if the local authority was doing its job; and for any reasonable purpose, any parent of any child in an ordinary school should already be able to expect a full Statement drawn up by appropriate professionals at any time (p. 15).

Sayer's point, then, is that any school which is doing its job should be able to provide a detailed picture of each child's educational needs. It follows, presumably, that formal assessment should be needed only when the school is manifestly *not* doing its job. Yet if that is the case, the problem will not be solved by issuing Statements on behalf of a small minority of children. At best the Statement might prod a reluctant LEA to provide extra resources. As Parliament granted LEAs no extra resources with which to implement the Act, this last point needs further discussion.

RESOURCES

Mainstream schools cannot be expected to accept greater responsibility for pupils with learning and adjustment difficulties without adequate support. This does not mean that all schools need a lot of extra staff, but that LEAs should be flexible enough in their allocation of resources to help particular schools to respond positively as and when special needs are identified. At present an 'all or nothing' approach is evident in what most LEAs can offer. Many educational psychologists and educational welfare officers can think of children from disadvantaged, stressful homes whose attendance would improve dramatically given taxi transport to and from school. This, however, can only be provided if the child is referred to a special school. Again, other children require intensive help with reading and numeracy skills. Given some temporary guidance and support, the school's own teachers might provide this. In the absence of any guidance or support, full-time indefinite special schooling becomes inevitable.

One way of developing expertise in mainstream schools is through schemes such as Sheffield's Centres of Integration in which one teacher and one child care assistant support up to ten children integrated into ordinary classes in a primary or secondary school. Providing staffing at this level to selected schools which had expressed an interest would not only extend the bank of expertise available in an LEA but also could enable some children to be taught successfully in the mainstream when their own schools were insisting on their transfer. The LEA would still, however, need to retain sufficient flexibility to provide extra resources to enable other schools to respond imaginatively to children with special needs.

We are not implying that the offer of extra resources should be open-ended, nor that it should be unconditional. We are simply arguing that the system should contain sufficient flexibility to provide extra resources for specified purposes and on mutually agreed conditions. At present such flexibility is often lacking.

The conditions would be negotiated in the light of each school's immediate, medium-term and long-term needs. There is little point in providing an extra teacher to help seven-year-old Jimmy, who has a severe perceptual handicap, learn to read if teaching of reading in the infant classes has been criticised by HMI as of generally low quality. An imaginative LEA response might well be able to offer the school some extra help with Jimmy, but to make this extra help conditional on a detailed review of the school's approach to the teaching of reading. This might seem like rather elementary common sense, but it flies in the face of existing administrative procedures in many LEAs. It suggests that resources should not be allocated on a strict *per capita* basis according to the number of children in the school; nor should additional funds simply be allocated for Statemented children. Our argument is that resources should be allocated in the light of the *school's* special needs and that they should have broader aims than helping individual children.

Children with learning and adjustment difficulties expose the tensions and shortcomings of their school's organisational structure, curriculum, pastoral care, teaching methods and techniques, and interpersonal relationships. Dealing with these tensions is likely to benefit all pupils, not simply those regarded as having learning or adjustment difficulties. It is also likely to benefit relationships with parents. The two-fold challenge for the LEA is: (a) to provide immediate help for children with special needs and for their teachers; (b) to see beyond the immediate problem to offer the in-service training, professional support and, if necessary, material resources to enable the school to respond constructively to similar situations in the future.

Chapter nine
CONCLUSIONS

OVERVIEW: CONSENSUS ON THEORY; DIVERGENCE ON PRACTICE?

There is remarkable consensus on many of the points we have discussed in this book. As the Fish Report so explicitly recognised, children become more or less handicapped depending on the reactions of others (ILEA 1985a). Progress or behaviour which in one school is taken as evidence of the need for special schooling is regarded in another as indicating the need for curriculum review.

In the first case the special needs department may be regarded throughout the school as catering for the 'dim' or 'thick' kids. In the other this department is seen as just one of the school's resources for catering for individual needs, like a ramp for a child in a wheel chair, coaching for the school sports teams or special help for high-flying pupils in certain examination classes. Teachers do not seriously dispute that children can live up, or down, to their reputation. Children whose teachers and peers regard them as problems often come to see themselves in the same light.

Nor is there disagreement that schools and units for children with learning and adjustment difficulties cater mainly for pupils from socially disadvantaged backgrounds and disproportionately for boys and minority ethnic groups. A similar picture applies to classes for special needs in the ordinary school. Concern is growing that the 1981 Education Act will result in larger numbers of children being placed in special needs departments where, for all the principal subjects, they will follow a separate and potentially disadvantaging curriculum. In principle at least, teachers would agree that schools should aim to bridge the social class divisions and reduce the inter-ethnic tensions in late twentieth-century Britain, not deepen them.

There is also broad consensus on the arguments in favour of separate special schools or units for children with learning and

Conclusions

adjustment difficulties. Some teachers in ordinary schools appear unaware of these pupils' needs, and it is probable that few recognise the full extent of the school's influence, for better or worse, on their behaviour and educational progress. A minority seems actively unsympathetic. Teasing by other children can be a problem. In practice teasing or bullying is usually symptomatic of deeper problems in the school's social relationships, but that is scant comfort for the children concerned. Just as important, an unsuitable curriculum can undermine the child's confidence and lead to behaviour problems in addition to the original learning difficulty. The final argument is that other children suffer when too much time is spent on children with problems.

On the other hand, some special needs cannot be met in separate special schools. The most obvious of these is the need to learn to live and work with other children. The shelter of a special school or unit is a bizarre kind of preparation for life in the wider community at the age of sixteen. A less immediately obvious need is for realistic understanding and acceptance of one's strengths and limitations.

Children learn from experience. Blind children have to learn to live in a sighted world. This may be a painful learning experience but is unquestionably a necessary one. Voluntary associations for the blind have long recognised that their children are not generally helped to achieve independence through the sheltering experience of long-term special schooling. The same principle applies to children with learning difficulties. They, too, need to learn to live with their limitations as well as to recognise their abilities. By removing them from the mainstream we remove them from learning experiences which may be painful but are nevertheless necessary if they are to achieve independence on leaving school.

In this connection an important pastoral task for every school is to help children to use the experience of success and failure constructively. Many children with learning and adjustment difficulties interpret failure as a message about *themselves*. This becomes more likely when they are placed in separate special schools, but is also evident from the low self-esteem of many pupils in the special needs departments of ordinary schools. The teacher's task is to show pupils that failure carries a message about the *task* and not about them. Criticism can then be used constructively as an aid to mastering the task in question. Diener and Dweck (1978) have argued that the ability to use criticism, and hence the experience of failure, constructively is as important as intellectual ability to a pupil's success as a learner.

The continued existence of special schools and units also has to be challenged on two further grounds. First, the curriculum is inevitably more restricted than in an ordinary secondary school. The claim that children with learning and adjustment difficulties cannot benefit from the ordinary curriculum is simply untrue. They may not opt for classics or modern languages, but the same applies to a sizeable minority of other pupils in all secondary schools. Both in the mainstream and in special schools individual teachers have demonstrated the ability of their most backward and most disturbing pupils to benefit from a wide range of subjects and to achieve work of excellent quality. The point is simply that special schools, because of their smaller size, inevitably offer a narrower range of subjects than is available in the mainstream. The same is even more true of units. Whatever teachers may think, the narrower curriculum is recognised by pupils as potentially disadvantaging.

The second point concerns the consistent evidence that children with learning difficulties make better educational progress in ordinary classes than in special schools or special classes. Those with adjustment difficulties may be contained in special schools or centres, but there is little evidence that they actually benefit. The research on pupils with adjustment difficulties is less extensive than on those with learning difficulties, but the overall picture is that the chances of spontaneous improvement are, if anything, reduced by special placement.

On purely logical and intellectual grounds, then, there is not a great deal to argue about. The present network of special schools and units in parallel with the mainstream is unsatisfactory and requires urgent review. Nor is it controversial that some ordinary schools are achieving impressive results with their most vulnerable pupils. The task facing teachers and LEAs is not to decide whether to integrate or segregate. The question is based on a false dichotomy. The task is rather to discover how to give the staff of mainstream schools the support, training, confidence and will to meet the special needs of *all* their pupils. That will not be achieved simply by provision of extra resources to extend existing provision in the special needs department or the on-site unit for difficult pupils. Extra resources will almost certainly be needed, but should be used to extend the school's policies in catering for the special needs of all its pupils. Our point is that the quality of education *throughout* the school is the principal influence on the progress and behaviour of the pupils we have been discussing.

POLICY MAKING AND PLANNING AT FOUR LEVELS

SCHOOLS

The precise relationship between school, family and community influences on children's educational progress and on their behaviour remains a matter for debate. What is not in dispute is that schools do

Conclusions

exert an important influence on their pupils' development, and particularly on their behaviour. Further, there are indications that this influence is strongest, for better or worse, in the case of pupils who receive little encouragement or support from home.

Schools can no longer pretend that children with special needs are simply none of their business. Ten years ago it was not unusual for secondary schools to appoint one part-time teacher to take 'remedial' pupils for a few sessions a week. Today almost all schools recognise the need for a coherent policy based on more generous provision. They nevertheless retain considerable scope for constructive innovation.

Those schools which have had the greatest success in educating their most problematic pupils are those which have moved beyond the minimal requirements imposed by the 1981 Education Act. They have established procedures which aim to recognise the special needs of all their pupils. To be effective, these require an ethos of evaluation (see Ch. 7) in which teachers see review of resources and methods for teaching children with learning and adjustment difficulties as an integral part of their job.

Unfortunately, very few LEAs have done much to encourage schools to undertake the wide-ranging review of curriculum and organisation which this requires. Indeed, a few schools have realised that the Act requires no fundamental change in school organisation or in the curriculum. Further, the Act can legitimise a policy decision to place increased numbers of slow-learning or uncooperative pupils in newly created special needs departments. Here nominal integration for non-academic subjects is combined with a separate curriculum for all subjects regarded as important by pupils and teachers alike.

We emphasise that this gloomy scenario applies only to a minority of schools. Similarly, only a minority have taken the initiative in establishing the 'whole school' policies for special needs that we described in Chapters 7 and 8. Between these two extremes the majority of schools have made some adjustments, but with no clear lead from their LEA have not developed these to any logical conclusion.

LOCAL EDUCATION AUTHORITY POLICY

Some LEAs have done little or nothing to the network of special schools and units for children with learning and adjustment difficulties that existed prior to the 1981 Education Act. The majority have tinkered with it, but have made no fundamental changes. The expedient of replacing separate special schools with designated units in ordinary schools is often little more than a crude attempt to make an educational virtue out of financial savings. Scepticism will remain the appropriate response until there is evidence that attempts are being made to achieve full functional integration for children placed in the units. At present the limited available evidence suggests that they spend all or most of their time in the special units. Hence, the units may incorporate the worst characteristics of separate special schools, together with lonely isolation both for teachers and for pupils within the host school.

In accepting the Fish Report ILEA (1985a) made an important statement of intent to provide equal opportunities in ordinary schools for all pupils. The Fish Committee claimed to be in no doubt that the right place to educate children and young people with special needs was with their contemporaries. Yet it is signficant that the report baulked at a formal recommendation to phase out the parallel special school system and envisaged a continuing role for special units attached to ordinary schools. Moreover, it appeared to overlook evidence from other LEAs in regarding adjustment difficulties as in some way inevitable, in effect recommending a change in policy from off-site to on-site units. Given the enormous variation between schools in their production of pupils with adjustment difficulties, relatively unexplained by catchment area factors, it is disappointing that the committee did not consider in greater detail the lessons to be learned from the organisation and teaching of successful schools.

The Fish Report could constitute the start of imaginative innovations in which ILEA could lead the way for other LEAs in developing a policy of equal opportunities within ordinary schools for children with learning and adjustment difficulties. The danger is that entrenched professional interest groups will ensure that ILEA, like other LEAs, merely tinkers with the system without altering it in any fundamental way. A strength of the 1981 Act is that it empowers, and would even claim to encourage, LEAs to make appropriate provision within the mainstream. Its weakness is that there has so far been little movement in this direction.

HER MAJESTY'S INSPECTORATE OF SCHOOLS

The inspectorate is independent of the DES in the sense that the Chief Inspector has direct access to the Secretary of State, and does not have to channel his views through the Permanent Secretary. Hence, HMI is in a position to criticise government policy in a way that would be unthinkable for civil servants in the DES. To their credit, inspectors have drawn attention in their reports to the effects on educational standards of declining resources in schools. Also to their credit they have given a much higher profile in recent years to pastoral care and to provision for children with special needs. They

Conclusions

have been critical of some fashionable trends, for example ILEA's expensive policy of off-site units for disruptive pupils, but behind the scenes can do a good deal to publicise and encourage successful innovations in meeting special needs. John Fish himself was formerly a staff inspector for special education.

In the last few years HMI has appeared to be moving away from the more advisory function it had been developing in the 1970s to the more exclusively inspectorial role of former years. This trend might make it difficult for individual inspectors to encourage LEAs to promote the kind of fundamental changes in special needs provision that we have advocated, even if they supported them. On the other hand HMI remains, in the old cliché, the 'eyes and ears of the Department'. Without the tacit, if not explicit support of HMI, changes such as those proposed by the Fish Report are unlikely to take place. Even if ILEA succeeds in implementing the report's recommendations, other LEAs are unlikely to follow suit without some kind of encouragement from the inspectorate. Policy cannot be made by HMI but can be influenced by it. More important, HMI's experience of plans to implement policy decisions can help LEAs avoid many of the worse pitfalls.

DEPARTMENT OF EDUCATION AND SCIENCE

The government provided no funds to assist LEAs in implementing the 1981 Education Act. Moreover some of the inconsistencies in the Act may be seen at least in part as a reflection on its confusion about the most appropriate education for children with learning and adjustment difficulties. The DES cannot tell LEAs how to organise provision for children with special needs. The only restriction is that local arrangements must be consistent with the 1981 Act. In practice the relevant clauses are so broad that it could be quite difficult to step outside them. Nor can the DES tell LEAs how to spend their money, again provided their decisions are consistent with the requirements imposed by Parliament. The DES nevertheless has considerable scope for influencing LEA policy.

Through its publications the department can indicate its official view on what constitutes good practice. A good example in special education was the DES (1975) circular on procedures for assessing special needs. This had no legal power, but constituted a very clear statement of the department's views. Local education authorities currently have little or no practical advice from the department on how, or indeed whether, to adopt a policy of integration in ordinary schools for all pupils, including those with learning and adjustment difficulties. Some detailed guidelines from the department are long overdue.

The question of resources also needs attention at departmental level. The Secretary of State has considerable flexibility within the education budget. He can encourage initiatives which promote the education of children with learning and adjustment difficulties in ordinary schools. A starting point could be to allocate priority on in-service courses in special education to teachers in mainstream schools. These could usefully be based on the experience of schools which have successfully developed their own policies.

At present people involved in special education seem to be caught in a web of inertia. Lacking a clear policy from the head and senior staff, teachers in many ordinary schools are understandably reluctant to add children with serious learning and adjustment difficulties to their existing problems and responsibilities. Lacking a clear policy from the LEA, headteachers have little incentive to do more than maintain the *status quo*. Lacking a clear policy from the DES, LEAs have little incentive to do more than meet their legal obligations as economically as possible. Consequently they have adopted the line of least resistance by tinkering with the *status quo* while doing little or nothing to change it. Initiatives can be taken at any level, but if we are to see any forward development into the 1990s a more active lead will be required from the Secretary of State and from his officers in the DES. At the time of writing there is sadly no evidence that such a lead is at all likely (see Swann 1985).

MEETING ALL PUPILS' NEEDS

RECOGNISING THE NEED FOR CHANGE

The former grammar schools cultivated a reputation for recognising and meeting the special needs of one group of pupils. These were pupils whose academic excellence seemed likely to bring credit on the school. Extra help and small classes were frequently provided for these high flyers. The same applies in comprehensive schools. Indeed it is possible that many of the problems in comprehensive schools may result from the divisions created by determination to maintain the grammar school tradition for academic pupils without corresponding attention to the special needs of those at the other end of the continuum.

Children with learning and adjustment problems play a valuable part in the social ecology of any school by exposing weaknesses. To take a fairly straightforward example, most children learn to read irrespective of the methods and materials used. The dreadful jerk-jerk chatter of Peter and Jane, Janet and John, and the other caricatures of children in some widely used reading schemes may be

Conclusions

linguistically inappropriate. They may also: (a) be devoid of anything to stimulate a young child's imagination; and (b) contain no figures with whom many of their readers could identify. Yet most children learn to read in spite of the awful materials inflicted on them. Their success reflects credit not on the reading schemes, but on teachers who manage to arouse their enthusiasm for even the most tedious books.

A few do not make progress. Many of these children respond to a fresh approach with intrinsically more interesting material. In addition the value of parental participation is now widely recognised, and was first established with backward readers (Hewison and Tizard 1980). This work has obvious implications not only for the partnership between parents and teachers but also for children's motivation and self-image. If all children made good progress, teachers would have little or no incentive to review their existing curriculum and teaching methods. More important, approaches which succeed for pupils with learning difficulties may also be appropriate for the majority.

This is clearly seen in the pastoral care network of some large comprehensive schools. Teachers agree that every child should feel that he or she has ready access to at least one teacher. They also agree on the need for someone to coordinate and disseminate all necessary information about a pupil with special needs. Purely for practical reasons the obvious choice is the form tutor (see Ch. 7). Yet the organisation of pastoral care sometimes leaves form tutors with no greater responsibility than the clerical task of completing attendance registers. Most pupils get along quite well in spite of this. A few do not. It is these pupils who provide the incentive for review and change.

CATERING FOR SIMILARITIES

Recognising that some pupils have special needs, schools sometimes fail to recognise the much greater similarities between them and their peers. To cater successfully for the similarities between children the ethos of a school must be one in which all children feel that they have something useful to contribute. Catering for similarities does not just imply token integration in PE and in other 'non-academic' activities. It implies a practical recognition that all children, from the most gifted to the least able, come to school for the same basic experiences.

The topics covered in the traditional curriculum constitute one set of children's experiences at school. In these areas some differentiation between pupils is necessary. Gifted mathematicians, for example, may need the stimulus that comes from working together on projects which would be beyond their class-mates. Similarly children retarded in reading need special attention for their particular difficulty. This does not, however, mean that a separate curriculum is needed. The special mathematics activities are most likely to be useful when seen as an extension to the work of the ordinary class. The reading programme is most useful when specifically related to the curriculum areas in which the child is having difficulty, so that it provides the opportunity for success in these areas.

Other experiences at school are just as influential on children's development as those obtained from the core curriculum. At school they exchange ideas and attitudes with other children and with adults. They learn, or fail to learn, to work and play cooperatively, to recognise and develop their own particular abilities and to prepare themselves for the next stage in their lives. When we consider how little of what we were formally taught at school, especially secondary school, we can actually remember, it is clear that the learning experiences which last are the ones influenced by the school's 'hidden' curriculum, the attitudes and relationships which determine the climate of the school and hence what children expect of themselves and of adults. In other words the most important learning experiences are those which children share with each other. This is true for all children, not only those with learning and adjustment difficulties. Teaching children to learn through mistakes and to use criticism constructively should be an essential part of every school's curriculum.

A separate point is what children in a school's mainstream learn about those with special needs. We know of numerous children whose life has been made miserable by teasing following their transfer to the 'thick class' in an ordinary school. We know other children attending special schools whose parents will not allow them to play outside the home because of teasing about going to the 'daft school'. Yet we also know schools which have successfully created a climate which accepts and respects exceptionality. These schools have created a cooperative climate in which attempts to cater for individual differences do not obscure the qualities and experiences which all children have in common. Children throughout these schools learn to accept without particular comment that some of their peers have special needs. We suspect that these children will be much more comfortable than many adults in the presence of people with severe disabilities.

EDUCATIONAL AND POLITICAL PRIORITIES

We have argued that a policy to cater for the children we have been discussing in an ordinary school requires a political decision from the

Conclusions

LEA's Education Committee. Such a decision will not be easy to make. The present system is administratively convenient and arouses few major protests either from teachers in the special sector or in the mainstream. An obvious, if cynical, explanation is that it helps to insulate mainstream schools from the critical self-appraisal which will be needed in order to cater effectively for all their pupils. The most disturbing minority can be referred to the special sector or to centres for disruptive pupils. Slightly less troublesome pupils can be contained in the special needs department. Motivation for review of policies and practices that may have contributed to these pupils' difficulties is thus minimised.

As the Fish Report so clearly recognised, a policy of integration implies equal opportunites for all pupils in ordinary schools, including those with learning and adjustment difficulties. This will not be achieved without a wide-ranging review of general organisation, pastoral care, curriculum, and teaching methods and techniques. Adjustment and learning difficulties reflect pupils' problems in the mainstream of the school. Logically, then, the mainstream must be the starting point in implementing a policy of integration.

We know from our work in Sheffield and in New Zealand that this is no idle dream. Schools which have tackled these issues are challenging, yet highly satisfying, places for teachers as well as for pupils. Since the overriding aim is to cater as effectively as possible for *all* pupils' needs, there is no question of catering for the most able at the expense of the least able, or vice versa. Catering effectively for pupils with learning and adjustment difficulties, as for all other pupils, requires a varied but flexible curriculum which challenges and extends them, irrespective of ability, and a social climate in which each individual knows that he or she is expected to, and will, achieve something worth while.

Teachers often feel expected to achieve ever higher standards with ever diminishing resources. In this climate they may well feel tempted to cling to what they have, resisting any attempt to reform the existing network of special schools and units, especially if reform might add to their already considerable workload. Without any real lead from HMI, the DES or their own LEAs, it is clear that individual schools have done a great deal to offer equal opportunities to all their pupils, including the most disturbing. With leadership from the head and senior management teachers can rise above their legitimate anxieties to offer a genuinely 'comprehensive' education.

A successful school is one in which senior staff encourage new ideas in response to continuous but constructively critical review of existing policy and practice. A successful LEA is one which encourages, stimulates and if necessary provokes its headteachers to review existing policies and to explore new ways of gaining pupils' active cooperation in their own learning. A successful education system is one in which LEAs receive encouragement and resources to explore new responses to pressing education problems. The developments we have advocated could lead to far-reaching advances in the quality of education for all pupils in many schools. In the short run these could be stressful. In the long term the benefits throughout the school system could be felt by pupils and teachers alike.

REFERENCES

Adams, F. (1984) *Implementation of the Education Act 1981*. Slough: Education Management Information Exchange.
Advisory Centre for Education (1980) *Survey on Disruptive Units*. London: ACE.
Advisory Centre for Education and Spastics Society (1983) Slow progress on integration, *Where*, **187**, 5–6.
Ainsworth, S. H. (1959) *An Exploratory Study of Educational, Social and Emotional Factors in the Education of Mentally Retarded Children in Georgia Public Schools*. Washington DC: US Office of Education.
Anderson, E. (1973) *The Disabled Schoolchild: A Study of Integration in Primary Schools*. London: Methuen.
Ascher, M. (1970) The attainments of children in ESN schools and remedial departments, *Education Research*, **12**, 215–19.
Atkinson, G. C. E. (1975) The Highfield experiment, *New Behaviour*, 10 July, 54–7.
Balbernie, R. W. (1966) *Residential Work with Children*. Oxford: Pergamon.
Baldwin, J. (1972) Delinquent schools in Tower Hamlets 1. A critique, *British Journal of Criminology*, **12**, 399–401.
Barton, G. (1984) Description of a therapeutic pre-school unit in Buckinghamshire, *Association for Child Psychology and Psychiatry Newsletter*, **6**, iv, 9–12.
Bennett, A. (1932) A comparative study of sub-normal children in the elementary grades, *Teachers College Contributions to Education*. New York: Columbia University Press.
Berger, M. (1979) Behaviour modification in education and professional practice: the dangers of a mindless technology, *Bulletin of the British Psychological Society*, **32**, 418–19.
Berger, M. (1982) Applied behaviour analysis in education: a critical assessment and some implications for training teachers, *Educational Psychology*, **2**, 289–300.
Berger, M., Yule, W. and Rutter, M. (1975) Attainment and adjustment in two geographical areas: II. The prevalence of specific reading retardation, *British Journal of Psychiatry*, **126**, 510–19.
Binet, A. and Simon, T. (1914) *Mentally Defective Children*. London: E. J. Arnold.

Blatt, B. (1958) The physical, personality and academic status of children who are mentally retarded attending special classes as compared with those who are mentally retarded attending regular classes, *American Journal of Mental Deficiency*, **62**, 810–18.

Blunkett, D. (1976) *The Disabled Person in the Community: Separate or Integrate?* Appendix to Report of the Special Education Working Party, submitted to Sheffield Education Department Schools Sub-Committee, 11 February.

Board of Education (1934) *Report of the Committee of Inquiry into Problems relating to Partially Sighted Children*. London: HMSO.

Board of Education (1938) *Report of the Committee of Inquiry into Problems Relating to Children with Defective Hearing*. London: HMSO.

Board of Education and Board of Control (1929) *Report of the Joint Departmental Committee on Mental Deficiency* (the Wood Committee). London: HMSO.

Bolger, A. W. (1983) Training in counselling, *British Psychological Society, Education Section Review*, **7**, ii, 33–8.

Booth, T. (1982) *Special Needs in Education: National Perspectives*. Course E241. Milton Keynes: Open University Press.

Booth, T. (1983) Creating integration policy. In T. Booth and P. Potts (eds) *Integrating Special Education*. Oxford: Blackwell.

Booth, T. and Statham, J. (eds) (1982) *The Nature of Special Education*. Milton Keynes: Open University Press.

Borland, N. R. (1962) Discipline and strain, *National Education (New Zealand)*, **44**, 165–70.

Boxall, M. (1973) Nurture groups, *Concern*, **13**, 9–11.

Breese, J. H. (1983) Special provision for difficult pupils: Does this prevent schools from improving? *Westminster Studies in Education*, **6**, 43–53.

Bromley Education Committee (1983) *Special Education Development Plan: Consultative Paper*. Bromley: Bromley Education Committee.

Brown, T. W. (1978) Shaping clear speech in a nine year old maladjusted boy using a structured procedure, contingent feedback and attention, *Newletter of the Association of Behaviour Modification with Children*, **2**, 23–29.

Burland, J. R. (1978) The evolution of a token economy in a residential school for maladjusted junior boys, *Behavioural Psychotherapy*, **6**, 97–104.

Burland, J. R. (1979) Behaviour modification in a residential school for junior maladjusted boys, *Journal of the Association of Workers with Maladjusted Children*, **7**, 65–79.

Burland, J. R. (1985) Survival skills for the comprehensive school, *Bulletin of the British Psychological Society*, **38**, A57.

Burn, M. (1964) *Mr. Lyward's Answer*. London: Hamish Hamilton.

Burt, C. (1937) *The Backward Child*. London: Hodder and Stoughton.

Carlberg, C. and Kavale, K. (1980) Efficacy of special versus regular class placement for exceptional children: a meta-analysis. *Journal of Special Education*, **14**, 295–309.

Carrier, J. (1977) *Social Influence on the Development of Scientific Knowledge: the Case of Learning Disability*. Unpublished Ph.D. Thesis: University of London.

Carrier, J. G. (1984) Comparative special education ideology, differentiation, and allocation in England and the United States, in S. Tomlinson and L. Barton (eds) *Special Education and Social Interests*. London: Croom Helm.

Cashdan, A. and Pumfrey, P. D. (1969) Some effects of the remedial teaching of reading, *Educational Research*, **11**, 138–42.

References

Cassidy, V. M. and Stanton, J. E. (1959) *An Investigation of Factors Involved in the Educational Placement of Mentally Retarded Children: A Study of Differences Between Children in Special and Regular Classes in Ohio*. Columbus: Ohio State University.

Chamberlain, J. (1973) Mentally handicapped children in ordinary schools: learning together. Paper presented at conference run by Campaign for Mental Handicap, April 1973.

Chandler, B. (1981) *Standard Education Almenac 1981–2*. Chicago: Marquis.

Charity Organisation Society (1893) *The Epileptic and Crippled Child and Adult. A Report on an Investigation of the Physical and Mental Condition of 50,000 School Children, with Suggestions for the Better Education and Care of the Feeble Minded Children and Adults*. London: Swan-Sonnenschein.

Children and Young Persons' Act (1969). Elizabeth II, Ch. 54.

Chisholm, B. (1977) Remedial help within non-streaming, *Forum for the Discussion of New Trends in Education*, **20**, 24–6.

Cleugh, M. F. (1957) (2nd edn 1968) *The Slow Learner*. London: Methuen.

Coard, B. (1971) *How the West Indian Child is Made Educationally Sub-Normal in the British School System*. London: New Beacon Books.

Coates, T. J. and Thoresen, C. E. (1976) Teacher anxiety: a review with recommendations. *Review of Educational Research*, **46**, 159–84.

Coleman, J. (1983) The concept of equality of educational opportunity, *Harvard Educational Review*, **38**, 7–22.

Coleman, J. S. *et al*. (1966) *Equality of Educational Opportunity*. Washington: US Government Printing Office.

Cooling, M. (1974) *Educational Provisions for Maladjusted Children in Boarding Schools*. M. Ed. Thesis. Birmingham University.

Cornish, D. B. and Clarke, R. V. G. (1975) *Residential Treatment and its Effects on Delinquency*. London: HMSO.

Cox, C. B. and Boyson, R. (1977) *Black Paper 1977*. London: Temple Smith.

Craft, M. (1965) A follow-up study of disturbed juvenile delinquents, *British Journal of Criminology*, **5**, 55–62.

Critchley, C. (1969) *An Experimental Study of Maladjusted Children*. M. A. Thesis. Liverpool University.

Dahl, M., Tangaud, T. and Vislie, L. (1982) *The Integration of Handicapped Pupils in Compulsory Education in Norway*. Oslo: Universitets Farlaget Oslo.

Dain, P. (1977) Disruptive children and the key centre, *Remedial Education*, **12**, iv, 163–7.

Davie, R., Butler, N. and Goldstein, H. (1972) *From Birth to Seven*. London: Longmans.

Dawson, R. C. (1980) *Special Provision for Disturbed Pupils: A Survey*. London: Macmillan.

Department of Education and Science (1966) *The Health of the School Child, 1964–65*. London: HMSO.

Department of Education and Science (1967) *Children and their Primary Schools* (The Plowden Report). London: HMSO.

Department of Education and Science (1972) *Aspects of Special Education: Education Survey 17*. London: HMSO.

Department of Education and Science (1973) *Special Education: A Fresh Look*. Reports on Education No. 77. London: DES.

Department of Education and Science (1975) *The Discovery of Children Requiring Special Education and the Assessment of their Needs.* Circular 2/75 London: DES.
Department of Education and Science (1976) *Statistics of Education 1976, Vol. 1, Schools.* London: HMSO.
Department of Education and Science (1978a) *Special Educational Needs.* (The Warnock Report). London: HMSO.
Department of Education and Science (1978b) *Statistics of Education 1978, Vol. 1, Schools.* London: HMSO.
Department of Education and Science (1979) *Aspects of Secondary Education in England: A Survey of HM Inspectors of Schools.* London: HMSO.
Department of Education and Science (1981a) Circular 8/81: The Education Act 1981. London: DES.
Department of Education and Science (1981b) *West Indian Children in our Schools* (The Rampton Report). London: HMSO.
Department of Education and Science (1982) *Statistics of Education 1982: Schools.* London: HMSO.
Department of Education and Science (1983) *Assessments and Statements of Special Educational Needs.* Circular 1/83. London: DES.
Department of Education and Science (1984) *Parental Influence at School: A New Framework for School Government in England and Wales.* London: HMSO.
Department of Education and Science (1985) *Education for All: The Report of the Committee of Inquiry into the Education of Children from Ethnic Minority Groups* (The Swann Report). London: HMSO.
Department of Health and Social Security (1968) *Report of the Committee on Local Authority and Allied Personal Social Services.* (The Seebohm Report). London: HMSO.
Diener, C. I. and Dweck, C. S. (1978) An analysis of learned helplessness: continuous changes in performance, strategy and achievement cognitions following failure, *Journal of Personality and Social Psychology*, **36**, 451–62.
Douglas, J. W. B. (1964) *The Home and the School.* London: MacGibbon and Kee.
Dunn, L. M. (1968) Special education for the mildly retarded – is much of it justifiable? *Exceptional Children*, **35**, 5–22 (reprinted in W. G. Becker (ed.) *An Empirical Basis for Change in Education.* Henley-on-Thames, Science Res. Associates).
Dyer, H. S. (1968) School factors and equal educational opportunity, *Harvard Educational Review*, **38**, 38–56.
Education Act (1921) 11 and 12 George V, Ch. 51. London: HMSO.
Education Act (1944) 7 and 8 George VI, Ch. 31. London: HMSO.
Education Act (1981) Elizabeth II, Ch. 60.
Education Department (1898) *Report of the Departmental Committee on Defective and Epileptic Children.* London: HMSO.
Eide, K. (1978) *Special Financial Provision for Compulsory Education in Norway.* Oslo: OECD Paper.
Elementary Education Act (1870) 33 and 34 Victoria, Ch. 75. London: HMSO.
Elementary Education Act (1876) 39 and 40 Victoria, Ch. 79. London: HMSO.
Elementary Education (Defective and Epileptic Children) Act (1899) 62 and 63 Victoria, Ch. 32, London: HMSO.
Ellenbogen, M. L. (1957) A comparative study of some aspects of academic and

References

social adjustment of two groups of mentally retarded children in special classes and in regular grades, *Dissertation Abstracts*, 17, 2496.

Farrington, D. (1972) Delinquency begins at home, New Society, 14 September.

Finlayson, D. S. and Loughran, J. L. (1976) Pupils' perceptions in high and low delinquency schools, *Educational Research*, 18, 138–45.

Fish Report (1985) See Inner Education Authority (1985a).

Fixsen, D. L., Phillips, E. L. and Wolf, M. (1973) Achievement place: Experiments in self-government with pre-delinquents, *Journal of Applied Behavioural Analysis*, 6, 31–47.

Flanders, N. A. C. (1970) *Analysing Teaching Behaviour*. Reading, Mass: Addison-Wesley.

Fogelman, K. (1976) *Britain's Sixteen Year Olds*. London: National Children's Bureau.

Ford, J., Mungon, D. and Whelan, M. (1982) *Special Education and Social Control: Invisible Disasters*. London: Routledge and Kegan Paul.

Frampton, O. (1981) *The Social Adjustment and Academic Achievement of Segregated and Integrated Slow-Learners in a Christchurch Secondary School*. Christchurch, New Zealand: University of Canterbury Education Department.

Francis, M. (1980) 'Sin-bins': Narrow and racist or working well? *Times Educational Supplement*, 5 December, 13.

Frederick, L. v. Thomas (1977) 419 F. Supp. 960 (E. D. Pa. 1976), aff'd, 57 F 2a 373 (3d Cir. 1977)

Frommer, E. (1967) A day hospital for children under five, *Lancet*, 1, 377–9.

Galloway, D. (1976) Size of school, socio-economic hardship, suspension rates and persistent unjustified absence from school, *British Journal of Educational Psychology*, 46, 40–7.

Galloway, D. (1982) A study of pupils suspended from school, *British Journal of Educational Psychology*, 52, 205–12.

Galloway, D. (1983) Disruptive pupils and effective pastoral care, *School Organisation*, 3, 245–54.

Galloway, D. (1985a) Meeting special educational needs in the ordinary school? Or creating them? *Maladjustment and Therapeutic Education*, 3, iii, 3–10.

Galloway, D. (1985b) *Schools, Pupils and Special Educational Needs*. London: Croom Helm.

Galloway, D. and Barrett, C. (1984) Off-site centres for disruptive secondary school pupils in New Zealand, *Educational Research*, 26, 106–10.

Galloway, D., Ball, T., Blomfield, D. and Seyd, R. (1982) *Schools and Disruptive Pupils*. London: Longman.

Galloway, D., Panckhurst, F., Boswell, K., Boswell, C. and Green, K. (1984a) The health of primary school teachers, *New Zealand Journal of Educational Studies*, 19, 136–42.

Galloway, D., Panckhurst, F., Boswell, K., Boswell, C. and Green, K. (1984b) Mental health, absence from work, stress and satisfaction in a sample of New Zealand primary school teachers, *Australia and New Zealand Journal of Psychiatry*, 18, 359–63.

Galloway, D., Boswell, K., Panckhurst, F., Boswell, C. and Green, K. (1985a) Sources of satisfaction and dissatisfaction for New Zealand primary school teachers, *Educational Research*, 27, 44–51.

Galloway, D., Wilcox, B. and Martin, R. (1985b) Persistent absence from school and exclusion from school: the predictive power of school and community variables, *British Educational Research Journal*, **11**, 51–61.

Garnett, J. (1975) *A Curriculum for Less Able Children*. Unpublished ACE course dissertation. Oxford University.

Garnett, E. J. (1976) Special children in a comprehensive special school, *Forward Trends*, **3**(i), 8–11.

Gath, D., Cooper, B. and Gattoni, F. E. G. (1972) Child guidance and delinquency in a London borough: Preliminary communication, *Psychological Medicine*, **2**, 185–91.

Gath, D., Cooper, B., Gattoni, F. and Rockett, D. (1977) *Child Guidance and Delinquency in a London Borough*. Oxford: Oxford University Press.

Gathorne-Hardy, J. (1977) *The Public School Phenomenon*. London: Hodder and Stoughton.

Gipps, C. and Goldstein, H. (1984) You can't trust a special, *Times Educational Supplement*, 27 July, 15.

Goldberg, D. P. (1972) *The Detection of Psychiatric Illness by Questionnaire*. Oxford: Oxford University Press.

Goodwin, C. A. (1974) Leicestershire: Countesthorpe College, *Remedial Education*, **9**, 16–18.

Gorrell-Barnes, G. (1973) Work with nurture-group parents, *Concern*, **13**, 13–16.

Graham, P. and Rutter, M. (1968a) The reliability and validity of the psychiatric study of the child: II. Interview with the parent, *British Journal of Psychiatry*, **114**, 581–92.

Graham, P. and Rutter, M. (1968b) Organic brain dysfunction and child psychiatric disorder, *British Medical Journal*, **3**, 695–700.

Graham, P. and Rutter, M. (1970) Selection of Children with Psychiatric Disorder. In M. Rutter, J. Tizard and K. Whitmore (1970) (eds) *Education, Health and Behaviour*. London: Longman.

Gregory, R. P. (1980) Individual referrals: how naive are educational psychologists? *Bulletin of the British Psychological Society*, **33**, 381–4.

Grosin, L. (1985) School ethos and pupil outcome, *Research Bulletin from the Institute of Education, University of Stockholm*, **11**, i, 1–33.

Grunsell, R. (1979) Suspensions and the sin-bin boom, *Where*, **153**, 307–9.

Grunsell, R. (1980) *Beyond Control? Schools and Suspension*. London: Readers and Writers.

Grunsell, R. (1985) *Finding Answers to Disruption: Discussion Exercises for Secondary Teachers*. York: Longman.

Haggerty, M. E. (1925) The incidence of undesirable behaviour in public-school children, *Journal of Educational Research*, **12**, 102–22.

Hall, R. V., Panyan, M., Rabon, D. and Broden, M. (1968) Instructing beginning teachers in reinforcement procedures which improve classroom control, *Journal of Applied Behavioural Analysis*, **1**, 315–22.

Hargreaves, D. H. (1967) *Social Relationships in a Secondary School*. London: Routledge and Kegan Paul.

Hargreaves, D. H. (1978) What teaching does to teachers, *New Society*, **43**, 9 March, 540–2.

Hargreaves, D. H. (1983) *The Challenge of the Comprehensive School: Culture, Curriculum, Community*. London: Routledge and Kegan Paul.

Hargreaves, D., Hestor, S. K. and Mellor, F. J. (1975) *Deviance in Classrooms*. London: Routledge and Kegan Paul.

References

Harris, R. (1978) Relationships between EEG abnormality and aggressive and anti-social behaviour – a critical appraisal, in L. A. Hersov, M. Berger and D. Shaffer (eds) *Aggression and Anti-Social Behaviour in Childhood and Adolescence*. Oxford: Pergamon.

Harrop, L. A. (1980) Behaviour modification in schools: A time for caution, *Bulletin of the British Psychological Society*, 33, 158–60.

Harrop, A. (1983) *Behaviour Modification in the Classroom*. London: Hodder and Stoughton.

Hegarty, S. and Pocklington, K. (1981) *Educating Pupils with Special Needs in Ordinary Schools*. Windsor: NFER Nelson.

Her Majesty's Inspectorate of Schools (1978) *Behavioural Units*. London: DES.

Her Majesty's Inspectorate of Schools (1980a) *Community Homes with Education*. London: HMSO.

Her Majesty's Inspectorate of Schools (1980b) *Educational Provision by the Inner London Education Authority*. London: Department of Education and Science.

Her Majesty's Inspectorate of Schools (1983) *Science in Primary Schools: A Discussion Paper Produced by HMI Science Committee*. London: Department of Education and Science.

Her Majesty's Inspectorate of Schools (1985a) *Education Provision by Dyfed Education Authority*. Cardiff: Welsh Office Education Department.

Her Majesty's Inspectorate of Schools (1985b) *The Effects of Local Authority's Expenditure Policies on Education Provision in England and Wales 1984*. London: Department of Education and Science.

Her Majesty's Stationery Office (1972) *Statistics Relating to Approved Schools, Remand Homes and Attendance Centres in England and Wales for the Year 1970*. London: HMSO.

Hewison, J. and Tizard, J. (1980) Parental involvement and reading attainment, *British Journal of Educational Psychology*, 50, 209–15.

Inner London Education Authority (1981) *Ethnic Census of School Support Centres and Educational Guidance Centres (RS784/81)*. London: ILEA Research and Statistics Division.

Inner London Education Authority (1984) *Improving Secondary Schools* (The Hargreaves Report). London: ILEA.

Inner London Education Authority (1985a) *Equal Opportunities for All?* (The Fish Report). London: ILEA.

Inner London Education Authority (1985b) *Improving Primary Schools* (The Thomas Report). London: ILEA.

Johnson, D. (1975) Girl of 11 may be sterilised. *The Guardian*, 5 June, 1.

Johnson, G. O. (1962) Special education for the mentally handicapped – a paradox, *Exceptional Children*, 29, 62–9.

Jones, A. (1980) The school's view of persistent non-attendance, in L. Hersov and I. Berg (eds) *Out of School: Modern Perspectives in Truancy and School Refusal*. Chichester: Wiley.

Jones, E. (1980) *The Carterton Project: a monitored account of the way a comprehensive school responded to children with special educational needs*. Unpublished M.Ed. Thesis, University of Birmingham.

Jones, E. (1981) A resource approach to meeting special needs in a secondary school, in L. Barton and S. Tomlinson (eds) *Special Education, Policy, Practice and Social Issues*. London: Harper and Row.

Jones, N. (1973) Special adjustment units in comprehensive schools: I. Needs and resources. II. Structure and function, *Therapeutic Education*, **1**, 2, 23–31.

Jones, N. (1974) Special adjustment units in comprehensive schools: III. Selection of children, *Therapeutic Education*, **2**, 2, 21–6.

Jones, N. (1983a) An integrative approach to special educational needs, *Forum for the Discussion of New Trends in Education*, **25**, ii, 36–9.

Jones, N. (1983b) The management of integration: The Oxfordshire experience, in T. Booth and P. Potts (eds) *Integrating Special Education*. Oxford: Blackwell.

Jones, N. (1983c) Policy change and innovation for special needs in Oxfordshire, *Oxford Review of Education*, **9**, iii, 241–53.

Jordan, A. (1959) Personal–social traits of mentally handicapped children, in T. G. Thurstone (ed.) *An Evaluation of Educating Mentally Handicapped Children in Special Classes and in Regular Classes*. University of North Carolina.

Kirp, D. L. (1974) Student classification, public policy and the courts, *Harvard Educational Review*, **44**, 7–52.

Kirp, D. L. (1983) Professionalisation as a policy choice: British special education in comparative perspective, in J. B. Chambers and W. T. Hartman (eds) *Special Education Policies: Their History, Implementation and Finance*. Philadelphia: Temple University Press.

Klemm, L. R. (1891) *European Schools*. New York: Appleton.

Kolvin, I., Garside, R. D., Nichol, A. R., MacMillan, A., Wolstenholme, F. and Leitch, I. M. (1981) *Help Starts Here: The Maladjusted Child in the Ordinary School*. London: Tavistock.

Kounin, J. S., Friesen, W. V. and Norton, E. (1966) Managing emotionally disturbed children in regular classrooms, *Journal of Educational Psychology*, **57**, 1–13.

Kyriacou, C. and Sutcliffe, J. (1977) Teacher stress: a review, *Educational Review*, **29**, 299–306.

Kyriacou, C. and Sutcliffe, J. (1978a) A model of teacher stress, *Educational Studies*, **4**, 1–6.

Kyriacou, C. and Sutcliffe, J. (1978b) Teacher stress: prevalence, sources and symptoms, *Journal of Educational Psychology*, **55**, 61–4.

Lane, D. (1977) Aspects of the use of behaviour modification in secondary schools, *Bulletin of the British Association for Behavioural Psychotherapy*, **5**, 76–9.

Larry, P. v. Riles (1974) 343 F. Supp. 1306 (N.D. Cal. 1972), aff'd, 502 F. 2d. 963 (9th Cir. 1974).

Laslett, R. (1984) *Changing Perceptions of Maladjusted Children 1945–81*. Portishead: Association of Workers for Maladjusted Children.

Lennhoff, F. E. (1960) *Exceptional Children*. London: Allen and Unwin.

Levitt, E. E. (1957) Results of psychotherapy with children: an evaluation, *Journal of Consulting Psychology*, **21**, 189–96.

Levitt, E. E. (1963) Psychotherapy with children: a further evaluation, *Behavioural Research and Therapy*, **1**, 45–51.

Lindsay, G. A. and Desforges, M. (1986) Integrated nurseries for children with special educational needs, *British Journal of Special Education* (in press).

Lovell, K., Johnson, E. and Platts, D. (1962) A summary of a study of the reading ages of children who had been given remedial teaching, *British Journal of Educational Psychology*, **32**, 66–71.

References

Lovell, K., Byrne, C. and Richardson, B. (1963) A further study of the educational progress of children who had received remedial education, *British Journal of Educational Psychology*, **33**, 3–9.

McFie, B. S. (1934) Behaviour and personality difficulties in school children, *British Journal of Educational Psychology*, **4**, 30–46.

McMichael, P. (1974) After-care, family relationships and reconviction in a Scottish approved school, *British Journal of Criminology*, **14**, 236–47.

Makins, V. (1975a) The story of Countesthorpe, *Times Educational Supplement*, 16 May, 17–18.

Makins, V. (1975b) Dividends of change, *Times Educational Supplement*, 23 May, 18–19.

Marland, M. (1980) The pastoral curriculum, in R. Best, C. Jarvis and P. Ribbins (eds) *Perspectives in Pastoral Care*. London: Heinemann.

Marland, M. (1983) Preparing for promotion in pastoral care, *Pastoral Care in Education*, **1**, 24–36.

Marshall, M. (1971) The effect of special educational treatment of maladjusted pupils in a day school, *Association of Educational Psychologists Journal*, **2**, 10, 23–5.

Mental Deficiency Act (1913) 3 and 4 George V, Ch. 28.

Mickleborough, P. J. (1980) *Atherstone Day Unit: Fifth Annual Report*. Atherstone: Warwickshire LEA.

Mills v. *Board of Education* (1972) 348 F. Supp. 866, 880 (D.D.C. 1972).

Milner, M. (1938) *The Human Problem in Schools*. London: Methuen.

Ministry of Education (1945) *The Handicapped Pupils and School Health Service Regulations* (S. R. and O. No. 1076). London: HMSO.

Ministry of Education (1953) Circular 269. *The School Health Service and Handicapped Pupils Regulations*. London: Ministry of Education.

Ministry of Education (1954) *Training and Supply of Teachers of Handicapped Pupils*, Fourth Report of the National Advisory Council on the Training and Supply of Teachers. London: HMSO.

Ministry of Education (1955) *Report of the Committee on Maladjusted Children* (The Underwood Report). London: HMSO.

Ministry of Education (1958) *Report of the Chief Medical Officer for the Years 1956–57*. London: HMSO.

Ministry of Education (1959) *The Handicapped Pupils and Special Schools Regulations* (SI No. 365). London: HMSO.

Ministry of Education (1961) Circular 11/61. *Special Educational Treatment for Educationally Sub-Normal Pupils*. London: Ministry of Education.

Mitchell, S. and Rosa, P. (1981) Boyhood behaviour problems as precursors of criminality: a fifteen year follow-up, *Journal of Child Psychology and Psychiatry*, **22**, 19–33.

Morris, J. M. (1959) *Reading in the Primary School*. London: Newnes.

Morris, J. M. (1966) *Standards and Progress in Reading*. Slough: NFER.

Mortimore, P., Davies, J., Varlaam, A. and West, A. (1983) *Behaviour Problems in Schools: An Evaluation of Support Centres*. London: Croom Helm.

Mullins, S. (1982) *A Study of the Role of the Support Teacher in Relation to Children with Special Educational Needs in Mainstream Primary Schools in Sheffield*. Unpublished M.Ed. Dissertation, University of Sheffield.

Murgatroyd, S. (1983) Counselling at a time of change and development, British Psychological Society, *Educational Section Review*, **7**, ii, 5–9.

Neale, M. D. (1958) *Neale Analysis of Reading Ability Manual*. London: Macmillan.
O'Leary, K. D. and O'Leary, S. C. (1979) (eds) *Classroom Management: The Successful Use of Behaviour Modification* (2nd edn). New York: Pergamon.
Osterling, O. (1967) *The Efficacy of Special Education*. Uppsala: Scandinavian University Books.
Panckhurst, F., Galloway, D. and Boswell, K. (1982) Stress and the Primary School Principal, *National Education* (*NZ*), **64**, 131–9.
Pase v. Hannon (1980) 74C3586 (N.D.Ill. 1980)
Phillipson, C. M. (1971) Juvenile delinquency and the school, in W. G. Carson and P. Wiles (eds) *Crime and Delinquency in Britain: Sociological Readings*. London: Martin Robertson.
Pollack, M. (1972) *Today's 3 Year Olds in London*. London: Heinemann.
Power, M. J., Alderson, M. R., Phillipson, C. M., Schoenberg, E. and Morris, J. M. (1967) Delinquent schools, *New Society*, 19 October.
Power, M. J., Benn, R. T. and Morris, J. M. (1972) Neighbourhood, school and juveniles before the courts, *British Journal of Criminology*, **12**, 111–32.
Pratt, J. (1978) Perceived stress among teachers: the effects of age and background of children taught, *Educational Research*, **30**, 3–14.
Pringle, M. L. Kellmer (1961) The long-term effects of remedial treatment: a follow-up study, *Educational Research*, **4**, 62–6.
Pringle, M. L. Kellmer, Butler, N. and Davie, R. (1966) *11,000 Seven Year Olds*. London: Longman
Pritchard, D. G. (1963) *Education and the Handicapped 1760–1960*. London: Routledge and Kegan Paul.
Public Law 94–142 (1978) 89 Stat. 773 (1975) (codified at 20 U.S.C. 1401–1461).
Rabinowitz, A. (1981) The range of solutions: a critical analysis, in B. Gillham (ed.) *Problem Behaviour in the Secondary School: A Systems Approach*. London: Croom Helm
Radical Statistics Education Group (1982) *Reading Between the Numbers: A Critical Guide to Educational Research*. London: BSSR Publications.
Reynolds, D. (1976) When pupils and teachers refuse a truce: the secondary schoool and the creation of delinquency, in G. Mungham and G. Pearson (eds) *Working Class Youth Culture*. London: Routledge and Kegan Paul.
Reynolds, D., Jones, S., St Leger, S. and Murgatroyd, S. (1980) School factors and truancy, in L. Hersov and I. Berg (eds) *Out of School. Modern Perspective in Truancy and School Refusal*. Chichester: Wiley.
Robins, L. N. (1966) *Deviant Children Grown Up*. Baltimore: Williams and Wilkins.
Robins, L. N. (1972) Follow up studies of behaviour disorder in children, in H. C. Quay and J. S. Werry (eds) *Psychopathological Disorders of Childhood*. New York: Wiley.
Roe, M. (1965) *Survey into Progress of Maladjusted Children*. London: ILEA.
Rowan, P. (1976) Short-term sanctuary, *Times Educational Supplement*, 2 April, 21–4.
Rudd, W. G. A. and Wiseman, S. (1962) Sources of dissatisfaction among a group of teachers, *British Journal of Educational Psychology*, **32**, 275–91.

References

Rutter, M. (1965) Classification and categorisation in child psychiatry, *Journal of Child Psychology and Psychiatry*, **6**, 71–83.

Rutter, M. (1966) *Children of Sick Parents: An Environmental and Psychiatric Study*. Institute of Psychiatry, Maudsley Monographs No. 16. London: Oxford University Press.

Rutter, M. (1967) A children's behaviour questionnaire for completion by teachers – preliminary findings, *Journal of Child Psychology and Psychiatry*, **8**, 1–11.

Rutter, M. (1972) *Maternal Deprivation Re-Assessed*. Harmondsworth: Penguin.

Rutter, M. (1977) Prospective studies to investigate behavioural change, in J. S. Strauss, H. M. Babigian and M. Roff (eds) *Methods of Longitudinal Research in Psychopathology*. New York: Plenum Publishing.

Rutter, M. and Graham, P. (1968) The reliability and validity of the psychiatric assessment of the child. I. Interview with the child, *British Journal of Psychiatry*, **114**, 563–79.

Rutter, M., Lebovici, S., Eisenberg, L., Snerzevskij, A. V., Sadoun, R., Broke, E. and Tsun, Yi Lin (1969) A triaxial classification of mental disorders in children, *Journal of Child Psychology and Psychiatry*, **10**, 41–61.

Rutter, M., Tizard, J. and Whitmore, K. (1970) (eds) *Education, Health and Behaviour*, London: Longmans.

Rutter, M., Yule, W., Berger, M., Yule, B., Morton, J. and Bagley, C. (1974) Children of West Indian immigrants: I. Rates of behavioural deviance and of psychiatric disorder, *Journal of Child Psychology and Psychiatry*, **15**, 241–62.

Rutter, M., Cox, A., Tupling, C., Berger, M. and Yule, W. (1975a) Attainment and adjustment in two geographical areas. I. The prevalence of psychiatric disorder, *British Journal of Psychiatry*, **126**, 493–509.

Rutter, M., Yule, B., Quinton, D., Rowlands, O., Yule, W. and Berger, M. (1975b) Attainment and adjustment in two geographical areas. III. Some factors accounting for area differences, *British Journal of Psychiatry*, **126**, 520–33.

Rutter, M., Yule, B., Morton, J. and Bagley, C. (1975c) Children of West Indian immigrants: III. Home circumstances and family patterns, *Journal of Child Psychology and Psychiatry*, **16**, 105–23.

Rutter, M., Graham, P., Chadwick, O. F. D. and Yule, W. (1976) Adolescent turmoil: fact or fiction, *Journal of Child Psychology and Psychiatry*, **17**, 35–56.

Rutter, M., Maughan, B., Mortimore, P., Ouston, J. and Smith, A. (1979) *Fifteen Thousand Hours: Secondary Schools and their Effects on Pupils*. London: Open Books.

Sampson, O. C. (1975) *Remedial Education*. London: Routledge and Kegan Paul.

Sarason, S. and Doris, J. (1979) The Education for All Handicapped Children Act (PL 94–142): what does it say? *Exceptional Parent*, **7**, iv, 6–8.

Sayer, J. (1983) Assessments for all, statements for none? *Special Education: Forward Trends*, **10**, iv, 15–16.

Scottish Education Department (1978) *The Education of Pupils with Learning Difficulties in Primary and Secondary Schools: A Progress Report by Her Majesty's Inspectorate*. Edinburgh: HMSO.

Shaw, O. (1965) *Maladjusted Boys*. London: Allen and Unwin.

Shearer, E. (1967) The long term effects of remedial education, *Educational Research*, **9**, 219–22.

Shearer, E. (1977) Survey of ESN(M) children in Cheshire. *Special Education: Forward Trends*, **4**, 2, 20–2.

Sheffield Education Department (1976a) *ESN(M) Schools in the Comprehensive System: Report of the Special Education Working Party*. Paper submitted to Schools Sub-Committee of the Education Committee, 11 February.

Sheffield Education Department (1976b) Minutes of Meeting of the Schools Sub-Committee (Education), held on 11 February.

Sheffield Education Department (1984) *Centres of Integration*. Unpublished paper submitted to the Education Committee by the Chief Education Officer.

Shuttleworth, G. E. (1888) The education of children of abnormally weak mental capacity, *Journal of Mental Science*, **34**, 80–4.

Silva, P. A., McGee, R. and Williams, S. (1985) Some characteristics of 9- year old boys with general reading backwardness or specific reading retardation, *Journal of Child Psychology and Psychiatry*, **26**, 407–21.

Simmonds, E. (1965) Testing results in the day maladjusted school, *Educational Review*, **17**, 144–50.

Stott, D. H. (1963) *The Social Adjustment of Children* (2nd edn). London: University of London Press.

Stott, D. H. (1971) *The Bristol Social Adjustment Guides*. London: University of London Press.

Swann, W. (1985) Is the integration of children with special needs happening? An analysis of recent statistics of pupils in special schools, *Oxford Review of Education*, **11**, 3–18.

Thurstone, T. G. (1959) *An Evaluation of Educating Mentally Handicapped Children in Special Classes and in Regular Classes*. Washington DC: US Office of Education.

Tizard, J. (1973) Maladjusted children and the child guidance service, *London Educational Review*, **2**, 22–37.

Tizard, J. (1978) Research in Special Education, *Special Education Forward Trends*, **5**, iii, 26–8.

Tobin, D. and Pumfrey, P. (1976) Some long term effects of the remedial teaching of reading, *Educational Review*, **29**, 1–12.

Tomlinson, J. (1980) The educational performance of ethnic minority children, *New Community*, **8**, 213–34.

Tomlinson, S. (1981) *Educational Subnormality: A Study in Decision-Making*. London: Routledge and Kegan Paul.

Tomlinson, S. (1982) *The Sociology of Special Education*. London: Routledge and Kegan Paul.

Topping, K. (1983) *Educational Systems for Disruptive Adolescents*. London: Croom Helm.

Tuckey, L., Parfit, J. and Tuckey, R. (1973) *Handicapped School Leavers*. Windsor: NFER (NCB Report).

Vacc, N. A. (1968) A study of emotionally disturbed children in regular and special classes, *Exceptional Children*, **35**, 197–204.

Vacc, N. A. (1972) Long term effects of special class intervention for emotionally disturbed children, *Exceptional Children*, **39**, 15–22.

Vaughan, M. and Shearer, A. (1986) *Mainstreaming in Massachusetts*. London: Centre for Studies on Integration in Education/Campaign for People with Mental Handicaps.

Warnock, M. (1982) Introduction, in J. Welton, K. Wedell and G. Vorhaus *Meeting Special Educational Needs: The 1981 Education Act and its Implications*. Bedford Way Papers 12, London: University of London Institute of Education.

References

Warnock Report (1978) See Department of Education and Science (1978a).

Weatherley, R. and Lipsky, M. (1977) Street-level bureaucrats and institutional innovation: implementing special education reform, *Harvard Educational Review*, **47**, 171–97.

Wechsler, D. (1949) Wechsler Intelligence Scale for Children (Manual). New York: The Psychological Corporation.

Wedge, P. and Essen, J. (1982) *Children in Adversity*. London: Pan.

Wedge, P. and Prosser, H. (1973) *Born to Fail?* London: Arrow Books.

Welsh Office (1978) *Statistics of Education in Wales*, iii, 1978, Cardiff: Welsh Office.

Welsh Office (1978) *Statistics of Education in Wales*, vii, 1982, Cardiff: Welsh Office.

Welton, J. Wedell, K. and Vorhaus, G. (1982) *Meeting Special Educational Needs: The 1981 Education Act and its Implications*. Bedford Way Papers 12. London: Institute of Education, University of London.

West, D. J. and Farrington, D. (1973) *Who Becomes Delinquent?* London: Heinemann.

Wheldall, K. (1982) Behavioural pedagogy or behavioural overkill? *Educational Psychology*, **2**, 181–4.

Wheldall, K., Merrett, F. E. and Russell, A. (1983) *The Behavioural Approach to Teaching Package*. Birmingham: Centre of Child Study, University of Birmingham.

Willis, P. (1977) *Learning to Labour: How Working Class Kids Get Working Class Jobs*. Farnborough: Saxon House.

Wills, D. (1941) *The Hawkspur Experiment*. London: Allen and Unwin.

Wills, W. D. (1945) *The Barns Experiment*. London: Allen and Unwin.

Wills, W. D. (1960) *Throw Away Thy Rod*. London: Gollancz.

Wills, W. D. (1971) *Spare the Child*. Harmondsworth: Penguin Books.

Wolf, M. M., Phillips, E. L. and Fixsen, D. L. (1975) *Achievement Place Phase II: Final Report*. Department of Human Development, University of Kansas.

Wood Commitee (1929) See Board of Education and Board of Control (1929).

Woods, P. (1984) *Parents and School: A Report for Discussion on Liaison between Parents and Secondary Schools in Wales*. London: Schools Council Publications.

Woolacott, S., Graham, P. J. and Stevenson, J. (1978) A controlled evaluation of the therapeutic effectiveness of a psychiatric day centre for pre-school children, *British Journal of Psychiatry*, **132**, 349–55.

Wright, D. M., Moelis, I. and Pollack, L. J. (1976) The outcome of individual child psychotherapy: increments at follow-up, *Journal of Child Psychology and Psychiatry*, **17**, 275–85.

Wrightstone, J. W., Forland, G., Lepkowski, J. R., Sontag, M. and Edelstein, J. D. (1959) *A Comparison of Educational Outcomes Under Single-Track and Two-Track Plans for Educable Mentally Retarded Children*. Washington DC: US Office of Education.

Ysseldyke, J. and Algozzine, B. (1982) *Critical Issues in Special and Remedial Education*. Boston: Houghton Mifflin.

Yule, W. (1973) Differential prognosis of reading backwardness and specific reading retardation, *British Journal of Educational Psychology*, **43**, 244–8.

Yule, W., Berger, M., Rutter, M. and Yule, B. (1975) Children of West Indian immigrants: II. Intellectual performance and reading attainment, *Journal of Child Psychology and Psychiatry*, **16**, 1–17.

INDEX

able children, provision for, 154, 178
absenteeism, rates of, 135, 136
accountability, teachers', 121–2
Adams, F., 19
adjustment difficulties *see* maladjusted *and* disruptive
adjustment groups, 59
administrative selection, LEA's, 9–12, 118–20
Advisory Centre for Education, 30
Afro-Caribbean children, 42–4, 134
Ainsworth, S. H., 64
Algozzine, B., 81, 86
Anderson, E., 47, 163
anti-school subculture, 136, 145
appeals committees for parents, 18
approved schools (community homes), 50
Ascher, M., 65
assessment of special needs
 ascertainment as ESN(M), xiii, 8, 9, 10, 44
 certification as feeble-minded, 6, 8
 circular 2/75 (DES), 11, 12, 13, 177
 class bias, 10, 11, 45–6, 48, 131
 'discovery' of needs, 27–8, 30
 formal assessments (1981 Act), 17–21, 97, 99, 116–18, 168–9
 progress misjudged, 54, 66
 sex bias, 44–6
 see also attribution, criteria *and* prevalance
Atkinson, G. C. E., 55
attendance rates, 135, 136
attribution of needs, individualised, 17–18, 41–8, 117, 126, 172

Balbernie, R. W., 52
Baldwin, J., 133
Banbury, integration in, 88, 94–9, 169
Barrett, C., 58, 140, 164
Barton, G., 61
behaviour disorders
 definitions of, 31, 32, 33, 35–6
 girls', 38
 intractability of, 61–2
 tests of, 40
 variation between schools, 129, 132–9, 151
behaviour modification methods, 53, 55, 142–6
Bennett, A., 63
Berger, M., 34, 37, 145
Bicester, special unit, 94, 95, 96
Binet, A., 5
Birmingham, reintegration in, 58
black pupils
 in Britain, 13, 24, 35, 42–4, 155–6, 164
 in the USA, 78, 82
Blatt, B., 64
blind children, integration of, 173
Board of Education reports, 7, 38
Bolger, A. W., 146
Booth, T., 89, 90, 91, 104, 105
Borland, N. R., 123
Boxall, M., 59
boys, high proportion in special education, 44–6
Boyson, R., 121
Breese, J. H., 49
Brislington School, Bristol, 59, 139
Bristol Social Adjustment Guide, 31, 40, 54–5
Bromley, integration in, 88–94
Bromley Society for Mentally Handicapped Children, 91, 93–4
Brown, T. W., 53
Buckinghamsire, follow-up study in, 62

197

Index

bullying, of segregated pupils, 107, 180
Burland, J. R., 53
Burn, M., 51
Burt, *Sir* Cyril, 38, 39

Cambridge Institute of Criminology, 133
Carlberg, C., 59, 67, 68
Carrier, J., 78, 79, 85
Carterton School, 96
Cashdan, A., 69
Cassidy, V. M., 64
catchment area factors, 91, 133–4, 158–9
categories of special need
   see under behaviour disorders, disruptive pupils, ESN(M), feeble-minded, handicaps, learning difficulties, maladjusted pupils, *and* psychiatric disorders
certification of mental defect
  in Britain, 6, 8, 10
  in the USA, 80, 84, 85
Chamberlain, J., 89, 91
Charity Organisation Society recommendations, 3
child guidance clinics, 57, 62, 109
Children and Young Persons' Act 1969, 50
Chisholm, B., 102
circulars
  11/61 (Ministry of Education), 10, 11
  2/75 (DES), 11, 12, 13, 177
Clarke, R. V. G., 51
class, social *see* social class
classes, school
  in Norway, 73–4
  ordinary, 88, 96, 157, 180
  special *see* special classes
classroom interaction, 136–7, 142–6
Cleugh, M. F., 44
Coard, B., 42, 44
Coates, T. J., 124
Coleman, J., 78, 138
communes (Norwegian LEAs), 72, 73, 74
community homes (approved schools), 50
comprehensive schools
  in Bicester, 95–6
  and grammar schools, 178
  in Norway, 72
  pastoral care in, 179
  reasons for creation, 163
  threat against, 1
conditions of service, teachers', 122
Cooling, M., 54

Cooper School, Oxfordshire, 94, 95–6
Cornish, D. B., 51
corporal punishment, abolished in sheffield, 130
counselling, 61–3, 146–51
Countesthorpe College, Leicestershire, 88, 99–104
Cox, C. B., 121
Craft, M., 51
Critchley, C., 54
criteria of special needs, 8–12, 37–41, 68
curriculum
  adapted for integration, 100–4, 160, 162
  'hidden', 49, 180
  in Norway, 73
  pastoral, 148
  restricted in special schools, xii, 58, 60, 154, 155, 172–4

Dahl, M., 74
Dain, P., 58
Davie, R., 34, 37
Davies, D. (Brislington School), 139
Dawson, R. C., 54, 58
day-schools, special, 54–6
delinquency
  residential schools for, 50–1, 61
  school influence on, 133, 137
Dendy, M., 5
Department of Education and Science
  circulars, 10, 11, 12, 13, 20, 168, 177
  and ethnic minorities, 44
  and health survey, 28
  and HMI, 176–7
  policy making, 177–8
  statistics cited, 45
Desforges, M., 113
Diener, C. I., 173
discipline, classroom, 143–6
  and pastoral care, 159
'discovery' of special needs, 27–8, 30
Disruption in Schools Scheme, 167
disruptive pupils, 32–3, 155–8
disturbing children
  effect of other pupils and teachers, 15, 17, 32–3, 45, 115, 155–8
  ordinary schools' provision for, Ch. 7
Doris, J., 83
Douglas, J. W. B., 136
Dunn, L. M., 64
Dweck, C. S., 173
Dyer, H. S., 138
dyslexia, 69

Education Act 1870, 1, 2, 4

Index

Education Act 1876, 1, 2
Education Act 1899, 5
Education Act 1914, 6
Education Act 1921, 9
Education Act 1944, xiii, 7, 8–10, 44
Education Act 1970, 90, 91
Education Act 1976, 13
Education Act 1980, 121–2
Education Act 1981, 16–25
  assessment under, 17–21, 116–18
  failure to effect real change, 1, 21, 22, 153, 168, 172, 175
  Oxfordshire (Banbury) scheme and, 97, 99
  parents' rights under, 16, 19–20, 121
  USA laws compared, 85–6
educational psychologists' role, 10, 11, 59, 109, 115, 125–9, 167
educational support services, 125–9, 167
Education Department's Departmental Committee on Defective and Epileptic Children, report, 1898, 4
Education (Handicapped Children) Act 1970, 90, 91
effectiveness of schools, 132–8
effects of special education, Ch. 3
  as counterproductive, ix, xii, 57, 67, 92, 154, 172
  pupils' progress *see* progress
egalitarianism and education, in USA, 78
Eichholz, A., 4
Eide, K., 75
Elementary Education (Defective and Epileptic Children) Act 1899, 5, 6
Ellenbogen, M. L., 64
employment prospects of special pupils, 54, 55, 57, 58–9
EMR (educable mentally retarded) pupils, 63, 65
epileptic children, 5, 30, 47
equal opportunities, 24, 78–9, 179
ESN(M) pupils
  assessment (1944 Act), 10, 44
  definitions of, xiii, 8, 15, 22, 27
  and moderate learning difficulty, xi, 22, 63–8
  numbers of, 28–9, 38
  in Sheffield, 107–10
  West Indian children, 42
ethnic minorities
  in Britain, 13, 24, 35, 42–4, 155–6, 164
  in the USA, 78, 82
ethos of schools, 135–8
Essen, J., 47
eugenicist theories, 5

examinations, school, 135, 136, 138, 156
exclusion from school, rates of, 60, 134

failure in school, children's adjustment to, 173, 180
family factors, 46–7, 51, 139
Farrington, D., 133
feeble-minded children, 3, 5, 6, 8
finance, educational, 57, 90, 97, 105, 113, 177–8
  in New Zealand, 140
  in Norway, 74–6
  in the USA, 79
Finchden Manor School, 51–2
Finlayson, D. S., 137
Fish, J., Report 1985, 23–5, 172, 176–7, 181
Fixsen, D. L., 53
Flanders, N. A. C., 143
Fogelman, K., 34
Ford, J., 66, 153
formal assessments (1981 Act), 17–21, 97, 99, 116–18, 168–9
forms for assessment under 1944 Act, 9, 10, 11
  under 1981 Act, 99
form tutors' role, 149–50, 160, 179
frame-hour-numbers, 74–5
Frampton, O., 67
Francis, M., 58
Freud, Sigmund, 142
Frommer, E., 60

Galloway, D., works cited
  1976, 134
  1982, 42, 48, 60, 113, 134, 139, 141
  1983, 155
  1984, 58, 123, 140, 164
  1985, 23, 134, 137, 141, 155, 167
Galton, *Sir* Francis, 5
Garnett, E. J., 95, 96
Gath, D., 133
Gathorne-Hardy, 38
gender bias, 44–6
Gipps, C., 39
girls, 38, 44–6
Goldberg, D. P., General Health Questionnaire, 123
Gorrell-Barnes, G., 59
Graham, P., 31, 35
grammar schools, 178
Gregory, R. P., 126
Grosin, L., 138
Grunsell, R., 134, 167

Haggerty, M. E., 38

199

Index

Hall, R. V., 143
handicaps
  definition of, 8, 10, 14–15, 39
  physical, 5, 30, 47, 173
Hargreaves, D. H., 124, 135, 136, 150, 154
Harrop, L. A., 142, 145
Haug Special School, Oslo, 73–4
headteachers
  judgement of pupils, 55–6
  policies for integration, 120
  training of, 97
health factors, 3, 47–8, 122–4
Hegarty, S., 77
Her Majesty's Inspectorate, reports
  curriculum, 122
  off-site units criticised, 58, 139
  remedial provision criticised, 66
  policy influence, 168, 176–7
  Scottish education, 2
Hewison, J., 179
'hidden agenda', 22, 125–6
'hidden curriculum', 49, 180
high flyers, provision for, 178
home background *see* family factors
Hugh Middleton School, 4
Hungerford Centre, 58

illness *see* health factors
immigrant children, 13, 24, 35, 42–4, 155–6, 164
Individual Education Programmes, USA, 80, 84, 85
influence of schools on pupils, 132–8, 145
Inner London Borough Study, 34–7 *passim*
Inner London Education Authority, 23, 24, 25, 53, 133, 176–7
in-service training for teachers, 96, 97
integration, 8, 13–25
  in Bromley, 89–94
  encouraging normal development, ix, 173, 180
  in Leicestershire, 99–104
  in Norway, 71–7
  in Oxfordshire, 88, 94–9, 169
  seldom achieved despite 1981 Act, 14, 16, 21, 22, 114–15, 130–1
  'whole school', 88, 97–104, 155–61
intelligence tests
  as criteria of special needs, 37, 68
  and reading ability, 37, 39, 44
  and streaming, 136
  in the USA, 78–9, 82–3
interaction analysis, 142–6

Isle of Wight study, 34–7

Johnson, G. O., 64
Joint Departmental Committee on
  Mental Deficiency 1924–9, 6, 7
Jones, A., 147, 151
Jones, E., 96
Jones, N., 59, 88, 98, 162
Jordan, A., 64

Kavale, K., 59, 67, 68
Kellmer-Pringle, L., 34, 69
Kent, special education in, 37
Kirp, D. L., 79, 86
Klemm, L R., 3
Kolvin, I., 62
Kounin, J. S., 143, 144
Kyriacou, C., 123

Lane, D., 58
Laslett, R., 46
law *see* legislation
learning difficulties
  defined, 14, 38–9
  mild, 66–8
  moderate, xiii, 63–6, 92–3
  specific, 68
legislation on special education
  in Britain *see under* Education Act
  in Norway, 71, 72, 73
  in the USA, 72, 79–80
Leicestershire, special education in, 3, 88, 99–104
Lennhoff, F. E., 46
Levitt, E. E., 61
'limpet' model of integration, 88–94
Lindsay, G. A., 113
Lipsky, M., 85
local education authorities
  and Act of 1899, 5
  and Act of 1917, 6
  and Act of 1944, 8, 9, 27, 32
  and Act of 1981, x, xi, 1, 18–23 *passim*, 118–20, 168–9
  and headteachers, 53, 178, 181
  in Norway, 72–3
  policy making, 90–1, 96, 98, 99, 104–6, 161–4, 175–7
  residential schools, 51, 53, 56–7, 61
  Sheffield, 108, 134
  and social service departments, 51, 56
  surveyed by the Advisory Centre for Education, 30
  and West Indian children, 42
London, 23, 24, 25, 35–6, 58, 88–94
London School Board, 1890–1900, 3

Index

Loughran, J. L., 137
Lovell, K., 69
Lyward, G., 51–2

McFie, B. S., 38
McMichael, P., 51
mainstream *see* ordinary
Makins, V., 100
maladjusted children
  day schools for, 54–7
  definitions of, xi, 15, 31, 32
  delinquency, 50–1, 61, 133, 137
  family factors, 46–7
  residential schools for, 51–4
Manpower Services Commission, 122
Marland, M., 148
Marshall, M., 56
Massachusetts, special education in, 84
medical factors, 47–8
medical officers' role, 9, 10, 27
Mental Deficiency Act 1913, 6
middle class children, 45
mild learning difficulties, 66–8
Mills v. Board of Education case, USA, 80
Milner, M., 38
Milton Street Board School, Leicester, 3
Ministry of Education regulations, 8, 27, 31
Mitchell, S., 62
moderate learning difficulties, 63–6, 92–3
Morris, J. M., 37
Mullins, S., 127
Murgatroyd, S., 146

National Association for Promoting the Welfare of the Feeble Minded, 5
National Child Development Study, 34–5, 46–7
Neale Analysis of Reading Ability, 36, 37, 43
needs
  compared with wants, 17–18
  special *see* special educational needs
  teachers', 106–31
neurological abnormalities, 47
New Zealand, 58–9, 67, 68, 123, 137, 154, 140–2, 164
Nordic Council, 72
Norway, special education in, 71–7
nursery school placement in Sheffield, 110, 113
nurture groups, 59, 139

off-site units, 57–8

O'Leary, K., 142
on-site units, 59–60, 139–42
ordinary classes, special provision in, 73–4, 88, 96, 157, 180
ordinary schools
  Bromley, 89–94
  disturbing children in, Ch. 7
  growth of special provision in, 59–60
  integration in *see* integration
  Leicestershire, 99–104
  Oxfordshire, 88, 94–9, 169
  return of segregated children to, 3, 4, 20–1, 53–4, 56, 58, 61, 70
  see also special classes *and* units
Oslo, Haug School, 73–4
Osterling, O., 67
outcomes *see* effects *and* progresses
Oxfordshire, special education in, 88, 94–9, 169

Panckhurst, F., 137
parellelism of special provision, 98, 120, 162
parents
  health, 47
  in Norway, 71
  participation with schools, 90, 121–2, 150, 160, 179
  rights in Britain, 9, 12, 16, 18–21, 121–2
  rights in the USA, 79, 81–2, 83, 86
pastoral care, 146, 148–51, 158–9
Pennsylvania Association for Retarded Children, 79
'persuasion model' of integration, 89
Phillipson, C. M., 133
physical factors in special needs, 5, 13, 30, 47–8
Pinsent, *Dame* Ellen
planning, administrative, LEA's, 118–20
Pocklington, K., 77
policies for special education
  central government, 10, 11, 12, 13, 168, 176–8
  local education authorities, 90–1, 96, 98, 99, 104–6, 161–4, 175–7
Pollack, M., 43
Power, M. J., 133
Pratt, J., 123
prejudice, racial, 44
pre-school children, 30, 60–1
prevalence of special educational needs, Ch. 2
  in the USA, 84–5
primary school children, 56, 61, 69
  in Bromley, 88–94

201

Index

Pritchard, D. G., 2
procedures for assessment *see* assessment
progress of pupils
  better, in ordinary schools, 174
  maladjusted pupils, 54–5
  with mild learning difficulties, 59, 66–7
  misjudged by headteachers, 54, 55, 66
  with moderate learning difficulties, 63–6
  with specific learning difficulties, 68–9
  temporary, in special units, 155
Prosser, H., 47
psychiatric disorders
  parents', 47
  pupils', 31, 36, 39, 46–7, 60
  teachers', 123
psychologists *see* educational psychologists
psychotherapy, 61–3
Public Law 94–142 (USA), 72, 79, 85
Pumphrey, P., 69, 155
pupil-teacher relationship, 142–6

Rabinowitz, A., 126
racial prejudice, 44
Radical Statistics Education Group, 134
reading performance, 37, 39, 68–9, 155
Red Hill School, 51
referral
  to school counsellors, 146–7
  to special schools, justification for, 165–6
  to support services, 125–6
regional variations in special education, 28–9
Rehabilitation Act 1973 (USA), 80
re-integration *see* return
remedial teaching
  in integration, 100–4
  for mild learning difficulties, 66–9 *passim*
  misconception criticised, xiii, 4
  resources for, centralised, 157
  temporary effect of, 155
research, inadequate, on special needs, 63–4, 163
residential special schools, 50–4
resources for special education
  flexible allocation needed, 169–71
  growth of, 21, 79, 113
  in Norway, 74–7
  in Sheffield, 108–9, 113
  in Victorian England, 3–4
  for 'whole school' integration, 97–104, 155–61
  see also finance

resources model of special education, Oxfordshire, 96–7
responsibilities, retained by teachers, 156–60
return to ordinary schools, 3, 4, 20–1, 53–4, 56, 58, 61, 70
Reynolds, D., 134, 135, 136
riots, in Victorian schools, 38
Robins, L. N., 62
Roe, M., 53, 54, 56
Rogers, Carl, therapy method, 62
Rosa, P., 62
Rowan, P., 139
Royal Commission on the Care and Control of the Feeble Minded 1904–8, 5
Rudd, W. G. A., 124
Rutter, M., 31, 35, 36, 55, 133–9 *passim*
Rutter Scale for Teachers, 35, 40, 42

St Paul Woods School, Bromley, 89
Sampson, O. C., 69
Sarason, S., 83
Sayer, J., headteacher, 97, 169
school climate (ethos), 135–8, 145
school differences in effectiveness, 132–8, 172, 176, 181
School Health Service and Handicapped Pupils Regulations, 27
school influence on pupils, 132–8, 145
schools
  approved schools, 50
  day schools, 54–6
  residential, 50–4
  special *see* special schools
school uniform, 130, 136
Scottish Education Department, 2, 66
Second World War, 9
segregation
  continuing after 1981 Act, 16, 21–2, 130–1
  counter-productive, ix, xiii, 57, 67, 92, 154, 172
  of feeble minded children, 5–6
  for the good of ordinary pupils, 15, 17, 32–3, 45, 115, 155–8
  increasing, xi, 14, 114–15, 172
  justified by some needs, 116
  racial, in USA, 78–9
  see also transfer *and* special schools
selection of children for special education, 9–12
  see also assessment *and* attribution
self esteem of pupils, 150, 179–80
sensory disabilities, 13, 30, 130
sex bias, 44–6

Index

Shaw, O., 46, 51
Shearer, A., 84, 85
Shearer, E., 65–6
Sheffield, integration in, 42, 47–8, 60, 106–20, 130–1, 154
Sheffield Working Party on Special Education, 153
Shuttleworth, G. E., 3
Silva, P. A., 68
similarity between children, 179–80
Simmonds, E., 54
Simon, T., 5
'sin bins', 59, 140
social class
  and school influence, 134, 138
  and special needs, 10–11, 45–6, 48, 130–1
social service departments, and LEAs, 51
Spastics Society, report, 30
special classes
  adjustment problems of, 67
  attainment lower in, 63, 64, 69, 70
  temporary removal to, 158
special educational needs
  attributed solely to pupils, 17, 18, 41–8, 117, 126, 172
  definitions of, xiii, 8–12, 14–18, 30–3
  as justifying segregation, 3, 12, 49, 116, 125–6, 165–6
special schools
  day schools, 54–6
  enrollment figures, 29–30
  in Norway, 71–7
  residential, 50–4
  transfer to, 1, 12, 14, 26, 49, 56, 125–6, 129, 165
specific learning difficulties, 68
spontaneous remission, 61–3
Stanton, J. E., 64
statements, under the 1981 Act, 18–21, 97, 99, 117–18, 165, 168–9
Statham, J., 89
Stott, D. H., 31
streaming, 72, 135–6
stress
  families', 46–7, 139
  teachers', 122–4
subnormality, educational *see* ESN(M)
successful schools, x, 132, 156, 181
support services, educational, 125–9, 167
support teachers, 111–12, 127, 128
suspension from school, rates of, 42, 60, 134, 135
Sussex, West, 59
Sutcliffe, J., 123

Swann, W., 29–30, 98, 178
Sweden, special education in, 67, 73

teacher-pupil ratio, Sheffield, 60
teacher-pupil relationship, 136, 137, 142–6
teachers
  accountability, 121–2
  competence, 144
  conditions of service, 122
  cooperation with colleagues, 124, 158, 159, 161
  cooperation with educational psychologists, 125–9, 167
  cooperation with parents, 160
  needs, 106–31
  qualifications, 2, 73
  responsibilities, 156–60
  stress, 122–4
teasing of segregated pupils, 107, 180
Technical and Vocational Education Initiative, 122
terminology of special needs, xi, xiii, 14–16, 30–33
Thoresen, C. E., 124
Thurstone, T. G., 63
Tizard, J., 57, 91, 163, 179
Tobin, D., 69, 155
'token economy', 55, 145
Tomlinson, S., 22, 41, 44, 153, 154
Topping, K., 58
transfer to special schools, 1, 12, 49, 56, 125–6, 129, 165
  increased, xi, 14, 26, 114–15, 172
  justified, 116, 165–6
treatment of special needs *see under* behaviour modification, counselling, integration, pastoral care, psychotherapy, *and* segregation
Tredgold, A. F., 22
Tuckey, L., 55
tutors' role, 146–51, 160, 179
types of special need *see* categories of

Underwood report 1955, 31
uniform, school, 130, 136
United States, special education in, 78–87
units
  off-site, 57–8
  on-site, 59–60
  in Sheffield, 109–10

Vacc, N. A., 59
variations, regional, in special education, 28–9, 172, 176
Vaughan, M., 84, 85

203

Index

Wales, South, 134, 136
wants, compared to needs, 17–18
Warnock Report 1978, ix–xiii, 12–16, 37–41, 85, 163
Weatherley, R., 85
Wechsler Intelligence Scale for Children, 36, 39, 43
Wedge, P., 47
Welton, J., 168
West Indian children, 13, 24, 35, 42–4, 155, 164
Wheldall, K., 142, 145
'whole school' integration, 88, 97–104, 155–61

Willis, P., 121
Wills, W. D., 46
Wiseman, S., 124
Wood Committee 1924–9, 6, 7, 38
Woods, P., 150
Woolacott, S., 60
working-class children, 130–1, 153, 164
World War 2, effect on education, 9
Wright, D. M., 62
Wrightstone, J. W., 64

year tutors, pastoral care by, 147
Ysseldyke, J., 81, 86
Yule, W., 37, 39, 42, 68